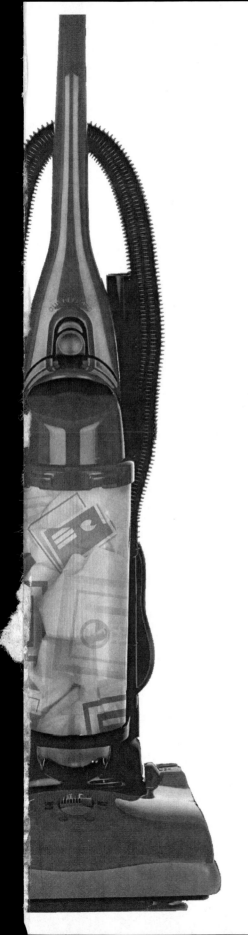

WHY MOST
POWERPOINT
PRESENTATIONS
SUCK

And how you can make them better

RICK ALTMAN

Why Most PowerPoint Presentations Suck

And how you can make them better

by Rick Altman

June 2007: First Edition
May 2009: Second Edition

Published by:
Harvest Books
1423 Harvest Rd.
Pleasanton CA 94566
925.398.6210
www.betterppt.com

Library of Congress Control Number
2007924582

ISBN
978-0-578-01805-8

Printed in the United States of America

To my four girls—beloved wife Becky, darling daughters Erica and Jamie, and loyal canine Missy. Once in a while, my household rank improves to fourth…

Contents

Foreword

*by Jim Endicott,
Founder,
Distinction
Communication,
Inc.*

www.distinction-services.com

My morning routine starts with a 7:00 am trip to my favorite local drive-thru latte stand and I've found that in just 10 minutes, I can be back in my office checking emails with a hot beverage in hand. Recently my favorite spot went belly up so I drove a block further to another stand. "Double tall 20 oz. mocha - light on the chocolate," I requested. As far as lattes go, this order is pretty much a no-brainer so I was frustrated to find that it didn't taste at all like my usual drink.

At lunch I tried another stand and was frustrated with yet another version of a light chocolate mocha. The whole experience left me scratching my head. Everyone used pretty much the same ingredients but the results were dramatically different. So, what's up? Much like life, the real magic is in the hands of the craftsperson, not the tools they use.

For the most part, presenters today have access to all the same tools as well. They have a version of PowerPoint that isn't more than a few years old, an image editing program and maybe even a vector drawing application. But much like my latte experience, given the same basic ingredients, presenters and presentation designers manage somehow to produce dramatically different outcomes. One person using an older version of PowerPoint produces a masterful work of personal communication art, while another using the latest software packages only manages to build a mind-numbing, convoluted, self-indulgent presentation that does little to accelerate information and ideas.

If audiences really are asking for more and we have a higher level of sensitivity to what doesn't work, why do so many still fail to deliver on those higher expectations? The answer is easy. Presenters and presentation designers still believe their presentations are all about them.

A reality check is in order. Audiences don't care about how much fun presenters are having with PowerPoint. Their collective brains go numb every time a presenter fills their screens with sub-sub-sub level bullets. Their use of animation is too often highly gratuitous and the pervasive stock flavor of everything on screen is a constant reminder that their presentations have been brought to us courtesy of Microsoft wizards, not a single original thought.

All this being said, take heart, reader. There are those out there who are helping us better navigate the presentation design process and within these pages, Rick Altman helps shed some much needed light on this important business communication process. He challenges what's all too easy but also provides some much needed insight into what does work and how to do it. If you're like most presenters or presentation designers, you're looking for resources to help take your presentation visuals to the next essential level. Read on and begin to fill up your personal toolkit with the kinds of fresh insights and creative skills you can put to use in your next presentation.

Your audiences want more. It's time to finally deliver for them.

Thanks To...

It might take a village to raise a child, and there are times when I feel a book cannot adequately be written without an entire community. I am fortunate to be part of a phenomenal one. The professional presentation community has many gathering points today, not the least of which is the PowerPoint Live User Conference, which I have hosted since 2003.

Each year, I have been privileged to have met some of the most passionate, enthusiastic, and dedicated presenters, designers, and content creators anywhere in the world. Their group energy is an almost intoxicating call to action for anyone who thinks out loud in public and I am so very grateful for having them in my head throughout this process.

And surprise, surprise, I don't have to venture past this group to assemble an excellent team of editors:

Chantal Bossé is a gifted trainer and presentations specialist from Quebec Canada. She was not only an eagle-eye through the text, but with English as her second language, she was a great reality check against some of my runaway jargon. She now knows what *bass-ackwards* means, so the relationship was of mutual benefit. **www.chabos.ca**

Geetesh Bajaj is one of the legions of the Microsoft Most Valued Professional team of dedicated volunteers who help PowerPoint users with issues and questions. A trainer and consultant based in India, Geetesh creates custom PowerPoint presentations and templates and is a featured speaker on presentation technologies. **www.indezine.com**

Sandra Johnson blends impeccable design sense, practical slide-making expertise, and fastidious attention to detail. In other words, she dinged me on bad-looking slides and misplaced periods—nothing that a bit of therapy won't solve... (Oh, and she doesn't like when I use ellipses.) **www.presentationwiz.biz**

Lisa Lindgren spots typos before I make them. Her gentle but firm eye acts like the perfect rudder for a ship whose captain would otherwise send it off like a drunken sailor.

Introduction

The word he used was *meshuga*, known by both Jews and non-Jews alike to mean "crazy." And my father was looking right at me when he said it.

"You're going to say *that* in the book?"

"Actually, Dad, I'm going to say it in the title."

"You must be meshuga!"

And there you have either the most compelling reason to, or not to, author a book without the assist of a large publishing house. I've written for Sybex Books, Peachpit Press, Que Publishing, and several others, and I have the distinct impression that, were I to have followed that path this time, you would now be holding a book in your hands of a different name. Pretty good chance, also, that a vacuum cleaner would not grace its cover.

My reason for choosing a private-label publisher was not because I sought an edgy title, although I do admit to enjoying the shock value that comes along for the ride. I did so because of a five-year-long frustration with being asked (make that required) by traditional publishers to include in any book proposal a clump of PowerPoint-centric topics that few in my intended audience find interesting.

Let's take a poll of one: Do you need to be taught how to create a slide? Did you buy this book because you don't understand how to make a string of text bold or how to make the bullet square instead of round?

If you bought this book for its intended purpose, it's because you have bigger issues.

- Your weekly load has now exceeded 200 slides and you are beginning to feel like a slide factory.

- Your presentations are not being received the way you were hoping they would and you're not sure why.

- You have good instincts but they need to be honed.

- Your co-worker keeps messing up your templates and you're about to scream.

- Your boss creates the most dismally-ugly slides and you don't know what to do about it.

- Or maybe...just maybe, it is you who needs a refresher in the principles of good presentation design.

Really, the potential market for this book is plenty vast without catering to the brand new user. How many horrible presentations did you sit through last month? In the face of how many colleagues or potential vendors would you like to shove this book and say "Here, please read this"?

I remember the first time I experienced it. I refer, of course, to the phenomenon we all know as Death by PowerPoint. The year was 1990, and three representatives from a well-known public relations firm wanted my partner and me to spend $10,000 on them to help us market a series of seminars.

They were smartly dressed, meticulously coiffed, and perfectly eloquent, as they proceeded to bore us out of our minds with drivel about value-added propositions, proactive initiatives, and positively-reinforced task-based personalization.

Every slide was read word for word, and each of us had a spiral-bound booklet that duplicated the slides.

Technically, this wasn't Death by PowerPoint; the software had not yet been invented. It was Death by Overhead Slide. Just as bad...

Who Should Read This Book?

As lead author, I would like to think that any presenter, presentation designer, or content creator would enjoy the pages of this book. The fact that I won't try to convince you of that is a sure sign that I have no future as a marketing consultant. From my annual conference and my on-going work as a presentations consultant and coach, I have a pretty good sense of the typical PowerPoint user. If I'm right, you fall into at least one of the following categories:

- You are thought of as the Slide King or Queen of your department and are called upon to crank out untold volumes of slides. Getting the job done on time becomes your sole focus.

- You are a presentation designer, where you have a bit more opportunity than the Slide King/Queen to consider the aesthetic side of content creation, but every project given to you is due yesterday.

- You are on the road a lot, giving sales presentations to audiences of various sizes. You have a well-worn template that fits you like an old shoe, never mind that it was designed from a wizard back in the 1990s. You have gotten pretty good at swapping in new content for old, but have begun to wonder what you are missing by not learning more about the application.

- You are an outside consultant brought in to work with people in the marketing department who have absolutely no idea how to refine a concept, crystallize an idea, or shape words into a message.

- You are hired to help terrified public speakers learn not to throw up all over themselves when in front of an audience.

- You work with the executives of your firm, and no matter how great the work is that you give to them before they board their plane, by the time they touch down at their destination, they've mauled your slide deck.

- You have worked your way into a position, created just for you, in which your expertise as a presentation professional is truly appreciated. You are given creative freedom and latitude, and are encouraged to cultivate your skills.

That last example is not fantasy; it only sounds too good to be true. There are just enough forward-thinking organizations and skilled presentation professionals to create optimism for the community at large. In fact, since our first edition, we have seen this trend quickening its pace. Even through the economic downturn that began in 2009, many of us who act as presentation consultants have seen an uptick in our businesses. Companies are indeed finally starting to get it.

In order for that community to grow and thrive, we need a universe of PowerPoint users who have moved past, as we describe in the first chapter, their first 30 minutes of training.

That is the thrust of this work. You don't need help with the basics of PowerPoint. You know your way around the program. You need someone to speak frankly to you about the issues, the challenges, the joys, and yes the perils associated with modern-day presentation creation and delivery. With this book, I accept that challenge.

How to Use This Book

There's an insulting headline for you. (*To use this book, start at the top of the page, read from left to right, and turn pages with your right hand...*) Proud authors like to insist that good books aren't used; they're read. But we in fields of technology know better. We know how people use computer books—lots of dog-eared pages, notes in the margin, table of contents brutalized—and I'm fine with that.

My hope, however, is that you do find it to be a good read. By design, it is written very unevenly. Some chapters are just a few pages long, others close to 40. Some topics we hammer and others we ignore. And I do not pretend that these 30 chapters are some sort of sterile, objective listing of "advanced tips," whatever that even means. This book is one person's view of the presentation community and the functions and nuances of PowerPoint that seem particularly relevant. It is full of bias and subjectivity and you are invited to disagree with it. In fact, if you agree with everything that I say here, this book's value is probably diminished.

In choosing my four editors, it was practically a prerequisite that they disagree with me on occasion. As a result, these pages alternate between first-person singular and plural enough to drive a grammarian nuts. And that is my prerogative—there are times when I speak for the team...there are times when I speak on behalf of a community of thousands. And there are times when I feel as if I'm on Survivor's Exile Island. It's all good.

To download a file, go to www. whypptsucks.com and find the file named after the figure that represents it.

But no book should be an island—it's challenging enough to ask static pages to cover a medium of motion. And that is why we consider the book's web site, **www.whypptsucks.com**, to be a full partner in this endeavor. You'll see our constant references in the margins to files that you can download, view, and dissect, and most of the time, the filename mirrors the name of the particular figure or illustration.

♦

There are no appendices to know about and there is no particular order in which you need to read this. **Part One** is where we bring the big hurt. We share our research and our conclusions about all that is wrong with the presentations industry and the software that is at its helm. Hopefully before the onset of depression, **Part Two** offers solutions to all of the pain we uncover in the chapters that precede it. **Part Three** channels the inner designer in all of us, providing strategies and advice for those who did not come from an academy of art. **Part Four** is devoted to skills and techniques that anyone can adopt to help become a better public speaker, whether you are a natural at it or not. And **Part Five** steps up the volume considerably and covers several truly advanced topics and ideas in which you can indulge.

What Version Do You Need?

In many cases, it matters little what version of PowerPoint you use, and we encounter hundreds of presentation designers every year still using Version 2000. A good designer needs only a blank slide; a good presenter could use a 1993 copy of Harvard Graphics.

Having said that, we'll make Version 2000 users drool over some of the advanced techniques possible with a more current version, which we define to be version XP or later.

Unlike the first edition of this book, version 2007 is given equal billing and full coverage, even though most of our readers are probably staying with version 2003 for the time being. Our conclusion is that there are two types of PowerPoint users today: those who are using version 2007 and those who are curious about it. And even if the second group is larger than the first, said curiosity is extraordinarily wide-spread. As a result, we are careful to deliniate the discussions and the step-by-step instructions that are version-specific.

If I have written this book correctly, it will prove to be bad for my business as a presentations consultant. A good chunk of my time as a hired gun is spent retraining, or untraining, to be precise. Many of the people with whom I work have read the reference guide and have taken some sort of introductory course, but never really learned any rules or guidelines for using the software.

By the time they bring me in, their slides often have dozens of unused placeholders, text boxes with bullets stuffed into them, random applications of animation, and multiple backgrounds.

Before I can teach them anything new, I have to strip off all of the old. I intend to provide you with the strategies, the techniques, and the tools for becoming completely proficient with the projects that you need to produce. I intend to leave you with a more complete understanding of how the program operates. And I intend for you to not have to rely upon consultants like me as often.

I guess you could say that this book attempts to reduce by half my billable hours.

◆

Finally, the wonders of print on demand are numerous, chief among them the agility with which we can print new versions...perhaps starring you. If you: a) have created a presentation that illustrates a technique discussed herein; b) disagree with an assertion that we make; c) have an alternative technique to propose; d) want to suggest a topic for us to cover or expand upon; or e) just want to comment on a passage, please write to me at betterppt@altman.com or at the betterppt.com web site. We will not hesitate to include noteworthy commentary in an upcoming version, which, if sales go well, could be as early as next month...

Part One

The Pain

This book is not about pessimism despite the somewhat bawdy title. In fact, this book explores quite the opposite: I maintain that the ultimate message contained in these 388 pages is enabling and optimistic.

Nonetheless, first there are dues to pay. As good friend and messaging guru Jim Endicott likes to remind us, good storytelling is often about first identifying the pain. And as tennis great Martina Navratilova once said to me personally, "No pain...no gain." She was talking about physical fitness, not creating slides, but I couldn't pass up a chance to name drop...

Chapter 1

The 30-Minute Syndrome

If only I could earn the proverbial nickel for every time I have heard the following. It could be any setting in which the conversation might turn to PowerPoint, which in my case is frequently.

"Oh," the person says, in response to almost any remark made about the software. "PowerPoint is easy. I learned it in about a half hour."

Let's start by acknowledging that the statement is generally true: PowerPoint is not difficult to pick up and begin using. Both of my daughters created slides for school projects before the age of 10, and indeed, a reasonably astute grownup can begin making slides within 30 minutes.

Microsoft might have you believe that this is a virtue of the software. In fact, it is bad. It is very, very bad.

Who Are These People?

Creating a presentation can be an extraordinarily creative experience, but it rarely starts out that way. And that is because PowerPoint's default settings are not very creative and because most PowerPoint users do not come to the software from a creative field. They start out elsewhere in the Office suite. They are Excel crunchers, Outlook gurus, Access junkies. They are used to software with a steeper learning curve and a point of entry that requires much more effort before they can do much of anything. When they encounter PowerPoint and discover that they can begin using the program with effect in less than an hour, they are like kids with new toys.

But again, this is not a good thing; it's a bad thing. These people declare themselves proficient after their requisite 30 minutes. These same people who get really good at their 30-minute skill set call themselves advanced. And those who get really fast at these same skills call themselves gurus. Those who teach it to others are gods.

But they don't get beyond those first 30 minutes of skills. And then they go forth and commit high crimes against innocent businesspeople everywhere. Yup...Death by PowerPoint.

▶ We point our finger of accusation at both of the two main camps that we speak to in this book: those who create presentation content and those who deliver presentations. Often, one person wears both hats, but there is plenty of blame to go around. Inexperienced content creators and ill-equipped presenters both contribute to the poor reputation endured by the software and the presentation industry in general.

The creative disconnect

Missing from the equation, of course, is the creative component. And you can't fault the typical number-crunching, word-processing Office user for not grasping that. These software programs are tools, wielded to perform tasks. You learn the tool well enough to perform the task, you go home for the day, and what happens in the cubicle stays in the cubicle.

But PowerPoint is different. With PowerPoint, you practice your craft in public, and this craft is forever linked with death and taxes as the three things humans fear most.

This is much more than the converted Excel user bargained for. It's possible, make that likely, that she had no experience at all speaking before a group; she simply taught herself how to make bullet slides.

And herein lies the biggest disconnect of all. The company that this innocent Excel-cum-PowerPoint user works for might spend millions of dollars on its brand. Expensive design firms to create glossy brochures...P.R. firms with lots of names on their door, hired to spin messages...high-powered marketing firms to ensure maximum exposure.

And this same company then sends someone out with 30 minutes of proficiency to make what will likely be a company's first impression: the presentation in a boardroom.

Why Is This Happening?

In the 1990s, Canada's Corel Corporation was flying high in the graphics world, owning the most heralded and most popular graphics

Figure 1.1
Corel's charting program was ahead of its time and not ready for prime time, but the graphic artists and illustrators who dabbled with it back in 1993 produced some very nice work.

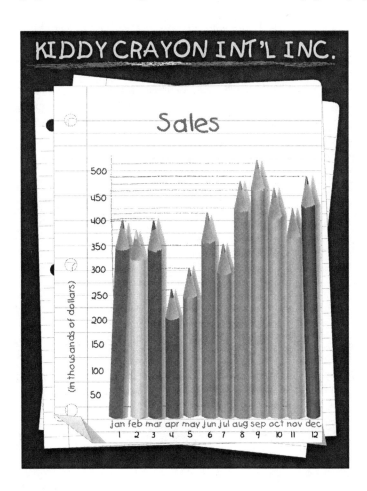

program around, CorelDraw. Back in 1993, Version 4.0 added two programs to the suite: Chart and Show, to facilitate the creation and animation of charts and graphs.

They went nowhere, they were full of bugs, and most Draw users ignored them. Two years later, they were out of the suite, banished to small footnotes in the history of a smallish software maker. But a few users did dabble with them and their creations were quite impressive, as you can see in Figure 1.1. They were like nothing that any PowerPoint slide or Harvard Graphics chart (remember that?) ever produced.

This was perhaps the first time that a presentation tool was placed into the hands of a creative professional, and this little story from the past speaks volumes about the dilemma that the presentation community faces today. The issue is two-pronged:

- People are thrust into a position of being the company's creative force even though they do not have a background in the arts or come from a creative field.

- Those who do have a creative background and are capable of producing excellent work with PowerPoint don't have a place in their company's org chart.

I would also like a nickel for every time that I have met a PowerPoint user with an obscure and obtuse title, or simply the "admin." Not to impugn in any way the workforce of administrative professionals; the title does not and should not imply that a graphically talented person is holding it.

Companies have simply not made enough of an effort to identify, define, and cultivate the role of the presentation professional. Therefore, it usually is assigned in haphazard fashion to anyone willing to step up to the plate, including the person who is simply good with Microsoft Office.

◆

Have I described you yet? Odds are, I'm in trouble one way or the other. If I have identified you as the person thrust into the role of PowerPoint jockey, I've either offended you or made you defensive. If you are the creative professional honing your craft with presentations, I've reminded you of your biggest frustration and now you're mad at me for that. There's pain in this part of the book for me, too!

There's hope for all of us...but we're not yet done with the pain. In other words, if I didn't offend you in this chapter, I have several more opportunities upcoming.

2

The Cram-Everything-In Obsession

Did you watch *Super Size Me*, the documentary on over-eating at McDonald's? ("A film of epic portions.") Both of my daughters vowed that they would never eat another Big Mac again, and one of them actually kept that vow for over a year. It espouses one of America's most robust sentiments: bigger is better, and more is more better.

I recently watched an episode of *The Apprentice*, where a handsome, well-dressed twenty-something young professional pleaded his case to Donald Trump by reciting every business slogan he could possibly think of, as fast as he possibly could, interspersed with the robotic "I'll be great for your organization, Mr. Trump." at every breath. And it worked: Trump fired the other guy.

This is a very real phenomenon in today's culture—the sense that it's better to say everything than risk forgetting to say the one thing that you really need to say. And nowhere is this more evident than in the typical slides that project onto the whiteboards and white screens of America today.

This plays out in a fairly predictable way by those who prepare their own slides for a presentation:

- They sit down at their desk.

- They open PowerPoint.

- They start thinking of every point that they need to make.

- Soon they start thinking of how they are going to make each point.

End result: they have written a speech.

I want to be fair here: If you have little or no experience speaking before a group of people, you have no idea that this is the wrong approach to take. This might seem like a perfectly logical way to prepare: write down what you want to say and then say it. And hey, there's this software program that will show you everything that you've written down, so your audience can see it, too. How cool is that?

This might not be such a bad proposition for the uninitiated public speaker; as we all know, it's a horrible proposition for her audience. The woman from Scottsdale AZ probably thought she was on the right track when she perpetrated the slide shown in Figure 2.1. It said everything she wanted to say.

No question about it: one of today's most acute pain points is when speakers use their slides as notes. In many cases, it is because they have no idea that the Notes view exists.

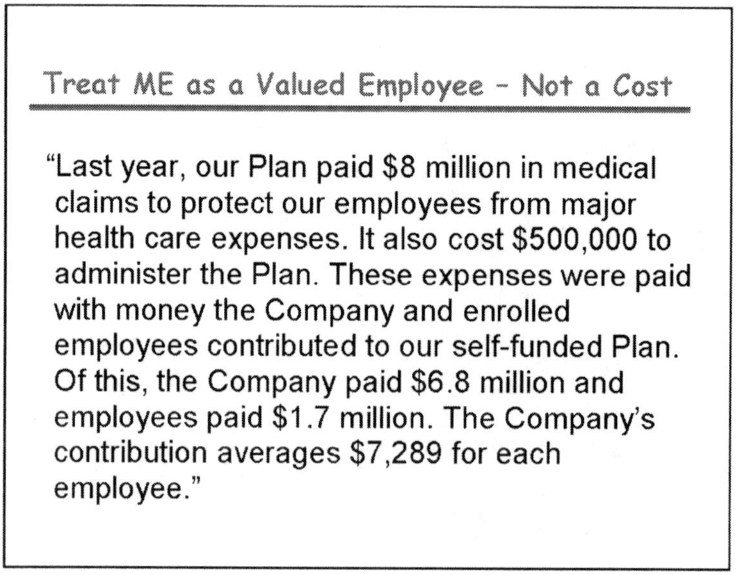

Figure 2.1
This slide says everything the speaker wants to say, so what's the problem?

> ## Treat ME as a Valued Employee – Not a Cost
>
> "Last year, our Plan paid $8 million in medical claims to protect our employees from major health care expenses. It also cost $500,000 to administer the Plan. These expenses were paid with money the Company and enrolled employees contributed to our self-funded Plan. Of this, the Company paid $6.8 million and employees paid $1.7 million. The Company's contribution averages $7,289 for each employee."

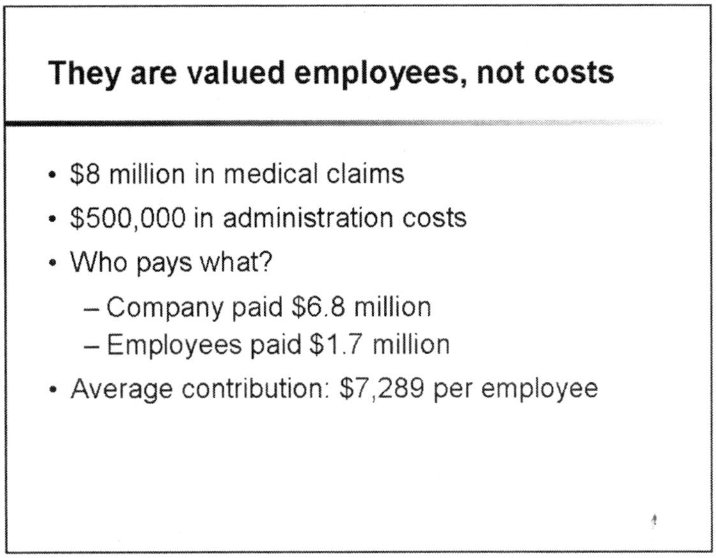

Figure 2.2
What a difference five minutes can make. You might actually stop and read this slide now.

They are valued employees, not costs

- $8 million in medical claims
- $500,000 in administration costs
- Who pays what?
  - Company paid $6.8 million
  - Employees paid $1.7 million
- Average contribution: $7,289 per employee

This leads to the first of several universal axioms that we will put forth across these pages. It is Universal Axiom No. 2 and it goes like this:

> **If a slide contains complete sentences, it is practically impossible for even the most accomplished presenters to avoid reading the entire slide word for word.**

Watch for it the next time you attend a presentation: the more verbiage a slide contains, the more likely is the speaker to read all of it. Talk about your double-whammy. We discuss strategies to work around this in Chapter 21, and they are important, because Universal Axiom No. 2 leads directly into Universal Axiom No. 3:

> **When you read your slides word for word, you sound like an idiot.**

Figure 2.2 is the result of a five-minute makeover. We did nothing more than parse out the main ideas and add a rule. If you take 10 seconds, you'll get the gist of what this presentation is about, but you probably would not have invested even one second trying to sift through the original slide.

More important, we might stand a chance of hearing the real person come out if she speaks to the second slide, as opposed to the drone who would have read the first slide. Gone is the compulsion to recite the slide verbatim; now she'll have to actually collect her thoughts and deliver them. Scary? Perhaps at first. But this five-minute slide makeover will also make her over into a better presenter.

But we're getting ahead of ourselves. First, more pain...

Chapter 3

Look at Me!!

It was the fall of 2003 and life as I knew it was about to change forever. We were in Tucson AZ for the debut of Power-Point Live, and Glen Millar had traveled from Australia to lead a session on animation. Glen is a brilliant designer of presentations who has dreamed up and forgotten more techniques than you or I will learn in our lifetimes.

And he was upfront about what he was about to show his audience. "You're about to see some really gratuitous stuff here," he said in his Down Under drawl, to which the audience laughed. "In order to discover the potential of what the software can do, sometimes you just have to experiment."

With similar irreverence, the slide was entitled "Absolute Nonsense," and it looked like Figure 3.1. You'll want to take a trip to the whypptsucks.com web site and download 03-01.ppt to see what Glen showed his audience that day. Gears turning, pistons pumping, paddles flapping, balls bouncing...all controlled by PowerPoint animation.

▶ To download any of the files referenced in this book, point your browser to www.whypptsucks.com and find the file by its figure number. You can either visit the above URL and browse the hyperlinks or you can download any file directly by entering www.whypptsucks.com/[filename].

In either case, you'll be prompted to choose between opening the file in your browser window or downloading it. In most cases, we recommend downloading the file to your computer and opening it in PowerPoint.

Finally, files with extensions of .ppt can be opened in either version 2003 or 2007. Files with extensions of .pptx are specific to version 2007.

Each of the elements on this slide are carefully timed to become part of a working, almost organic, system of motion. Most in the audience had never seen anything like this and had never considered the use of animation in this way. If you look up *epiphany* in the dictionary, it really should reference Glen's October 18, 2003 workshop on animation.

Figure 3.1
When the audience saw Glen's animation contraption in 2003, their lives changed. They saw an entirely new dimension to the potential of attracting the attention of their audience.

The buzz lasted all day; I knew the impact of this presentation would be more lasting. And I was a bundle of conflict. After all, what better advertisement for a conference in its rookie season than 200 disciples returning to their colleagues and saying, "I can't wait to show you what I learned at PowerPoint Live!"

But the specter loomed of those same disciples returning to their places of work and wasting not a moment finding an occasion to use their new skills. This tendency is remarkably human and cuts across all disciplines and all ages. My wife Becky and I can remember as if it happened yesterday the moment that our six-month-old daughter Erica discovered that she could flex a muscle in her throat and emit a sound. The cause and effect relationship was captivating to her and nothing short of a tranquilizer would stop her from demonstrating her new skill that night. And I'll show you the very essay in which our other daughter Jamie, then in third grade, discovered adjectives.

In software parlance, I refer to this as use of a feature based on recency of discovery, not appropriateness to the task. You use it because you just learned it. Rounded corners on rectangles back in the desktop publishing boom of 1986…dressing up your `C:\>` prompt in 1988…drop shadows in 1993…related database fields in 1997…Excel pivot tables in 2000…and "absolute nonsense" in 2003.

The urge to place into operation that which you have just learned might be one of the finest human traits ever. Imagine the innovation that has come from this tendency and the advances across all disciplines and pursuits. Intellectual curiosity is a wonderful thing; watching it play out in human achievement is even more wonderful.

Unless, of course, you practice your craft in public. Then it has potentially lasting implications of a different sort. You can usually tell when a person has just learned, say, how to make bullets go dim after appearing, or how to make a title fly in letter by letter, or how a motion path can turn static objects into ambulatory ones. When you see the effect in action, but it has no context or purpose whatsoever, there's a good chance that recency of discovery is the driving force behind its use.

I should note that we who considered ourselves Glen's colleagues that day were not left out of the epiphany. When he showed a little-known trick of hiding the background and showing pieces of it through other objects (see Figure 3.2), he sent us all scurrying to our notepads or notebooks.

To this day, many of us on that debut teaching team in 2003 still look for excuses to use this background trick, even if it is not suitable to the

Figure 3.2
Even the experts at PowerPoint Live learned something new when Glen Millar showed how to place a photo on the background, cover it up with a full-sized rectangle, create an object on top of the rectangle (the ellipse), and fill it with the background image.

The insatiably curious among our readers can deconstruct this cool technique by downloading 03-02.ppt (which can be opened in either version.

context of the presentation. We too cannot resist saying "Look at me!" in public.

By its nature, PowerPoint is an extroverted activity. People turn to it for the purpose of communication—often in person, often to large audiences. You put your ego on the line when you do this, so it helps to have a healthy one. In fact, showing off is almost part of the essential nature of the discipline and should not be viewed as an entirely negative trait.

But there are right ways and wrong ways to get attention, and there must always be purpose behind it. This chapter's pain is brought to you by the compulsion to add gimmicks to PowerPoint-driven presentations when there is absolutely no reason to do so. *The fact that you just learned how to do it does not change anything.* If it doesn't contribute to the message, it has no place on your slides. Let's say that again:

> **If it doesn't contribute to your message,**
> **it has no place on your slides!**

Chapter 14 discusses some of the healthier ways to show off in public.

Chapter 4

Is Your Message Upside-Down?

When you enter a room to give a presentation, what are you thinking and feeling? Are you comfortable? How will audience members perceive you? Will they like you? What can you say about yourself to instill confidence in them right from the start? How can you credential yourself right from the start?

If you actually address these questions, it could mean that you are one of millions of people speaking before groups who just doesn't get it. It could mean that you are guilty of sending a message to your audience that is completely upside-down.

That's pretty harsh, you might say—all you were doing is caring what your audience thinks about you. How did that turn into such an unpardonable sin?

Read on to learn about one of the most common misconceptions about presentations today and one of the least understood dynamics. It might compel you to take an entirely different approach to your presentation content and delivery. Or it might cause you to swear at me and throw this book in the trash. That's okay, too...

It's All About Whom?

"Hello, my name is Susan Sorenson, and today I'm going to talk to you about my five-step approach to home loans and how it has become the talk of the industry. First, let me tell you a bit about myself and my business..."

If you are like most, you have probably heard openings like that dozens of times, and perhaps you have employed something similar during your own presentations. It is as common as coffee; it has become the accepted backdrop for modern-day presentations.

And it is all wrong.

Let's imagine Susan's audience entering the room for this seminar. Do you suppose that a single one of them is looking forward to getting to know her? Are they hoping to become friends with her?

Not likely. They are probably wondering what they need to do to stay in their homes! They are hoping that they're going to learn something that can help them through these difficult financial times. They are wondering how Susan is going to help them with their own situation.

"Hello, my name is Susan Sorenson, and I know why you're here..."

Unless your mother is in your audience, you can't expect that anybody enters the room caring a lick about you. Forgive the candor, but it's simply not their job or their place to. They have their own issues and their own concerns, and your welfare is not likely to be one of them.

**It's not their job to care about you;
it's your job to care about them.**

It is your job to understand, recognize, appreciate, and connect with the issues and concerns that they have.

"Hello, my name is Susan Sorenson, and I know why you're here. You're afraid of losing your home, aren't you? I don't blame you—my sister just lost hers and I live with her pain nightly."

Notice how different the focus is between this intro and the one at the top of the page. In the first one, our fictional speaker tells her audience how (1) she is going to talk about (2) her approach to lending, but first (3) she is going to talk about (4) herself and (5) her business.

You have probably become so accustomed to the standard opening that you no longer notice, and you've probably witnessed a few hundred times the presentation that begins like the one in Figure 4.1.

There is nothing wrong with having slides like this in your deck, but what does it say about you if these are the first three slides after the title

Figure 4.1
If these three slides are batting leadoff in your slide deck, it tells your audience members that you care more about how great your organization is than you do about their own welfare.

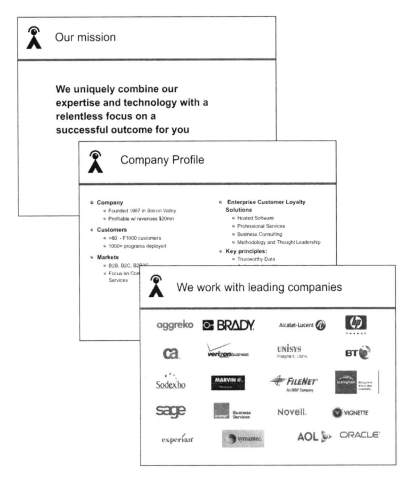

slide? What does it say about your priorities and your ability to connect with your audience? At a minimum, it certainly does not convey to your audience members that you identify with their concerns or that you understand their pain.

And yet, few things in the world of presentation are more important than that. Apologies in advance if you read this more than once; I'll probably write it a dozen times:

Audience members rarely make decisions to act because of what they hear or see. They act on what they feel. The gut guides them more than the brain.

In order to create an emotional connection with them, you have to show that you understand and care about them. You do that by talking about them, not about yourself.

"Hello, my name is Susan Sorenson, and I know why you're here. You're afraid of losing your home, aren't you? I don't blame you—my sister almost lost hers and I live with her pain nightly.

"I know this concerns you; it concerns me too. You're going to get answers today, this is certain. But I also want you to get some encouragement that you can do something to improve your situation. In addition to the tactics and strategies that we will discuss, I want you leaving here feeling that your future is within your control."

Although the second paragraph has several "I" sentences in it, they are all directed outward. I expect you...I want you... This creates a fundamentally different feeling among the audience—it is at the core of an audience-centric message, which is what you should aspire to deliver every single time you speak in public.

The promised land for you is this: instead of you offering up your credentials on Slide 2 and your customer list on Slide 3, your audience members become so compelled by your message that they want to know these things and they ask you about them during Q&A. At that point, seeing how they asked, you click a hyperlink on the slide (see Chapter 27 to learn how) and call up those credentialing slides.

◆

It does not take a Sally Field moment to understand that people want to be liked. If you are a living, breathing person, you would prefer for your audience members to like you, respect you, care about you, etc. You get there not by credentialing yourself, but by showing them those same emotions and feelings that you would like them to show you.

If you show that you care about them, they'll care about you. That is the order in which this must happen.

Chapter 5

Bitter Backgrounds

As we continue through the sources of pain, annoyance, and angst around presentation content, we note the cruel irony of the fate that all too often befalls the skilled presenter with engaging content. What could go wrong with that scenario, you ask? How about slide backgrounds that drown out the content on them? Indeed, little is more frustrating than slides that could have legitimate appeal but cannot be easily read.

If you know that a presentation sucks, you can leave the room or start texting your friends ("lol, omg this sux ur lucky ur not here...l8r"). When the speaker is good and the content actually interesting, it could be even more frustrating when the visuals work against him or her.

Invariably, this happens when content creators louse up with their backgrounds, and this usually can be traced to a fundamental lack of understanding about what makes a good background.

Backgrounds Shouldn't Be in the Foreground

We can put this entire problem to rest with one sentence:

Put black type against a white background.

Done. Problem solved. Stop reading, go home. If you're already home, go out to a movie. In the history of presentations, no deal has ever been lost, no contract not awarded, no grant not granted because a presenter used black text on a white background. It's the ultimate chicken soup for PowerPoint: it couldn't hurt. (That's pronounced "it cuddnt hoit," for those looking to brush up on their Jewish-mother accent.)

At the same time, we pundits have been telling you that photos can make a world of difference for your presentations, so it's no surprise that many of you choose to integrate them into the backgrounds of your slides. And today, you all have digital cameras; you're all content creators. The problem is that sometimes you choose photos that are too good!

Witness Figure 5.1. This is a well-composed photo of a Silicon Valley building—nice angle, very cutting edge and modern. It would vibrate well with just about any businessperson today.

I would love to use it in a presentation...I could envision burning type into it for dramatic effect...I might pan across it...I could even set it to music.

Figure 5.1
Great photo, lousy background.

But I wouldn't use it as my presentation's background, certainly not in its present form. It steals the show; it refuses to stay in the background. It does the one thing that you don't want your background to do: it takes attention away from your foreground—your text. Once you do that, you're done.

Now if the photo *is* the message, that's different. If the photo conveys your message without the need for text, that's the holy grail of presenting! But that doesn't happen very often, and most of us need to be content with integrating a photo with our text-based message.

Figure 5.2
This photo has too much contrast and too many points of interest. Bullets don't stand a chance and you cannot pick any one color of text that would have sufficient contrast against this photo.

Looking for Contrast in All the Wrong Places

Integrating standard bullets into this photo would be exceedingly difficult. Where would you put them? Figure 5.2 shows the folly of trying to approach this design from a conventional perspective—there's no traditional layout that is going to give you readability.

The culprit here is contrast and it is the single most misunderstood concept among those just starting to get experience blending imagery with standard PowerPoint content. If you had to sit through 30 slides that looked like this one, you wouldn't care if the speaker was the incarnate of Albert Einstein. You'd tune out.

The most important interplay between foreground and background is contrast. In short, you want a lot of it! You want dark text against a light background or vice-versa. People who had this mantra hammered into their heads sometimes go on auto-pilot and hear the singular message "look for high contrast." They find photos with high contrast and then get frustrated when their designs don't work properly.

A photo that has high contrast is going to work against your efforts to create appropriate contrast between foreground and background, and Figure 5.2 illustrates this problem perfectly. In order for you to rely on your background photo to provide good contrast with your foreground content, that photo itself must have low contrast.

As someone who acts as a commentator to the presentation community, I love that content creators are beginning to integrate visuals into their work. And as with any other discipline, there are right ways and wrong ways to do this.

See Chapter 13 for an in-depth exploration of integrating photos, mastering contrast, and understanding transparency, including version 2007's robust recolor, brightness, and contrast controls.

Chapter 6

The Scourge that is Custom Animation

There I sat, not three feet away, and I couldn't believe what I was hearing. I the consultant, he the client, trying to determine the best course of action with a slide whose content was not communicating the right message.

"It seems that we're not quite getting to the central point," I said to him. "It's not just that you save your customers time, they also benefit from a sales team that speaks a dozen different languages. I think we need to make that point stronger."

I swear I'm not making this up, his response to me: "How about if we make those bullets fly in when I say it?"

"_____"

"Rick? Are you okay?"

Okay, so that last part of the exchange was made up. I didn't actually go comatose. No doubt, though, a camera focused on me would have captured a look of utter bewilderment at the notion that gratuitous animation applied to a clump of words was actually the answer. However poorly this reflected on my client's sensibilities, it was even more insulting to his theoretical audience whom he hoped would be persuaded to take action as a result of bullets flying onto the screen.

That, in one 30-second exchange, sums up our national obsession here in the United States. We prefer television to radio, movies to books, and slides that move to ones that don't. We learned this at our first conference when the seminar on animation overflowed into the hotel foyer; now we offer that session in the general ballroom that can hold over 200 and we don't even consider offering any other seminars at the same time.

The irony of this situation is delicious. Earnest PowerPoint users are so completely taken with animation, they would gladly stand in the back of a hotel ballroom for 60 minutes in the hope of picking up a new trick or two. And at the same time, every single poll ever taken about PowerPoint's most annoying characteristics (Google "PowerPoint" and "annoying" to see how many polls have actually been conducted) lists bad animation in the top five, without fail.

This much is clear: whatever skills people learn in those first 30 minutes of training, restraint and good taste with animation do not seem to be among them.

Your Audience is at Your Mercy

There is a reason why this topic strikes such a raw nerve among those who suffer through poorly-crafted presentations, and to understand it, we will now introduce Universal Axiom No. 1:

> **When something moves on screen, your audience has no choice but to watch it.**

This is a response that occurs at a subconscious level. We are like moths drawn to a light; we cannot help ourselves.

In response to a skeptic at a recent seminar, I prepared the following experiment. I stood off to the side of the room, about 25 feet from the screen, and began to talk about this topic. In mid-sentence, careful not to take my eyes off of the audience, I sent a gear flying across the screen, just as you see in Figure 6.1.

Everyone looked.

Figure 6.1
For better or for worse, you have no choice but to watch objects as they move on screen.

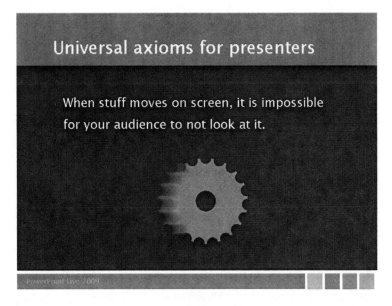

"Hey, I'm over here," I said playfully, as the audience returned their gaze to me. Five seconds later, a photo that was on screen suddenly drifted off.

Everyone looked.

"You see what I mean? You can't help it!"

At that point, I had a smiley face appear and disappear in a blink. There wasn't enough time for anyone to take their eyes off of me, but they all still saw the flashing ellipse in their peripheral vision and responded by looking over. Everyone laughed and I knew that I had made my point.

Your Covenant with the Audience

This implies a tremendous obligation on our part as presenters and content creators. Our industry needs its own variation of the Hippocratic Oath: Above all, we shall practice no excess.

If we know that our audience is compelled to track movement on the slide, it is incumbent on us to make sure that we use that power wisely and responsibly.

That rarely happens.

More likely, inexperienced PowerPoint users apply animation in knee-jerk fashion. If they haven't applied animation to something on the slide, they feel as if they haven't done their jobs. Our creative editor,

Sandra Johnson, was told this quite succinctly by the CEO of a large corporation: "The slide is incomplete without animation."

I don't have to go further than a nearby bedroom, the one occupied by my 16-year-old daughter, to witness this dynamic first-hand. We live in an environment in which multimedia distractions are part of the background noise. I truly believe that today's teenagers feel somehow disfunctional without them. It seems that we have created that same environment for our presentations. If a slide consists solely of bullets, we are compelled to animate them. An otherwise ordinary ruling line below a title is inflated in importance by a Fly In From Left. Slide transitions can't just fade; they must dissolve. We have created the implication that if an object just sits there, it must not be very important. It must move; it must exude some level of energy.

How Much is Too Much?

Some animations are worse than others, and now you know the barometer by which it should be measured: are audience members forced to track motion across the slide? The ones that move the most are the most potentially intrusive.

We have prepared the Official Rick Altman Pain Scale for you, to be consulted whenever you feel the urge to make something move:

Animation	From / To	Pain Quotient (5 is the worst)
Boomerang, Spiral, Swivel	Anywhere	6
Fly	From side to side	5
Fly	From bottom to top	4
Zoom Out	Anywhere	4
Fly	From left edge to one inch onto the slide	3
Zoom In	Anywhere	3
Wipe Slowly	n/a	2
Wipe Quickly	n/a	0
Fade	n/a	0

And every single time we do it, our audience is compelled to watch.

Chapter 14 continues the discussion of proper use of animation. When done correctly, animation can enhance rather than distract.

Exercising restraint with animation is not easy, as thousands of annoyed members of PowerPoint audiences each day will readily attest. And of all of the characteristics that define pain, misused animation is one of the most important to avoid. When you use animation gratuitously, you call into question your own sensibility. This undermines your entire reason for being in front of an audience.

Chapters and 15 perform fairly deep dives into animation. Please come back and read this chapter before starting in on either of them.

Because we are environmentally conscious, we have chosen not to kill a tree writing about all of the annoying animations that exist within PowerPoint, but you get the idea.

Animations that force your audience to track an object all the way across, up, or down the slide are the most invasive. The more lateral or vertical movement, the more visual tracking is required of them and the higher the annoyance quotient.

If an object flies all the way from the right to the standard starting point for bullets on the left side, that's really bad. An object that flies in from the left to that same point is not as bad. Zooming Out could fill the entire screen—that's bad—but zooming in does not grow the object beyond the size that it is ultimately going to be, and that's not so bad.

Similarly, Wipe and Fade take care of their business inside the boundaries of the object. They do not require that the audience track any motion across the slide, and as such, they earn a place at the bottom of the Pain Scale, where no pain exists. We said this earlier, we're saying it again, and we'll surely say it several more times: you can't be hurt by Wipe or Fade.

♦

Meanwhile, you had better have a very good reason to use Spiral, Boomerang, or Pinwheel. And if you ever find a legitimate reason to apply it to text, please email me at you're_lying@bull****.com.

Chapter 7

Can PowerPoint Make You Stupid?

One of the most inflammatory ideas circulating among PowerPoint skeptics has received quite a bit of credible press in the past few years. In a widely-circulated 2004 article, *New York Times* columnist Clive Thompson all but blamed the space shuttle Columbia accident on the use of PowerPoint. (www.betterppt.com/shuttle).

And the ever-bombastic Edward Tufte has essentially made a living out of attributing many of society's communication problems to Microsoft's venerable slide-making tool.

It's hard to imagine that a software program could be credited with something as profound as affecting one's intellect, but read on—there is a real dynamic at work here, making up the final chapter identifying PowerPoint pain.

Where Good Ideas Go to Die

Two years ago, my friend Lon came to me for assistance with a keynote address he was giving to a group of professional tennis teachers. These teachers were working with some of the most talented junior players in Northern California, so they were well beyond teaching the fundamentals of tennis. Their jobs were to turn these kids into seasoned athletes, help them land college scholarships, and maybe prepare them for professional tennis.

Lon had some innovative ideas to share with these teachers about how to turn kids with raw talent into strong competitors and winners. Over a beer, he was amazing, fluent with such heady concepts as the ideal performance state, living in the present moment, and his most novel theory, having to do with calming the mind to maximize the body's energy.

I'm an avid tennis player and loved hearing him speak about it. These were novel and bold ideas about helping exceptionally talented athletes reach beyond their potential. When his ideas were flowing, he was a joy to listen to.

Now he needed to distill all of his wonderful ideas into a 60-minute after-dinner talk, and he wanted to show me the PowerPoint slides that he had created so far. My first reaction surprised him.

"Why do you need to show slides?"

"I'm sure that they're expecting it."

"I'm expecting you to do the unexpected."

Figure 7.1
Can this slide help a coach talk to other coaches? Not likely...

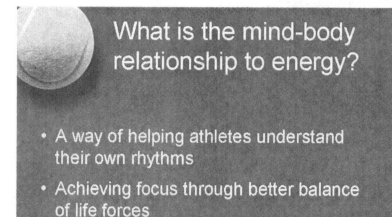

Figure 7.2
This slide did not inhibit Lon's ability to articulate his thoughts.

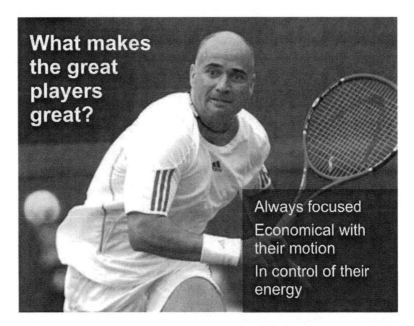

Once he untangled himself from my circular argument, he insisted that slides would make his talk go smoother.

He was wrong. Figure 7.1 showed his weak attempt to fit his thoughts onto a bullet slide. It sounded like mumbo-jumbo, something his ideas never did when he spoke about them informally. Worse, when he practiced his speech with his slides, he found himself trying to explain the meaning of the words on the slides, instead of just sharing the thoughts in his head. I call this "going on defense" and it is a sure sign that you are at risk for committing Death by PowerPoint.

Ultimately, I convinced Lon to go with Figure 7.2 instead. His ideas were more than enough to carry the hour; all he needed were a good image to evoke an emotional response and a few talking points. And when he realized that his original slides were doing him no good, he decided to forego slides altogether. Good call, Lon.

This was the classic example of good ideas getting torpedoed by Power-Point. Lon's ideas were far too nuanced to be contained within one title and three bullet points. Most good ideas can't survive such a boiling down, yet that is the default medium for sharing ideas in public. When smart people try to represent their good ideas with such a limiting medium, they come off sounding less smart.

PowerPoint does indeed dumb them down.

One chapter from now, you will read about my prescribed "three-word challenge"—a call to distill long bullets down to short ones. This might sound like a contradiction to the point I am making here, and it certainly won't be the last time you feel that way. I will explain the difference more fully then; for now, I will specify that the danger here is trying to use bullets to *explain* an idea, instead of just *represent* it.

Talking Points Can Create Talking Heads

Unless presenters practice with their material and with the medium, even simple and succinct bullets can derail them. I witnessed a good example of this just the other day, watching a volleyball match on ESPN. (Two sports anecdotes in one chapter? Get used to it! Ask anyone who knows me: sports is my metaphor for everything in life.)

Calling the action were Chris Marlowe, an experienced play-by-play professional, and Vince, a former Olympic player. Each of them was required, at various times during the broadcast, to comment on a statistic or a notable fact being displayed in a graphic.

One of Vince's assignments was to discuss the factors that he thought were significant during a particular match. The graphic displayed three items: return of serve, ability to set a double-block, and free-ball passing. With only a few months of experience as a television commentator and no formal training or background, Vince did nothing more than read, word for word, the three items in the graphic. He would have done far better if he were instructed to describe, in his own words, the three key elements of the match. The audience didn't need to see the graphic, but when ESPN showed it, it paralyzed Vince, reducing him to a cue-card reader.

Chris Marlowe is much more experienced in these matters. The graphic he was asked to elaborate on showed how many times UCLA, the top-ranked team in the nation at the time, had won games after being down game point. While the graphic showed the percentages and statistics, Marlowe said, "You don't win four championships in six years without playing the big points well, and here is why so many consider UCLA to be one of history's most successful teams."

Now that's the way to speak to bullet points! Marlowe didn't insult his audience's literacy by reading the graphic. Instead, he made the moment greater than the sum of its parts by telling us something more than just the raw facts.

Even though he is on live television and the stakes are high, Marlowe actually has an advantage over the person giving a speech. As a play-by-play announcer, Marlowe does not know what is about to happen, he does not work off of a script, and often he doesn't have any idea what he is going to say next. That promotes spontaneity and creativity, two of the most important ingredients of good public speaking.

While inexperienced with talking points, Vince proved to be an acute analyst of the game. When allowed to simply react to what he was watching, he was articulate, relaxed, and confident.

I suspect there are many executives and corporate speechmakers who are like Lon or Vince: astute, well-spoken, but ultimately hampered by the implicit (or explicit) requirement that all high-tech speeches be accompanied by a PowerPoint slide show. I had lunch recently with a Silicon Valley-based executive and he summed up the situation perfectly. First, he acknowledged that most of his colleagues are too busy to spend more than a half-hour working on their slides.

"Is it so important that they have slides?" I asked.

"Today," he replied, "you can't give a talk in this business without showing slides."

"But what can you do in 30 minutes?"

"Copy and paste your notes into the bullet holders."

"But if you just turn your notes into slides, your slides will be the same as what you say."

"That's right."

"That's sad."

"That's right."

You can't give a talk today without showing slides. Those are some of the most distressing words I have ever heard. *Too busy to spend more than 30 minutes on their slides.* Executives with good speaking skills don't necessarily need slides as they speak, and if they do, their slides should elaborate on their ideas, not repeat them. And executives who lack speaking skills make the situation worse with bad slides that compel them to read their speech instead of deliver it.

The Wrong Place to Start

Where do people go wrong? Often, their fatal errors are made in the first 10 seconds of a project: they put the mouse in their hand, after which it becomes exceedingly difficult to think creatively.

Even though it doesn't involve PowerPoint, a recent experience I had crystallized this issue for me. On a flight home a few years ago, I sat inbetween two businessmen, both using their notebook computers. I couldn't resist spying on them.

One of them was using CorelDraw, a graphic drawing program that I have been using since its inception in the late 1980s. The other was composing in Microsoft Word. The man using Draw was producing some sort of flier or publicity sheet, and he was struggling. He kept creating objects and text strings, fiddling with them, and then deleting them. He appeared to have no direction or objective.

I couldn't see what the other man was writing about, but what struck me was that he spent half his time making notes on a yellow legal pad. Funny, I thought, why doesn't he just use Word to keep his notes, and I asked him that very thing.

"This is the way I've always done it," he said, "and I can't break the habit. I always make my outlines longhand before writing."

Well, the irony of this situation was delicious. The man who least needed to use pencil and paper before embarking on a computer-based project couldn't work without them, and the man who desperately needed to do a bit of sketching or scribbling was trying to create a drawing using an eraser head to move the cursor.

Why do we computer users do this to ourselves? I think I know the answer, but first, let's point out the obvious: when you embark on a task—any task—first you decide what it is you want to do, then you determine how you are going to do it, and then you do it. That's how people do things in real life. All too often, however, users of creative software, like CorelDraw or PowerPoint, go about everything bassackwards. They sit in front of the computer, place their hand on the mouse, and start creating objects, hoping that a finished piece will spontaneously occur. In no other aspect of their lives do they expect to achieve success in this manner, but they hold exempt from natural laws their relationship with their software applications.

People come to graphics and presentation software from so many different professions and pursuits, it's impossible to generalize about work habits. But one thing is clear: most users do not arrive at the software with a formal background in any creative field. They have not had significant experience with sketch pads, light tables, dark rooms, or any other traditional creative tool. Their software is likely the only tool for working on a creative project that they have been exposed to, so it's only natural that they would use it for the entirety of a project.

This was certainly the case with the man in 16C. He knew that he had to produce a flier on a particular topic, but I doubt that he started with much more direction than that. He kept drawing shapes, creating text, moving them around, stopping, thinking, stretching, rotating, filling, deleting, redrawing...and all the while growing visibly frustrated. He expected CorelDraw to act as his sketch pad, or better yet, to magically produce the flier for him.

We see this same dynamic among PowerPoint users, usually to the same detriment. The cold hard fact is that programs like CorelDraw, Photoshop, Dreamweaver, and PowerPoint are the wrong tools for the beginning phases of a project, totally wrong. This is not a criticism of PowerPoint and the others—let's please just acknowledge that these programs are finishing tools, not starting tools.

PowerPoint lets you do a lot of things quickly and easily, but sketching or roughing out a creative concept is not one of them. There's way too much temptation to make everything perfect, and that's exactly what you don't want to do at the initial stages of a project. When starting work on a presentation, experienced content creators look to get ideas out as quickly as they think of them. This is the time to open the creative canal as wide as possible—to scribble, cross out, throw away, start over, blab to colleagues, and do all of that all over again. It is not the time to be thinking of transitions, animation choices, backgrounds, or color schemes. In fact, it's not the time to be handling the mouse at all.

The man in 16A had the right idea. While only creating a word-processed document, he realized that he's better off mapping out his route on paper first. Even Word offers too many temptations to make a first draft perfect, what with spell and grammar checkers, document controls, and paragraph formatting tools. He just wanted a brain dump, and the best dumping ground is the legal pad. He didn't have very

Map Your Mind

If you are insistent on beginning a project on the computer instead of on a legal pad, at least turn to software that is designed for that purpose. Programs like OneNote or MindMapper allow you to rough out ideas, refine concepts, create sketches, and then export finished ideas to an outline that PowerPoint can import.

We still think old fashioned tools are better, but applications like these help bridge that creative gap for those who are tethered to their mice.

Figure 7.3
Even the pros begin
with pencil and
paper, not with
slides.

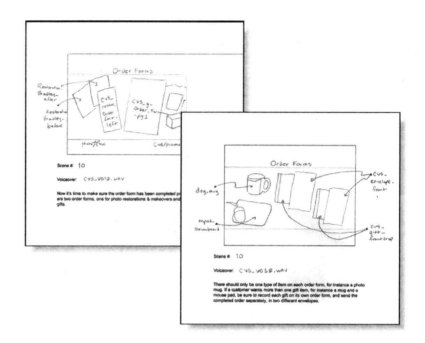

Figure 7.4
Proof positive that
your pre-slide
sketches don't have
to look
like much.

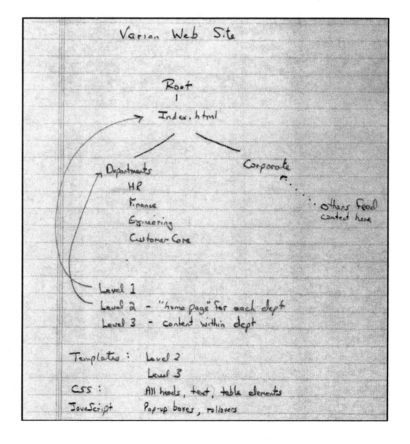

good handwriting; I doubt that he got an A in third grade penmanship. But that is of no consequence during the idea stage.

Figure 7.3 shows a sketch of a presentation prepared by Julie Terberg, one of the most prominent and talented presentation designers in the world. She is a regular at PowerPoint Live, where she shares her vast knowledge of design theory and how it is best applied to the presentation medium. Many in the audience were surprised when she showed this sketch, but in her own words, "I always start with pencil and paper. I'm freer that way."

Her sketches are probably nicer-looking than many of your or my finished products, but that is unimportant. Witness my chicken-scratching in Figure 7.4 about creating a PowerPoint-based tutorial on website design. It's a mess! But it is every bit as useful to me as Julie's sketches are to her.

It is not the product of your sketching that is so important to the process, it is the *act* of sketching. Sketching...doodling...free-associating...these are the secret ingredients to brilliance!

Kind of funny when you think of it. One of the secrets to using Power-Point effectively is knowing when not to use it.

◆

As we conclude our definition of everything wrong with modern-day PowerPoint usage, we have already produced for you one recipe for creating pleasing and potentially effective presentations:

- Organize your thoughts away from your computer

- Use black text

- Create white backgrounds

- Use only wipes or fades

If you confine yourself to those four practices, if you don't read past this point, if you *throw this book in the trash right now,* I'll be satisfied that we have reduced by one the number of people in the world who might commit Death by PowerPoint with annoying and obnoxious presentations.

The Solution

If you're still with me after the first seven chapters, you're in need of a good catharsis, and the rest of this book seeks to provide just that. If you have reached the conclusion that yes, most PowerPoint presentations do indeed suck, rest assured that there are solutions at hand.

We won't shy away from the direct tone that we adopted in Part 1; each of us remains just one poor choice away from committing Death by PowerPoint. But from here on, our objective is to arm you with the tools, strategies, principles, and perhaps above all, the philosophy behind the creation of truly excellent presentations.

Chapter 8

Surviving Bullets

We have chosen the order of these first few chapters carefully. Exhaustive articles have been written on the evils of bullets. My colleague, Cliff Atkinson, wrote an entire book, *Beyond Bullet Points*, espousing alternative approaches to creating content slides.

I disagree with neither the sentiment nor the philosophy behind this argument. Presentation content creators who go on auto pilot often crash and burn. The world does not need any more bullet slides in order to prosper.

But we have to be pragmatic here. Irrespective of your opinion about bullets, there is no escape from them. They are as inevitable as colds in the winter and mosquitoes in the summer.

Even were you to conclude that bullet slides are evil, there are two reasons why you might not be able to deliver yourself from them:

1) Many of you, we predict almost half, create presentations for others, in many cases your bosses or clients, and you are not at liberty to make those kinds of wholesale design changes arbitrarily.

2) You did not come from a design background and so you lack the confidence that you could create slides that are not just standard bullets. (You obviously haven't read Part 3 yet!)

Instead of trying to eliminate bullets from your slides, you might be better off trying to make your bullets as effective as possible, and that is the focus of this chapter.

Three Words

What if a law were passed prohibiting bullets from exceeding three words in length? Could you abide by it? Perhaps not, but humor me on this one, because it stands as one of the best exercises you can do, whether you are the presenter, the content creator, or both.

▶ This section pertains to presentations delivered live via a presenter. Presentations designed to be sent electronically and read on screen by the recipient are not subject to the same verbiage issues. In short, it's okay to be wordy with a self-running presentation, because those are the only words available to the recipient.

Fresh off all that pain in Part 1, you probably don't need a reminder about Universal Axioms 2 and 3, but you're getting one anyway:

> **If a slide contains complete sentences, it is practically impossible for even the most accomplished presenters to avoid reading them word for word.**

> **And when you read your slides word for word, you sound like an idiot.**

Figure 8.1 is a classic culprit. Somebody simply did an idea dump right into his or her slides, and anyone who tries to speak to this slide is doomed to become a drone.

Before you read on, I want you to clean this slide up by mentally reducing each bullet point down to three words. Ditch the adjectives, jettison the pronouns, eliminate the flotsam.

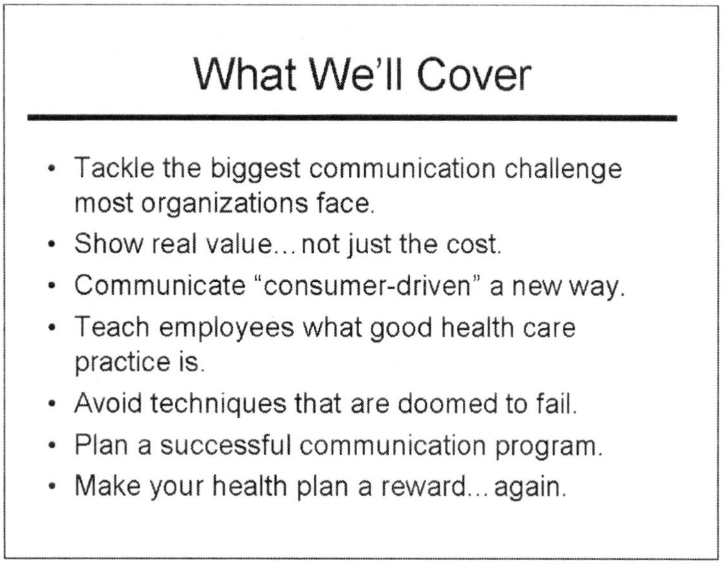

Figure 8.1
Pity the poor presenter who has to work with this slide.

What We'll Cover

- Tackle the biggest communication challenge most organizations face.
- Show real value... not just the cost.
- Communicate "consumer-driven" a new way.
- Teach employees what good health care practice is.
- Avoid techniques that are doomed to fail.
- Plan a successful communication program.
- Make your health plan a reward... again.

Even with your sharpest knife, you might not be able to cut all the way down to three words, but the reward is in the effort.

Figure 8.2 shows our attempt with the three-word challenge. You can see that we failed with one of the bullets, but the sum of our effort and our failure was an unqualified victory. The slide is much stronger now, and even though I have no familiarity with the subject, having gone through this process, I feel as if I could almost present on it now.

Several important things take place when you make an earnest attempt to get within three words:

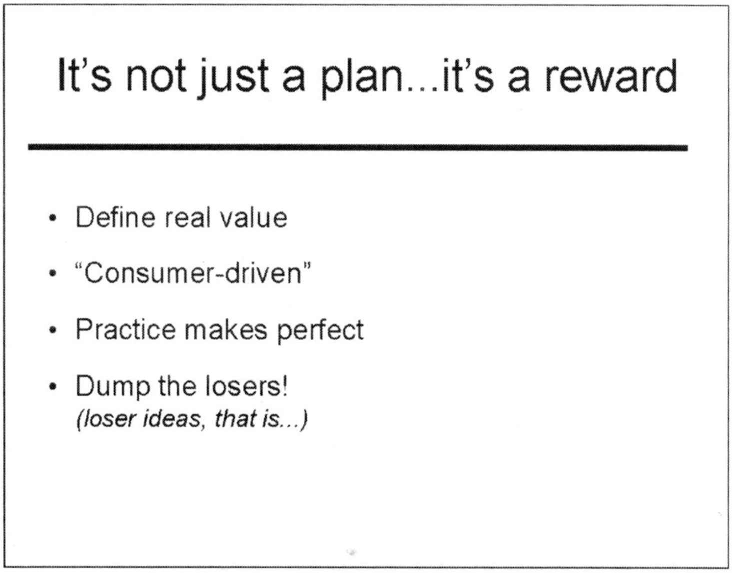

Figure 8.2
This slide no longer gets in the way. It frames the subjects and allows the presenter to find his or her natural speaking rhythm.

It's not just a plan...it's a reward

- Define real value
- "Consumer-driven"
- Practice makes perfect
- Dump the losers!
  (loser ideas, that is...)

Your slides are friendlier

With just that one task, you create slides that are much easier on the eyes of your audience. Eye fatigue is the silent killer of presentations. When you ask your audience to sit in a dimly-lit room for 30 or 60 minutes, their eyes are going to be the first to go. The more words each slide contains, the quicker the onset of fatigue. Fewer words, less fatigue. Your bullets might not be as descriptive, but that's okay—it's your job to do the describing.

Your pace improves

Something almost magical happens when you reduce the amount of words on a slide. Everything seems snappier. The slide draws more quickly, audience members absorb the information more efficiently, and you most likely project more energy.

You create intrigue

In three words, you are not going to be able to fully explain your points. But that's not bad; it's good. In fact, it's terrific! Without even trying to, you create mystique and intrigue. You invite audience members to use their imaginations. Once you get good at the three-word rule, you will become a better writer of bullets. You will begin to write with color and humor; you could become coy, even mysterious. These literary techniques serve to command attention. They help to engage your audience on an emotional level. And that, dear reader, is the holy grail of presenting.

You learn your material better

Of the many bad things associated with dumping complete sentences onto slides, perhaps the worst is how lazy it makes the presenter, whether it is you or someone for whom you create slides. Excess verbiage sends a subtle but powerful message that you don't need to prepare as much, because everything you want to say is already there.

Parsing the words increases your burden as a presenter, but once again, this is a noble burden. Adhering to the three-word rule forces you to learn your content at a level you otherwise might not have reached.

One of my favorite quotes about presenting comes from Mark Twain:

> **"If you want me to speak for an hour, I am ready today.**
> **If you want me to speak for just a few minutes, it will**
> **take me a few weeks to prepare."**

The three-word challenge is a microcosm of the wonderful dynamic that Twain articulated. In order to get down to three words, you really need to study the text. You need to truly understand what you intend to communicate and you need to pick three words that create the perfect backdrop for your ideas. Getting down to three words requires that you practically get intimate with your text.

Looking back on Figures 8.1 and 2, there are a few things to note:

- We eliminated altogether the two bullets about communications. This is purely subjective, but good communication is so fundamental to this topic, it doesn't need a bullet. As the theoretical presenter, I have made a mental note to discuss its importance in my opening remarks. Seven bullets on one slide is too many, anyway.

- The point of the "consumer driven" bullet is that the phrase is being redefined. The quote marks around the words imply that, so no other words are needed. If I were the presenter, the quotes would be all the reminder I would need about this topic.

- The final bullet has been promoted to title. If I were the content creator, I could see planning the entire presentation around that catchy phrase. In fact, if the company were looking for a marketing catch phrase, this could be it. At a minimum, it serves well as the title for this slide.

> For more ranting about leave behinds and further discussion about reducing text on your slides, see Chapter 17.

- Finally, our revised slide will not function nearly as well as a leave-behind document. Good. Great! You should never try to create one deck for these two purposes.

In the case of bullets, less is so much more. Taking the three-word challenge is one of the best devices to get you to less. It took four passes and over 45 minutes to create the revision. Mark Twain would have been proud...

Brief bullets, stupid bullets...what's the difference?

In Chapter 7, we wrote how ill-conceived bullets could keep you from fleshing out your ideas. (Actually, we wrote that they could make you stupid.) How is the three-word challenge different? This is a legitimate question and detractors of this strategy would argue that coy or evasive bullets offer no guarantee that an important idea will be shared, while a verbose bullet at least ensures that the idea will be made public.

In the previous chapter, we also warned against verbose bullets taking over your responsibility of telling your story, and that is the central point, as far as I am concerned: bullets that try too hard to tell your story rob you of the chance to tell it yourself. That in turn robs audience members of what they came to hear.

When the Words Must Display

We know of several organizations that require that bullets be fleshed out into complete thoughts and displayed for the audience. (One company actually suffered through litigation based on the charge that it did not divulge visually specific information to an audience of shareholders...oy vey.)

So how do we overcome Axiom Nos. 2 and 3? You might be required to show the text and recite the text, but must you do it in that order? Probably not, and when you avoid that, the experience is altogether different.

If you are the one tasked with presenting this fictitious report to your fictitious shareholders, start with this basic slide:

We hit our stride in 2008

- Our sales team rocked
- Incredible employee loyalty
- Training, training, training
- One terrific partner
- Fenway Park, here we come!

Now say everything that you are required to say about these five points. When you are done, then transition to this slide:

We hit our stride in 2008

- Our sales team rocked
  Sales were up over 200% in every region where we have a local presence.
- Incredible employee loyalty
  New hires have stayed on board for an average of 48 months since 2001.
- Training, training, training
  Renewed spending on internal training has created a vested and well-prepared work force.
- One terrific partner
  Acquisition of BrightLight Plastics more than doubled our production capacity.
- Fenway Park, here we come!
  We finally beat Synoptics in the annual softball game!

This slide could be word-for-word what you just told your audience, but when you say it first and display it afterward, it is an altogether different experience for your audience.

The axiom about being an idiot for reciting a slide only applies if the slide is present while you are reciting it. If the words appear afterward, you're not an idiot, you're omniscient.

Say it first, then display it. That's the solution for situations that require both.

The three-word challenge does not excuse you from fleshing out your ideas; it *demands* it. By distilling a slide down, you take ownership of the content—if you don't share your ideas, they don't get aired. This is as it should be. You are the presentation; your ideas are the main attraction.

From this perspective, it is obvious that slides that have been *three-worded* will support the presentation of ideas better than ones that drone on.

The War Against "On Click"

There is a battle of wills being fought in the boardrooms and in the trenches where America creates its presentation content. (Overseas as well—our technical editor, Geetesh Bajaj, from India notes the same battles there.) The controversy has raged on for over five years and numerous articles and scathing editorials have been written about the bitter battle. We refer, of course, to the issue of bullet advancement: do you display them all at once or click by click?

I come down on a particular side of this issue and I'm pleased to report that my side is winning: advancing one by one through bullets is losing favor. In this section, I will tell you why the all-at-once choice is the better approach to take and how to best incorporate it.

We understand the appeal for advancing slides "On Click." It could make pacing easier and it assures that everyone in the room will be on point. More likely, you simply accepted the default choice of On Click when applying animation to the bullet placeholder. But there are three significant downsides to this approach that you must take into account:

Loss of context

When you reveal ideas one by one, you ask the audience to absorb each piece of information by itself, and this often results in less-than-total understanding of the concept you are trying to share. As the presenter, you understand the connection between Bullets 1 and 3, but when you remove the forest and only show the trees, one by one, the audience doesn't get the same chance to connect the ideas.

Where's the end?

When you advance bullets one by one, you might lose the forest yourself! You increase the chances that you will forget which bullet is the last one and then have to do the advance-oops-sorry-go-back shuffle. Not the end of the world, but a needless disruption of your flow.

Figure 8.3
"You're not smart enough to keep up with me, so I will employ Sesame Street-type measures to help you."

How dare you!

Most important, when you spoon-feed simple information to your audience, you could actually be insulting them. Some of your audience members could infer from this approach that you lack confidence in their ability to follow along. They see it as commentary on their intelligence. In the polls that we have taken, about one in 15 have reacted this way. If you're speaking to a room of 100, you would be offending six people just by the way you have created your bullet slides.

Figure 8.3 represents the nadir of this design approach—dimming bullets after you're done with them. This is downright condescending and will be felt on a conscious or subconscious level by more than just one in 15. Not only do you imply to your audience that they are not worthy of seeing what you have to say next, but that they need to be told when to stop paying attention to the last point.

You didn't mean any of that. You were just trying to be helpful. Or perhaps you just learned how to do all that stuff with the dimming feature of the Custom Animation task pane and you wanted to try it out. How did this get so out of hand?

Life is Too Short

Bullets on slides are just not worth this kind of trouble. Everyone's life is made easier when you display your bullets all at once and then speak to them. You insult nobody and you eliminate the risk that you might lose your own place.

This is especially true if you have successfully three-worded your text. They're now short and sweet, so just get them out there! You make your life easier as the presenter, too—one click and you're there. No pretense, no false drama, no unnecessary commotion.

Nay-sayers will argue that audience members will run ahead and stop listening to you. Get real. How far ahead can they go? Do you have 22 bullets on the slide? I know presenters who refrain from distributing their handouts for this reason, and that is a legitimate point of view. But if your audience is having trouble paying attention to you, don't blame your bullets. It's your job to keep your audience on point.

When you liberate your bullets in this way, you also get the opportunity to practice one of my favorite animation techniques for text blocks: the "cascading fade," performed the same with any version of PowerPoint from 2002 (XP) forward:

1. Select the bullet placeholder and apply a fade for an entrance. Set Start to With Previous and Speed to Fast.

2. Click the downward-pointing arrows to expand the animated elements into their individual bullets, and if necessary, right-click on one of them and choose Show Advanced Timeline.

Not seeing the downward arrows? Your text is probably in a text box instead of a placeholder. Right click the animation and select Effect Options. Click the Text Animation Tab. Use the drop-down arrow to change the Group Text option to By 1st Level Paragraph, then click

OK. Now you should see the arrows and be able to proceed.

3. Click and drag the second bullet's duration (its orange bar) to the right by .2 seconds.

4. Drag each subsequent bullet to the right an additional .2 seconds.

5. Press Shift+F5 to play the current slide and witness your masterpiece.

This is one of the most elegant treatments of text animation that we know. It is softer than a standard fade and very pleasing to the eye. It has only one drawback:
because it involves different animations to the same level of bullets, it cannot be programmed onto a slide master; it can only be created on content slides. Therefore, I do not employ this technique when I am looking to automate a 300-slide presentation.

▼ Download 08-04.ppt from whypptsucks.com to see the effect.

The Art of Compromise

There will be occasions when you are either compelled by specific circumstances or by certain people (who sign your paycheck) to either advance bullets one by one or do the dreaded dim thing. And to be fair, we can think of situations in which it is appropriate to advance bullet by bullet or to highlight the specific idea that is being discussed. Here are a couple of recommended strategies for those times.

Is this the last bullet on your slide??

If you are compelled to display bullets one by one, here is a trick that will insure against your inadvertently advancing beyond the last bullet and switching to the next slide before you wanted to. The steps are the same across all modern versions of the software.

Asking for Directions Would be Wonderful

As the sayings go, men refuse to ask for directions and women don't realize they need to. Gender aside, we hope that Microsoft's development team learns how to. It would make the lives of advanced users oh-so-much more enjoyable.

Let's consider the technique that we just showed, the one we refer to as the "cascading fade." This name is made up; PowerPoint does not refer to it in any way and does not really acknowledge that anyone would want to employ it. To be candid, we don't think that the development team imagined anyone wanting to do it, and we do not fault them for this oversight—hundreds of thousands of users have developed techniques well outside the fundamental construct of the program.

Back to the cascading fade. (This is a sidebar; we're allowed to digress. See, I just did it again.) Those are semi-involved steps that you would have to undertake to create the effect, and after awhile, it becomes tedious. I willingly deal with the tedium because I like the effect so much. However, I'd love to not have the tedium.

I could get my wish, too, if the development team would add one modest setting to the Fade animation: direction.

Imagine if you could ask that a headline Fade In From Left? That would eliminate the weird and awkward workaround that many undertake using Zoom and Fade together. And if I could set my bullets to Fade In From Top, they would naturally cascade down the slide.

That would put my technique out of business, and I would happily mourn its passing. Two clicks for a set of bullets instead of multiple clicks for each bullet? That's a no-brainer.

Best of all, because that would be an action performed on an entire bullet level, it could be programmed into the slide master. No more going slide to slide.

I'm not sure this qualifies as my No. 1 wish-list item—animation styles would still get the nod over this—but it's close. Very little was done to the Animation engine in version 2007, and it is my hope that the next version will see notable new features with animation. In anticipation, I will start whining and kvetching for direction to be added to Fade in the next version of the software.

1. Open the slide in question and make note of its background color. In our example, it is a blue gradient.

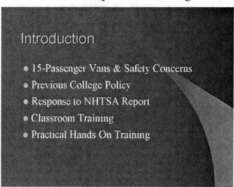

2. Create a thin rule in an out-of-the-way place, close to the color of the background. We placed ours along the bottom of the slide and filled it with a blue that is a bit lighter than the background.

3. Animate it, using the generic Appear for the type and After Previous for the Start. Make sure it is at the bottom of the animation sequence.

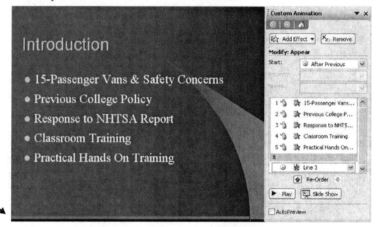

▼ Download 08-05.ppt to see this tactic in action.

Now when you show this slide, that thin rule will inconspicuously appear immediately after the last bullet appears. You know that your bullets for that slide have all displayed and you can focus on your ideas, without having to wonder if you dare click your remote one more time. It's an opportunity to reduce by one the things a presenter has to think about while in front of an audience.

Your audience probably won't notice your end-of-slide cue, but it's not a problem if they do. In fact, I know presenters who display a prominent "End of Slide" text box on their slide, in full view of everyone, after the last element appears. I don't think there is any problem at all allowing your audience to see the plumbing in your PowerPoint house. That just shows that you have given this some thought and are striving to create a smooth experience for everyone.

You are here

Should it become necessary to highlight the particular bullet you are speaking on, there are right ways and wrong ways to do it.

- Dimming everything except that bullet is the wrong way.

- Showing everything and then highlighting the current one is the right way.

▼ Download 08-06.ppt to see this effect in action.

The following example assumes that you need to show a lengthy list and discuss many of the points on that list. Our slide has 20 items on it, so we used the side-by-side layout, requiring that the following steps be performed twice.

Figure 8.6
Lengthy lists like this one are good candidates for a double animation that highlights the current point.

1. Animate your bullets however you normally do. We have chosen to create a fade on the master slide, set Fast, After Previous.

2. On the slide, select the bullet placeholder and add the Change Font Color emphasis. Pick a color close to the font color. With our white text on a dark background, we chose yellow.

3. From the Effects dialog box (right-click on the object in the Animation task pane to get there), set the After Animation to be the original color of the bullets.

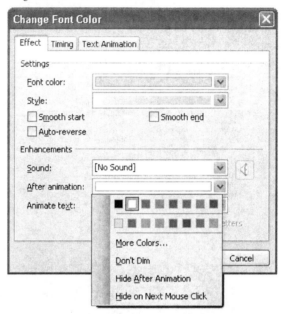

To summarize, there are two animations applied to the text. The first one is a conventional fade that brings all of the bullets in at once. The second animation, set On Click, changes the color of each bullet with each click of the mouse or remote. And while each click changes a bullet's color, it also sets the previous bullet's color back to its original.

I vastly prefer this to dimming or spoon-feeding the text. This double-animation technique gets all of the text out there at once and then allows you to highlight each one without being condescending.

We spent many minutes coming up with an example that we think justifies this type of treatment—the lengthy list of countries in Figure 8.6. Here it would be completely appropriate to highlight each country that you intended to speak about as you addressed it.

We might only employ this technique once a year. Please do not use it without good cause!

Chapter 9

Be the Master of Your Own Slide

The name of this chapter can be interpreted two ways: one, to be so adept at the mechanics of slide creation that you can pump them out in record time; two, to be smart and use the built-in tools that automate slide formatting.

We accept either interpretation.

This chapter focuses on the potentially dramatic control you can wield over your work by using the Slide Master engine.

It is also the first chapter requiring that we depart from our practice of *versionlessness*. Those still using PowerPoint from Office 2000 will suffer version envy through much of this discussion of slide masters, and those using PowerPoint 2007 will find this component to be entirely redesigned, so much so that it gets its own chapter, right after this one.

A Semantic of Questions

Wait, shouldn't the headline at left be "A Question of Semantics?" Yes, it should, just like Microsoft should have chosen between calling them *slide masters* and referring to the *master slide*. It is one of several instances of lazy language on the part of the program developers, which serves to inhibit total understanding of this otherwise fine tool. So let's begin with a definition of terms, courtesy of PowerPoint's on-line Help:

Slide Master
An element of the design template that stores information about the template, including font styles, placeholders, sizes, positions, background design, and color schemes.

Master Slide
See Slide Master.

Design Template
This file contains all of the following: the styles in a presentation, including the type and size of bullets and fonts; placeholder sizes and positions; background design and fill color schemes.

Title Master
Contains placeholders for a title, subtitle, and headers and footers.

◆

These definitions seem perfectly fine on their face, until you dive into the program. At that point, you will discover:

- Slide masters do not live just inside of a design template; they are a part of every PowerPoint file created. More to the point, there is no intrinsic difference between a PowerPoint template and a regular PowerPoint file.

- The program interface refers to individual slide masters as templates.

- The Title master is not a separate master onto itself but part of a set of masters.

- The most intuitive maneuver for applying a specific master to a particular slide will actually apply that master to every slide in your presentation, which most of the time is not what you would want.

Once you overcome these cognitive hurdles, working with slide masters is not difficult. But we know from surveying hundreds of content creators that these hurdles keep many from becoming one with slide masters. Therefore, one focus of this chapter will be to help you overcome the gotchas and the confusing terminology.

Understanding the Slide Master

At its core, the slide master is a global control: elements that you place on it will be present on the individual slides of your presentation. Similarly, formatting that you apply to those elements will affect the look and behavior of individual slides.

Object creation and formatting are carried out the same on a slide master as on a regular slide, so half the battle is in finding your way:

View | Master | Slide Master

That takes you to the relatively simple interface shown here in Figure 9.1. With very few exceptions, everything you can do on a normal slide can also be done here:

- Format titles and bullets

- Choose a background

- Add photos

- Create an animation scheme

▶ Does my interface look different than yours? That's because it has been customized to suit my every whim, and to help readers follow along with instructions. See Chapter 25 to learn how you can do it, too.

Figure 9.1
The slide master's first impression is not much different than that of a standard slide.

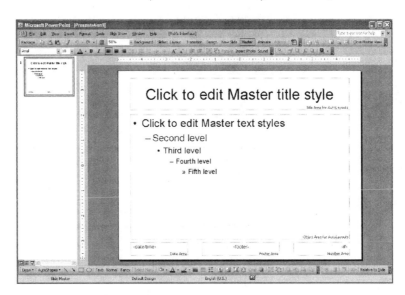

Part Two: The Solution

The one significant difference in behavior is a friendly one: it's much easier to format the placeholders. Local text formatting inside a placeholder has no meaning on a slide master — you can't drag across two or three words of the sample text ("Click to edit Master text styles") and make any meaningful changes to them. Those words get replaced by the actual content on your slides, so nothing that you do to individually selected words matters at all.

Therefore, any formatting you do inside a placeholder is done to the entire level that is selected. Plant your cursor anywhere and PowerPoint assumes you are formatting the level, not a word on that line. In fact, when you first plant your cursor, you'll notice that the entire level is initially selected.

So a single click is all you need to tell PowerPoint what to change.

The Title Master

Creative editor Sandy Johnson recommends the following analogies to help with this confusing terminology:

Title Master = Cover slide

Master Title = Headline

The first point of confusion that befalls users is the direction that appears in big letters:

Click to edit Master title style

They see the word "title" in Figure 9.1 and think that this has to do with their title slide. It doesn't. Most slide formats include a title—this placeholder controls the appearance and function of the title on any slide in the presentation that uses this slide master.

In order to create a specific design for the title slide(s) in your presentation, you would create a "title master," easily achieved by right-clicking on the slide thumbnail and clicking New Title Master.

Not so fast, though. The key to creating your title master is not the how, but the *when*. When title masters are born, they inherit the attributes of the slide master, but as they grow up, they have lives of their own. Most changes made to the slide master do not affect the title master, and vice-versa.

We hope that you seek an integrated design throughout your presentation, both title and content slides. To accomplish that, your two masters would share many attributes, such as background, color scheme, font choice, etc. If you were to create your title master from the presentation in Figure 9.1, it would look just as plain as the slide master does.

Figure 9.2 shows a more refined design, the one that we used as the standard template for all presentations given at PowerPoint Live a few years ago. This is the right time to create the title master, which, as you can see by its thumbnail, picks up all of the elements designed into the slide master.

Figure 9.2

Wait until you have finished designing the major elements of your slide master (top thumbnail) before creating your title master (lower thumbnail)—it will eliminate much repetition.

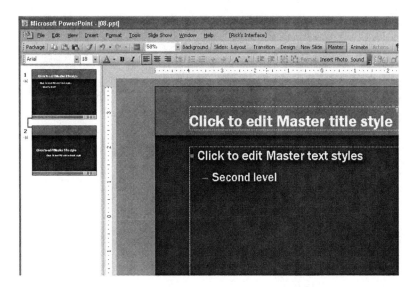

▶ Deb Shenenberg of Scottsdale AZ designed this template and submitted it to the annual PowerPoint Live Design Contest. As the winning entry, Deb won a free pass to the conference. To enter the contest, visit www.pptlive.com.

There is one attribute that is linked between the two masters...sort of. If you format the Master Title style in the slide master, that change will be reflected in the title master. The reverse is not true, however, and this bedevils unsuspecting users who see their titles change seemingly randomly. So again, go as far as you can with your slide master design before creating the title master.

Creating Multiple Masters

At this point, have you created one master or two? Simple question...complicated answer. In the thumbnails of Figure 9.2, there is a gray connector line linking the two slides. That is your cue that these two masters are joined at the virtual hip. It is better to think of them as a single set of masters. Hover the mouse over either one and you will see that they are named the same (Default Design).

Since PowerPoint XP (the one previous to PowerPoint 2003), ambitious users can create additional sets of masters, proving invaluable for those seeking maximum flexibility through minimal effort. We'll walk through one of the classic examples right now: the creation of a "print master," to facilitate the printing of a presentation. (While it is fine for

Figure 9.3
If you want a new master to look like an existing one, don't use the New Title Master command. That will get you a plain slide and buy you a lot of extra work.

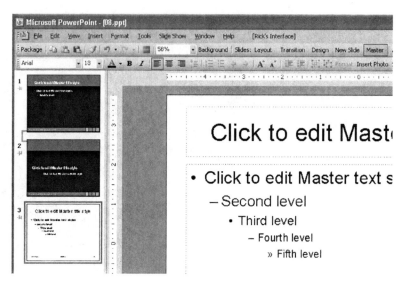

projected presentations to be white text on black, it is far better for printed presentations to be black text on white.)

If you were to create the second master according to conventional instructions, you would not be a happy camper. Figure 9.3 shows the result of right-clicking in the thumbnail area and choosing New Slide Master: a plain vanilla master with none of your design elements. Instead, do this:

1. Select one of your master thumbnails and copy and paste it (Ctrl+C and Ctrl+V), or press Ctrl+D to duplicate it.

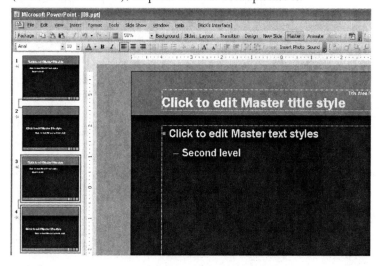

2. Individually, select the new title master and delete it.

Why would you do this? For the same reason that you would

delay creating a title master in the first place—so that it can inherit the formatting you perform on the slide master.

3. On the new slide master, select the entire master text style placeholder. In other words, don't just drop your cursor onto one of the text levels; select the boundary for the placeholder that houses all of the text levels. The easiest way to accomplish this is to press and hold Shift while you click the text. If your cursor is already planted in the text, press Esc to change the selection to the placeholder.

4. Set the text to black. It will promptly disappear against the black background.

5. Change the slide background to white, being careful to click Apply, and not Apply to All, which in this case would change the background for all masters.

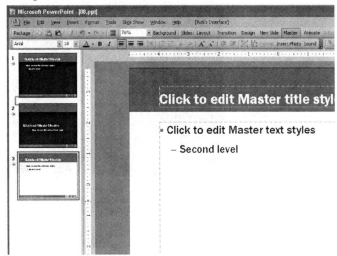

6. Right-click the new master thumbnail and choose New Title Master, at which point the only tweak that is needed is to set the title to black and perhaps center it in its placeholder.

7. Right-click either new master thumbnail, choose Rename Master, and call it Print.

▶ At your discretion, consider changing the face to a serif type, generally regarded as more readable for printed output. See Chapter 18 for more discussion about typeface usage.

You now have a set of masters tuned for printing out your presentation. How do you use this second set of masters?

1. Return to Normal view.

2. Go to Format | Slide Design to invoke the Slide Design task pane.

3. From the section entitled "Apply a design template used in this presentation," right-click your new slide master, entitled Print, and choose Apply to All Slides.

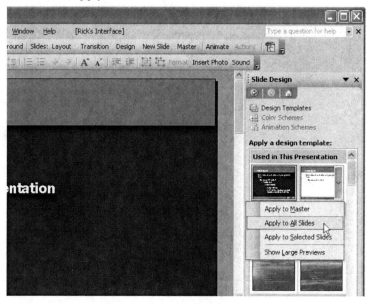

This change is instantaneous across every slide in your presentation: they all immediately take on the look of the Print master.

Changing out an entire presentation is simple; ironically, applying a new slide master to just one or two slides is not as easy. For reasons known only to the developers, the default action when you click on a new master in the Slide Design task pane is to apply it to *every* slide in the presentation. And the command is called "Apply to Master," which makes no sense to most of us. How do you apply a slide master to the master? What does that even mean?

If you aren't aware of this quirk, it could have a negative impact on your career. To apply a slide master only to the selected slide, you must right-click the master (or click the downward-pointing arrow) and choose Apply to Selected Slide.

Once you understand that quirk of the interface, you can make peace with slide masters and how they are used.

Mixing and Matching

There are countless examples of opportunities to create additional sets of slide masters. I have colleagues and clients who have designed:

- Quote masters with a large quote mark tinted into the background and room for a photo and attribution

- Section divider slides to signal changes in topic

- Question slides with large question marks or just the words "Any Questions?"

- Ending slides that prominently display contact information and company URL.

If you download columbus.ppt, you will see an example of how Christopher Columbus might have made use of multiple slide masters when trying to get funding from the Queen for his big voyage. There are four sets of masters in that file:

Standard: Conventional design with basic Wipe Right applied to the bullets.

Print: Designed specifically for printouts.

Self-Running Presentation: Columbus isn't certain that he will be able to get an audience with the Queen in person, so he designed a set of masters in case he needs to, um, email his presentation to her. This set offers a bit more animation (without a live presenter, the slides need to work a bit harder) and includes prompts for when to advance to the next slide.

Just the Facts: The Queen is a very busy lady who doesn't have time for things to spin, fly, wipe, or even fade. This set of masters displays each slide with no motion at all.

We noted earlier the unfortunate choice to make the default action be that of applying a slide master to every slide in the deck instead of just the current one. The other obtuse aspect of slide masters is the developers' decision to refer to them as "design templates" in the Slide Design task pane. A template file lives on a different rung of the conceptual ladder from a slide master (slide masters are a part of every presentation file; a template *is* a presentation file). Granted, you can import the slide design from a template or from a different presentation file in the same way that you swap out a slide master. Nonetheless, the decision to refer to a slide master as a template has served to confuse more than enlighten.

▶ There are two other types of masters in PowerPoint: the Handout master and the Notes master, both of which we plead guilty to ignoring. If you print handouts regularly, it is worth taking the time to explore the ways in which the standard layouts for handouts can be customized. And consult Chapter 17 for an unconventional suggestion for the use of the Notes master.

Understanding Design Templates

Apologies in advance if this section comes off as glib or flippant.

> **To create a template,**
> **rename the extension to .pot.**

That, ladies and gentlemen, is the entire difference between a regular presentation file and a template in versions 2003 and earlier. You can turn any presentation file into a template by changing its extension. When you double-click a .pot file, Windows does not open it directly; instead, it imports the content into a new, untitled, unsaved presentation.

▶ If you wanted to directly edit a template file, use the Open command within PowerPoint and change the Files of Type filter to Design Templates.

Any PowerPoint file, regardless of its extension, can be used as a template to spawn other presentations. All of the choices are available from the Slide Design task pane:

- Slide masters within the current presentation

- Presentation templates that live on your hard drive, either because you created them or because they were placed there during the program's installation

- Templates that you download from the Microsoft Office web site

- And via the Browse button, any presentation file—.ppt, .pot, or even .pps extension—that you can find within your network of computers

The Best Templates are .ppt Files Loaded with Content

In observing the behavior of hundreds of clients over the years, we have concluded that template files (.pot files) are best left for the cookie-cutter templates that come with the product. When you create your own templates, make them .ppt files, not .pot files. It makes life easier for all.

When you start a project by applying a .pot file, PowerPoint loads the slide masters, but no content. That's the idea of a template, to provide a starting point.

But most people prefer a starting point that has content. Boilerplate text, slides that represent typical ideas, builds of specific graphs, skeleton org charts, etc.

Well-conceived templates should include this type of springboard content to jumpstart the creative process and the simplest way to do that is to just use a .ppt file. No matter how you open it, all of your content appears, ready for you to begin tailoring it for the specific project.

At right are four slides from a recent redesign project that included four slide masters and 25 slides of sample content. Having all of this content as part of the template is standard operating procedure for any job that we take. We consider it an indispensible part of any design project.

The only risk to using .ppt files as templates: if you forget to perform a Save As command before embarking on a new project, you overwrite the template. Make the .ppt template a read-only file to insure against this happening.

Master Miscellany

With any version later than 2000, the idea of creating more than one set of masters within your presentation file takes you to a new plateau of productivity and it is worth the investment of time and creative effort to try to anticipate your future needs and build masters that would address them.

- How many ways do you present your company logo?

- Do you regularly create segue slides between sections or topics? Would you rather not simply reuse the title slide layout?

- Do you like to design your own "blank" slide?

- Do you create nice watermarked backgrounds but still regularly need to work with a flat background?

These are a few of the scenarios that are addressed with the creation of more than one set of slide masters in a presentation. Start to take advantage of them and you officially graduate from the School of the First 30 Minutes.

Chapter 10

Thriving with Version 2007 Masters and Layouts

There are myriad reasons why Office 2007 has not exactly taken the world by storm, and we who interact with corporate America see the chief reason on a daily basis: corporate wheels turn oh-so-slowly and many large organizations are not yet ready for the migration path and the learning curve of a new office suite.

(The aside to this is telling: many of these same companies have not been ready to make that move for years; hence, the number of them who are still using Office XP and even Office 2000.)

Office 2007 is a stroke from a completely different brush. Ribbons replace menus and groups stand in for toolbars. Unlike Vista, which has earned its disdain due to poor performance, most of the resistance to Office 2007 is due to its *otherness*.

This is a quality that many do not appreciate in their basic computing tools, and we understand that sentiment. If, for the past 20 years, you have counted upon Word, Excel, a screwdriver, a can opener, your shoelaces, or the faucet at your sink to function a certain way, how excited would you become if everything about its appearance and function changed?

This is all notwithstanding the fact that PowerPoint 2007 is a sound piece of software with very few bugs plaguing it and several compelling new features gracing it. And the most compelling of all? In the eyes of many, it would be the new paradigm for global formatting: slide masters and their corresponding layouts.

The Design / Layout Disconnect

As strong as global formatting has been since Version XP, one element of needless complexity has been the relationship between slide masters and layouts. Consider what you have had to do in order to apply a new master to a slide and change its layout:

1. Select the slide.

2. Open the Slide Design task pane.

3. Choose the desired slide master, taking care not to inadvertently apply that master to every slide in your deck.

4. Then switch to the Slide Layout task pane.

5. Choose the desired layout.

6. And more often than not with existing slides, right-click the layout and click Reapply.

Indeed, slide masters and layouts have lived in completely different neighborhoods—masters being thought of as global design elements, layouts being thought of as mere holders of slide attributes.

Version 2007 changes that relationship entirely, offering both increased control and much better access. In short:

You no longer apply a slide master to a slide
The slide master identifies a group of layouts, any one of which is applied to a slide.

The layout is now the primary formatting tool
While you have always had plenty of layouts to choose from in prior versions, you had little control over their appearances, and most went

unused and even unnoticed. In V07, you have complete control over them. You decide what they are called, what elements are placed on them, and how many to keep within a given slide master.

You choose the placeholders

Previous versions offer various combinations of title, subtitle, and up to two text placeholders, forcing even moderately ambitious designers to place repeating elements on the slide itself. The classic example being the title slide designed to hold a speaker's name, her position, and maybe a photo. There has been no provision for those common elements on the masters, so you have had to build them on the slide itself, and then take care to maintain consistent formatting across those slides that are to be formatted that way.

In V07, you can create placeholders on the Title layout for those elements, ensuring their consistent placement, size, and format.

One-stop shopping for your designs

You no longer have to jockey between the Slide Design and Slide Layout task panes to format your slides. When you pull down the Layout gallery, every layout contained within any slide master is available for selection, and you no longer have to worry about inadvertently applying one of them to every slide in the deck. In my opinion, it is the single most important interface improvement offered by version 2007.

Finding Your Way Around

Locating even familiar commands in V07 can be a chore, so we can relate to the potential frustration in learning an entirely redesigned set of commands. And I don't have to go far to find people who have not completely embraced the whole Ribbon thing—several of them are on our editing team and the jury is still out with our lead author, yours truly.

Your instincts would be entirely correct if they told you to look for something that said Slide Master, but unlike the reliable View | Master | Slide Master command in V03 and earlier, it will not always be in the same place. This is due to the context-sensitive Ribbon that offers you different groups of commands and functions depending upon what you are doing and what you have selected. So remember this:

- You will find access to the three masters—slide, handout, and notes—on the View tab of the Ribbon.

- You can access the View menu by pressing Alt+W, and once you do, you can press M to enter Slide Master view. And you do not need to wait for the View ribbon to appear before pressing M, so a quick Alt+W M will always get you into Slide Master view.

■ If the keystroke shortcut from previous versions (Alt+V M S) has been forever burned into your consciousness, just do it—it will still work. The interface will not react much when you start typing this shortcut, so it's best to not even look. Just start typing those keystrokes and when you're done, PowerPoint will figure out what you meant and execute the command, just as if you were still in a previous version.

Using the Quick Access Toolbar

version 2007 does not have the same ability to customize the interface offered by previous versions. While the more you use it, the more shortcuts you will discover, the only way to add your favorite commands to a permanent visible location is with the so-called Quick Access Toolbar (QAT). And you might need your reading glasses nearby—the icons are small!

The QAT lives either above the Ribbon or below it (above by default) and just about any command available across the program can be added to it. Commands cannot be shown by text, so you will need to memorize location or learn which icon represents which command.

You can customize the QAT by right-clicking the Office button or any part of the Ribbon (it's part of the redesigned PowerPoint Options super dialog). Once there, you can search for any command and add it to the QAT.

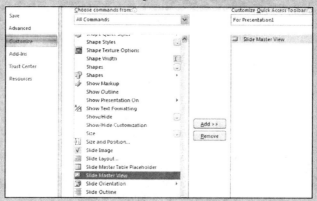

If you prefer to drive with the mouse, you should waste not a moment adding Slide Master access to the Quick Access Toolbar so it will always be available, regardless of context (see sidebar below).

Once in Slide Master view, you can proceed with design building and formatting as you would if working directly on the slide—which probably means slowly and methodically. Few among us are so fluent with V07 that we whip around the interface as fast as in V03. If you feel as if you are still stumbling around, rest assured you have lots of company! Most do get comfortable with the interface over time.

You can also add commands to the QAT by finding them on the interface, right-clicking, and choosing Add to Quick Access Toolbar. So to add Slide Master view to the QAT, click View and right-click on Slide Master.

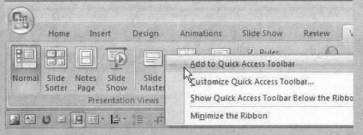

We recommend one additional step: place Close Master view on the QAT, as well. The command lives on the Slide Master ribbon, which activates as you enter Slide Master view. But as you begin earnest formatting work there, the Ribbon will inevitably change, and the command will disappear from view. Adding Close Master view to the QAT ensures that you can always access it, regardless of context.

Alt+M C will always close Slide Master view, as well, irrespective of context. Perhaps more important, press Alt and note that every item on your QAT is assigned a number. Remember those numbers and the Quick Access Toolbar truly lives up to its name.

The Relationship Between Slide Masters and Layouts

Upon entering Slide Master view, the thumbnails on the left reveal a clear parent-child relationship, with the slide master appearing larger than the layouts underneath. Formatting applied to the slide master is reflected on the layouts:

- Set the title bold and all title placeholders in all layouts become bold.

- Increase the typesize of bullet text and most text placeholders adjust.

- Add animation to a level and you'll find it on all layouts that have that level of text.

- Add a logo to the lower-right corner and you'll instantly see it on every layout.

Any layout can be overridden with local formatting and some layouts do not follow the slide master. For instance, if you change the size of bullet text, the two-column layouts will not reflect that change—perhaps the developers felt that these layouts would have an identity all their own, and that makes sense to us.

Once you address the most global of questions like typeface, style, size, basic alignment and the like (the ones that would be addressed on the slide master itself), you will then dive into the layouts, where you will find more control than ever before. It is here where you make the decisions that have the most direct and basic affect on your slides.

There are layouts for a dizzying array of scenarios. And if any one of them is not quite right, change any aspect of it. Perhaps more important, create your own layouts, based entirely on the needs and demands of your slide design. This is light years from the blunt distinction between title master and slide master or the rigid layouts that could not be tailored.

▶ Selecting thumbnails in version 2007 is tricky and Microsoft has done no favors for its contingent of color-blind users. In all views of the program, the selected slide is shown with an orange gradient background. If you hover over a slide, it takes on a yellow-to-orange gradient, which persists for as long as the cursor is atop it. We're not sure the benefit of the hover background, but it does keep us on our toes.

Figure 10.1
This slide deck contains three slide masters and 17 layouts. All 17 are available to be applied to the current slide.

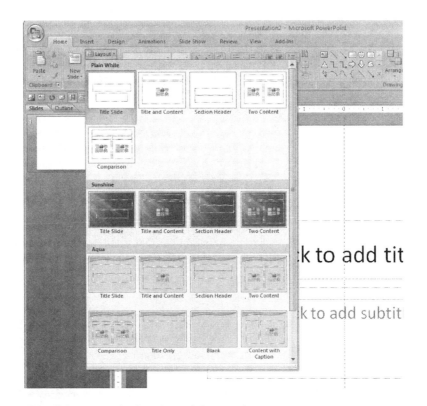

The Slide Master is the King of the Castle

From its perch, the slide master presides over all of its layouts, but it does so like a king over his country: with aloofness. While a slide is identified as belonging to a particular master, you do not overtly apply the master to a slide. It is not actually possible. Instead, you choose a layout, from any slide master that exists in the file. It doesn't matter how many slide masters there are or how many layouts each might contain—every layout that exists in a file is available for use, as you can see in Figure 10.1

The Layouts are the Royal Guards

Reporting directly to the king, the layouts are the real power brokers in the royal court. They directly control how a slide looks, feels, and behaves. They are much more powerful than slide layouts of previous versions; in fact, they are more like V03 slide masters than layouts.

The Slides are the People

As with previous versions, the slides themselves are governed by those higher up in the power structure. As with any constituency, the masses have little authority but without them, nothing would be possible.

The mechanics of working with layouts involves skills that any capable PowerPoint user already possesses, regardless of version. Once in Slide

Master view, you can select, rename, create new, and delete layouts all with right-clicks. You edit them by adding elements. There are plenty of nuances, and we'll get to them, but the core fundamentals of object creation and placement are no different than regular slide work.

▶ You can only delete a layout if no slide is using it. This is wise insurance for new users, and a source of irritation for advanced users.

Being Smart With Layouts

Layouts can take on any design motif imaginable—different typefaces, different colors, different animation schemes, different backgrounds. Elements can be moved anywhere on the slide and formatted with all of the robust controls available across the application. It is possible to make layouts of the same slide master look entirely different from one another.

Possible, yes. Wise…perhaps not. Smart designers resist making these types of wholesale changes to a layout, preferring instead to use the same basic design for all layouts of a given slide master. If a set of slides is to have a radically different look, they create a second master. (And if it really is a single slide that warrants unique treatment, you can just format the slide itself.)

As with previous versions, there is a lot of flotsam in the layout choices. But unlike previous versions, you can jettison any unwanted layout, and more important, create new layouts. As we observe people using V07's Slide Master view, we note two things:

- Some are hesitant about removing a layout for fear that they might decide later on that they want it after all.

- Others keep all the layouts in place and have difficulty wading through all of them.

Our advice is to make the interface as easy to work as possible and that argues for removing layouts you do not intend to use and making room for your own layouts. We think the more layouts you build from scratch, the more deft you become with the process.

Figure 10.2
Does the presence of a photo warrant the use of a separate layout in version 2007? Maybe...

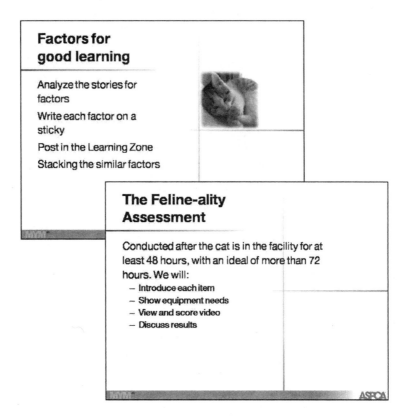

▶ If you remove a layout and later decide you want it back, you can retrieve it from a new presentation with a simple copy-and-paste maneuver. Layouts copy from one presentation to another just as slides do. A pasted layout takes on the attributes of the slide master that it now belongs to.

Flexibility vs. universality

One of the pleasant problems created by V07 layouts is the question of just how specialized to become. For instance, what if you were creating a slide design that called for some slides to have standard left-aligned text under the title and other slides to have photos to the right of the text? Figure 10.2 shows these two different designs. But should they literally be different designs? Do they need two separate layouts?

■ If you create two layouts for them, you might be able to create the slides faster (more flexible).

■ If you use one layout for both of them, you can control formatting changes more easily by not having to repeat those changes across two layouts (more universal).

In the top slide, the placeholder's right margin is tighter to allow for the photo, while the bottom slide allows the text to stretch further to the right. With a dedicated layout for the slide with the photo, you would have less slide fiddling to do, no question about it. However, with a criterion as exacting as this, you are liable to create many layouts, making control over them more difficult.

You enjoy far more control than in previous versions, no matter which way you go—whether you group multiple designs around a common layout or make layouts for every design permutation.

We're not ready to offer definitive advice to this question as usage patterns are still new and evolving. Instead, we suggest you ask two questions of yourself as the litmus test:

- Can I save time and/or effort by creating an extra layout?
- Will I create more work for myself if I have to manage two or more layouts when one layout might do the job?

We will say if you regularly backsave to V03, think twice about creating many layouts. There is no clean translation of them back to V03 and the usual result is a tremendous mess of redundant slide masters.

The other quirk we are tracking is behavior with a V07 template file that has had some of its original layouts removed. When that file is applied to a deck that still has those layouts, the results are unpredictable. If this has happened to you, we'd love to hear about it so we can add to the collective wisdom on this issue.

Ordering, naming, and identifying

In previous versions, slide layouts were displayed in a pre-ordained sequence, irrespective of your usage or preference. Version 2007 allows you to determine the order of the layouts and we suggest you take full advantage of that. Furthermore, while you used to be stuck with the names that the developers devised, now you can create your own names and give them much more context than "Title, Content and 2 Content."

See the upcoming case study on the ASPCA for some strategies for layout creation and implementation.

The ASPCA case study also addresses the one aspect of layouts that we think was handled poorly: identifying them. While tool tips identify each layout in Slide Master view, there is nothing to tell you which layout is used when in Normal view. The Status Bar only identifies the name of the Slide Master used by that slide (and it incorrectly refers to it as a "theme"). This is not nearly as useful as knowing which layout is being used.

Adding Placeholders

We plead guilty to burying the lead: down here on the 11th page of this chapter is perhaps the most valuable aspect of 2007 layouts—the ability to add additional placeholders to slides.

Let's return to the classic example we alluded to earlier: the title slide that is to serve to introduce each seminar and person speaking at a multi-day conference. Figure 10.3 shows one of the slide designs we used at PowerPoint Live 2008, created by Lindsey Stroebel, the winner of our Design-a-Template contest for that year.

This title slide has five elements that should all be consistently format-ted across three days and over 40 presentations. In previous versions, those elements would have to be placed on the slide and constantly checked against accidental repositioning, reformatting, or other hazards that could befall them. Not so in version 2007. Here is how we built this layout:

1. On the slide master itself, we placed all of the background ele-ments: the photo, the transparent gradient over it, the compass logo, and a subtle swoosh at the top that is probably not visible in black and white.

Figure 10.3
There are five elements on this slide whose content will change every time, but its formatting should never change. This is a job for version 2007's Layouts.

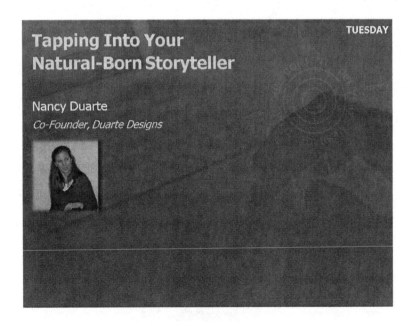

2. While still on the slide master, we assigned basic formatting to the title and text placeholder: 28pt Tahoma Bold for titles, 24pt Tahoma Normal for text.

3. On the Title layout, we moved the title to the top and changed the placeholder text to read "Title of presentation..."

   In version 2007, when you change the placeholder text on a layout, it displays that text on the slide. We're big fans of doing that to better simulate a title's appearance.

4. As we did not plan on having subtitles for the seminars, we deleted the subtitle placeholder.

5. From the Slide Master ribbon, we clicked Insert Placeholder to get a drop-down menu of our choices.

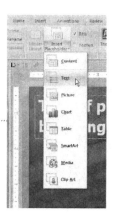

6. We chose Text and then dragged a marquee in the general location we had laid out for the name of the presenter.

Good thing we can change the placeholder text—what a mess with all five levels of bullets being anticipated. We wish we could change the default for that; next best thing is to remove them and enter our own placeholder text.

7. We fine-tuned the size and location of the placeholder and repeated the process for the speaker bio and day of week. For the latter, we used V07's All Caps setting to ensure consistent formatting.

8. We then added a *picture placeholder* to this layout and sized and placed it to taste.

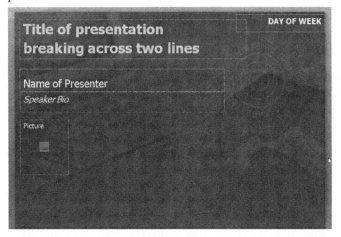

This exciting new feature allows you to define a place on a slide where a photo will go, but be able to make it a different photo on each slide.

Each of these five placeholders gets replaced with unique content on a new slide. The custom placeholder is the element that really makes layouts sing. With them, you can be, at the same time, a better designer and a more efficient content creator.

Odds and Ends with Layouts

Here is a collection of thoughts, discoveries, and miscellaneous musings around slide masters and layouts.

Applying a layout to every slide in a deck

One of our biggest complaints with version 2003 is how easy it is to inadvertently apply a slide master to every slide in the deck when you were intending to apply it to just one slide. Ironically, the opposite is the case with version 2007...and we'll take the trade.

Look at the Cute Doggy on the Slide...

When the American Society for the Prevention of Cruelty to Animals approached me to redesign its slide decks, I knew it would be a perfect opportunity to use version 2007's layouts. With so many different slide types and so few controls in place, the Society's existing slides were, um, a bit of the dog's breakfast. **1**

I created 16 layouts for the ASPCA and the first challenge came with the title, designed differently than the rest of the slides. The title has a larger footer and none of the crossing lines. **2 & 3**

I first created a separate slide master for the title, isolating it from the other layouts. The alternative was to cover up the elements with white rectangles and place the title elements on top. Then Sandy Johnson reminded me about the Hide Background Graphics checkbox, which in this case worked great, as I wished to remove all of the background graphics. If I need to swap out just one or two, the dual-master strategy works.

My client's favorite slide was the three-topic slide, with placeholders governing size, shape, and placement. She admitted that trying to keep these consistent with earlier software versions was frustrating and tedious. **4**

And my favorite trick was borne out of necessity as V07 does not indicate the layout used in normal slide view. So I began including a text box off to the side, displaying the name of the layout. This, too, I can already tell will become standard operating procecure. **5**

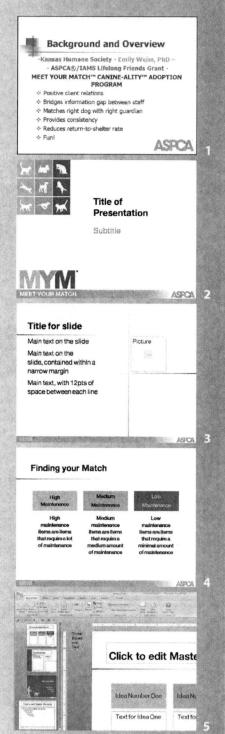

Hallelujah that we are delivered from the one-false-move threat of ruining a slide deck with a runaway slide master! But if you *want* to apply a layout to every slide, you won't actually find an Apply to All command. Instead, you must actually select every slide. You can do this in the Slide pane (the thumbnails on the left) without too much trouble.

The mysterious vertical layouts

The standard arrangement of layouts shows two intriguing layouts that run 90 degrees clockwise from the others. These so-called vertical layouts (below left) are ideal for turning a slide into a printout (below right), but you are likely to find something peculiar about them: they are probably unavailable to you, refusing to show up on the Layout menu. We discovered that they only show up if you have enabled support for Chinese, Japanese, or Korean languages. Say what??

We see value in these layouts far beyond support for languages that read 90 degrees opposite English. If activating one of these other languages is outside your comfort zone, do this:

1. Duplicate the Blank layout.

2. Go to the forbidden layout and copy the placeholders.

3. Return to your new layout and paste.

4. Design the rest of the layout to taste.

This new layout will now show up in the Layout menu, even though it is essentially identical to the one that won't. Go figure...

Figure 10.6

Using the vertical layouts can be quite useful—as long as you learn the secret password...

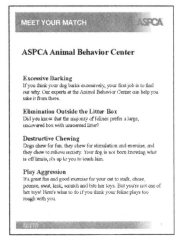

Apply layouts via the QAT

The Layout gallery is located on the Home ribbon, which is designed as the location for the most popular commands across the program. Yet Murphy's Law usually demands that I am always on a different ribbon when I want to apply a layout to a slide.

So I have placed the entire Layout gallery on the Quick Access Toolbar. This is most easily done with a simple right-click on the menu. It takes up the sixth position on my QAT, so I have committed to memory that Alt+6 will open it. With my fingers already on the keyboard, I then navigate through my layouts with the arrow keys and then press Enter to apply the one I want.

Much faster and easier than finding it with the mouse.

Right-click your way to a layout

You can also reach the Layout gallery from the context, or right-click menu. You can right-click on an empty part of the slide or on the thumbnail.

Your own custom notes in the slide margin

On the previous page, I shared the trick of creating a text string just off the slide to identify the layout in use. Let's do that maneuver one better with a place to write notes of your own. Just create a text placeholder off the slide, close enough to the edge so that you can see it while editing the slide. Keep the placeholder narrow and the text small, like about 12pt, and pick a color with good contrast (white if the placeholder is near the bottom where the color is dark or black if you have parked it near the top).

Figure 10.7
Placeholders off the slide can be useful too. This one is for notes to self or commentary to others.

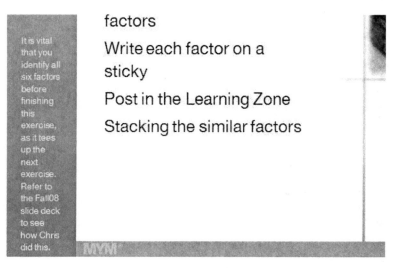

With this placeholder, any slide can now contain notes, instructions, comments, complaints, general whining, and the like. They can be notes to a collaborator or notes to yourself. I have found this preferable to using the Notes window at the bottom, which might or might not be visible or deep enough. On my wide-screen monitor, though, I rarely lack horizontal space so the area to the left or right of the slide is always visible. Figure 10.7 shows an example.

Two clicks get you a new slide and a layout

The New Slide command on the Home ribbon does just what you would expect it to do. But if you click the lower-half of the icon, the part with the downward-pointing arrow, you are taken to the now-familiar Layout gallery, allowing you to designate which layout your new slide is to have.

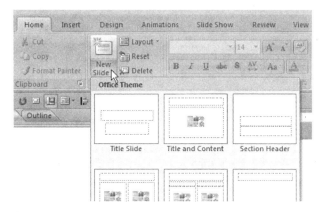

Chapter 11

The Theory Of the Theme

If slide masters and layouts represent the most significant change from older versions of PowerPoint, the idea of the Theme is the most dramatic, and perhaps the most glitzy. With a theme, you can not only create a fully-branded look and feel for your slide decks, you can extend it out to your other Office documents.

While themes work as promised, we remain unconvinced that many users will make the effort to understand and use them to capacity. It reminds us of the way that most users approach color schemes of earlier versions: with uncertainty and a lack of confidence.

In fact, when we first wrote up this part, we had it tacked on to the end of the previous chapter and it wasn't until almost press time that we chose to give it its own chapter. The irony there is that we could probably write an entire book on this topic...

Just Make It Look Good!

At the simplest level, applying a theme is an easy way to spiff up a slide deck, with easy-to-apply designs that are much more integrated, coordinated, and attractive than the .pot template files that came with previous versions. The Design ribbon offers a gateway to 20 themes and you can hover over any one of them to see how the current slide would look with that theme applied to it. You can also get one-click access to dozens of professionally-crafted themes, such as the two in Figure 11.1.

Although a theme is a better starting point than the old .pot files, we'd be happier if you created your own themes around your company branding. Just like the ocean/sunset template, these too are likely to become clichés, and if they do, they don't speak well of those who use them.

One Theme Equals Three Schemes

A theme contains slide masters and layouts and is further comprised of three distinct elements that together define the total look and feel of a slide deck.

- A set of theme colors, containing 12 color definitions—four more than in previous versions but otherwise similar

- A set of theme fonts, a simple pairing of two typefaces—one applied to titles and one to text

Figure 11.1
Two themes from the Office website, downloaded and applied to slides in about 30 seconds.

■ A set of theme effects, holding information about fill patterns, outlines, special effects, and backgrounds

▶ You can apply these theme effects to a slide deck all at once or you can
apply any one scheme by itself. The first two schemes mentioned above
are user-servicable, sure to be the source of delight for advanced users.
More on that soon.

Themes are the next generation of templates and can be used as starting points for new slide decks or applied to existing ones. Like a standard V07 file, they are written in the XML language, making them
very portable and pliable. Theme files have .thmx extensions and if you
were to study a .pptx and a .thmx file, you would find many similari-
ties in content and structure. In fact, you can tell PowerPoint to load a
theme from a .pptx file and it will do so with no backtalk at all.

If you can get a theme from a PowerPoint file, why bother with theme
files? Their value is in their portability, to other people and to other
applications.

Send a theme to a colleague

If you create a slide deck that is to serve as the model for others, you
can save it as a .thmx file (File | Save As | Office Theme) and send it to
a client or co-worker. This is largely similar to sending a .pot file, and
our advice from Chapter 9 holds: it is often better to send a regular
PowerPoint file than a content-less template file. Nonetheless, when
you share a .thmx file with another, you send that person every master,
every layout, the color scheme, and font and special effects
information.

Send a theme to your Office

The more interesting twist to this is the extensibility with other Office
2007 applications. The theme you create in PowerPoint can be applied
to a Word document, an Excel worksheet, and Outlook stationery.
This is branding on steroids: logos, backgrounds, type choices, color
palettes—they can all be standardized across your Office documents.

Each V07 app has a Themes button that contains a Browse for Themes
command. Use that in your other apps to retrieve a theme from
PowerPoint and you're on your way to a more unified look and feel
across your documents.

Part Two: The Solution

Figure 11.2
The Colors drop-down is loaded with well-crafted color themes, as well as ones that you can create yourself.

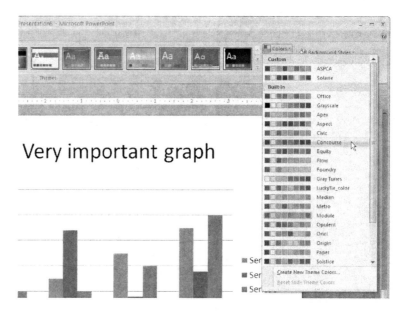

As interesting and as impressive as this intramural feature is, I have my doubts that many users will go this extra mile with themes. Here is why I feel this way:

- I have seen how users wrestle with color schemes in Verson 2003, a simpler paradigm than themes, and I suspect that they will be content to create slides that look good onto themselves.

- I wonder how important coordinated documentation is to most organizations. Is it vital that Word files look like PowerPoint slides? Perhaps it is enough that the logo is there. If you think I'm out of whack on this, I'd like to hear it.

48pt Heads in Word?

While it might be appropriate to have large titles on a slide, the same format applied to a headline in a document would constitute Death by Word. And what if you created a theme with a dark background and then used it within Excel—would every cell become reversed out?

No, thankfully.

Themes have many soft definitions built in, so the receiving application can use a bit of discretion. Word automatically dials back the title size when determining point size for Heading 1, and both Word and Excel will adjust colors to work with white backgrounds.

Even if we all get stage fright around extending themes out to our other Office apps, there is considerable value in being able to coordinate the elements of a slide deck. When you use a properly-created theme, you ensure that there is good contrast between foreground and background, that accent colors work well together, and that typefaces are complementary.

The question of color

If you agree with me that the most important contribution of the theme is to ensure better-looking slides, you will find much to like with the reworked color schemes. While colors are integral to a theme, you can deviate from them and not find yourself in design purgatory. If you go fishing in the Colors drop-down menu, like in Figure 11.2, you can choose between a host of color schemes, all of which provide nice complementary and contrasting color combinations.

▶ PowerPoint alternates between using "theme color" and "color scheme." They mean the same thing and can be used interchangeably.

You can also create your own color schemes, and this of course, you do at your own risk. If you set a pink background for your white text, no theme is going to be able to save you. Nonetheless, to create your own color scheme, do this:

1. From the Colors drop-down, click Create New Theme Colors. You'll be greeted with an intuitive dialog box for changing each of the colors that make up the scheme.

2. Edit each color swatch as desired and then provide a name for the scheme.

The color scheme in 2007 is tremendously matured over previous versions, in which color schemes would accumulate like hangers in the closet and discourage users from truly connecting with them. When you save a color scheme in V07, two important things happen: 1) the scheme shows up, identified by name, in the Custom section of the menu; and 2) an .xml file is created and stored on your computer.

Unlike with previous versions, the color scheme is not document-centric; it will be available across the application, for as long as its .xml file resides in the folder on your computer in which it was created. Any color scheme I make for any project will be available for other projects.

Judging from Figure 11.2, I have files by the name of ASPCA.xml and Solavie.xml on my computer (indeed, two recent client projects). And they are not complete jibberish—here is what one of them looks like:

```
<?xml version="1.0" encoding="UTF-8" standalone="yes"?>
<a:clrScheme
xmlns:a="http://schemas.openxmlformats.org/drawingml/20
06/main" name="ASPCA">
    <a:dk1>
        <a:sysClr val="windowText" lastClr="000000"/>
    </a:dk1>
    <a:lt1>
        <a:sysClr val="window" lastClr="FFFFFF"/>
    </a:lt1>
    <a:dk2>
        <a:srgbClr val="1F497D"/>
    </a:dk2>
    <a:lt2>
        <a:srgbClr val="C2C4C6"/>
    </a:lt2>
    <a:accent1>
        <a:srgbClr val="F79239"/>
    </a:accent1>
        <a:accent2><a:srgbClr val="6B2C91"/>
    </a:accent2>
        <a:accent3><a:srgbClr val="9BCD65"/>
    </a:accent3>
        <a:accent4><a:srgbClr val="8064A2"/>
    </a:accent4>
        <a:accent5><a:srgbClr val="4BACC6"/>
    </a:accent5>
        <a:accent6><a:srgbClr val="F79646"/>
    </a:accent6>
        <a:hlink><a:srgbClr val="0000FF"/>
    </a:hlink>
        <a:folHlink><a:srgbClr val="800080"/>
    </a:folHlink>
</a:clrScheme>
```

This is not exactly like reading the cartoons, but many web designers and most programmers will recognize the structures and the statements here. The six characters after the "val=" are the hex values of each color, and you could edit them directly if you were so inclined.

Of course, to edit the file, you would have to find it, and in our collective opinion, that is the biggest challenge of this entire chapter. However, in order to fulfill the potential of the new color engine—sharing your colors with others—find it you must. There are three potential locations for color schemes:

If you are using Vista

Your custom color schemes are housed in

c:\Users\[UserName]\AppData\Roaming\Microsoft\Templates\Document Themes

If you are using XP

Your custom color schemes are housed in

c:\Documents and Settings\[UserName]\Application Data\Microsoft\Templates\Document Themes

In both versions

Color schemes that shipped with the product are in

c:\Program Files\[location of office 2007]\Document Themes 12\Theme Colors

The simplest strategy for sharing colors is to email the file to your co-worker and instruct him or her to place the file in the third location shown here, the one under Program Files. Instead of appearing in the custom section, the color scheme will appear in the Built-In section. But it is much easier to locate and you don't have to address the whole Vista/XP question.

▶ If you receive a color scheme from someone else, all you have to do is place the file in the proper location. That color will immediately appear on the Color menu. You do not even need to restart PowerPoint.

A lighter shade of pale

If you go to apply a color, you will see many more colors available than in previous versions. Each of the 10 colors (the two hyperlink colors do not appear on the color menus) is given a set of variants—shades of the color. PowerPoint uses these shades at its own discretion for shadows, glows, transparencies, etc., and you can use them as you see fit. All in all, version 2007 boasts an entirely improved engine for handling color.

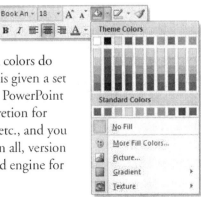

Font schemes...yawn

The engine for managing typefaces is not nearly as interesting. It performs identically to colors: you can select a font scheme, you can create your own, they are stored as .xml files, and you can share them. However, it only tracks two typefaces and makes blunt distinctions for their use across a slide deck.

Furthermore, many of the schemes call for two typefaces, including a serif face for main content. Few of us really need to use two typefaces, and if we did, we should be very cautious about choosing a serif face for text that could drop below 18pt.

Our advice is to choose your own typeface, make it san serif, and use it exclusively. Do not rely on a scheme to make that decision for you.

▼ Download the Theme Builder at www.codeplex. com/openxmlthe mebuilder.

Finally, creating effect schemes requires programming know-how (or the free Theme Builder add-in, that lets you change effects and more with a friendly interface). You cannot save variations from the Effects menu and the files are stored in binary format. So enjoy all of the new effects from in front of the interface, and if you want to share them with others, send the entire theme to them.

Backstage Pass

For the insatiably curious, the exceptionally ambitious, or the people who want to drive IT departments mad, PowerPoint theme files can be explored, dissected, reverse engineered, and even edited. Its file format

Figure 11.5
A theme file is actually a .zip file in disguise. Rename the extension and you can head inside...

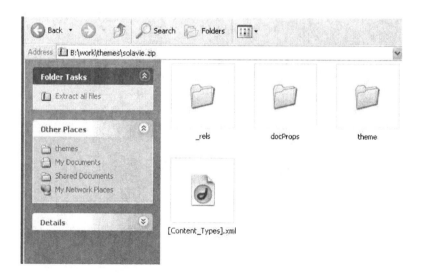

is actually a .zip file—the compressed archive format that can contain many files and folders within.

To get inside, you need only turn to your preferred .zip file manager or use the one built in to Windows. To do this, you need to rename the extension to .zip. Once done, you can see the structure and the contents of the file, as in Figure 11.5.

Most of the information in the file is way above our pay grade, so our tour will be very cursory.

In the docProps folder, you will find a thumbnail that depicts the colors and the background of the theme. The thumbnail is based on the first slide master in the file. If the first slide is not representative of the deck, you could replace this thumbnail with a better one.

The theme folder is where the action is:

■ The media subfolder contains all graphics that are placed on the slide masters. They are named generically and sequentially.

Part Two: The Solution

PPTX Files Like to Misbehave When you Email or FTP Them

Those who regularly cart around PowerPoint 2007 files have already discovered that their files behave differently than version 2003 files, and this has everything to do with the fact that they are actually .zip files masquerading as something else. Therefore, email and download links often identify them incorrectly, treat them like .zip files, and proceed to serve up garbage. To address this issue, there is a perfect solution and a bandaid.

The perfect solution is to contact your IT team or your ISP and ask for the Office 2007 file types to be added to the list of kosher formats. In geek speak, this is called a MIME table.

If the thought of that produces a migraine, here are two bandaids for you: 1) Place the V07 file inside of a .zip file (yes, a .zip within a .zip) and send that file off, with the instructions to unzip it on the receiving end; or 2) Rename the .pptx extension to .zip, send it off, with the instructions to rename it back upon receipt.

Of the two bandaids, Door No. 1 is the safer route, given that most people know what to do when they see a .zip file. Door No. 2 involves an easier procedure (renaming as opposed to unzipping), except that it is not clear that this is the course of action unless there are instructions accompanying the file, and many Windows systems remain in the default condition of hiding extensions.

- The slideLayouts folder houses all of the layouts.

- The slideMasters folder contains the masters.

- The theme subfolder contains a combined color/font/effects information file, one for each master.

XML programmers can build themes completely outside of PowerPoint. Likewise, reckless users can ruin themes outside of PowerPoint.

So create a backup. And don't forget to rename the extension back to .thmx when you're done...

Chapter 12

Creating Shows Within Your Show

If you were to poll 20 experts in PowerPoint usage, it is entirely likely that exactly none of them would list the topic of this chapter as among the most vital. And that is the beauty of writing a book that is designed to be uneven: I can indulge in the arcane and burrow into the obscure, and there's nothing you can do about it!

Lucky you, because while doing all of that burrowing, I have unearthed a topic that is one of PowerPoint's unsung heroes.

You might go weeks at a time without using it. You might only use it in specific situations. But the fluent practitioners of their craft recognize the creation of the custom show as one of the jewels that combines flexibility with economy of effort.

One File, Many Shows

At its core, the Custom Show engine is a means by which you can create a subset of a presentation. By implication, that means you can also create a superset presentation: you can develop all of the slides that you anticipate that you might *ever* use on a given topic, and then slice and dice it for any given presentation.

By creating custom shows, one presentation file can contain several combinations of slides. Slides 1-5...slides 2, 5, 12, and 80...slides 54, 53, 52, and 10...slides 3, 4, 4, 4, 5, 5, and 6. Any combination, any order, any sequence. Change any slide in the presentation, and it changes for all the custom shows that use it. Imagine the time you could save by not creating multiple versions of the same presentation.

Creating a custom show is not unlike hiding a group of slides, but it is more flexible. While you can only hide/unhide one group of slides at a time, you can create many custom shows:

1. Go to Slide Show | Custom Shows, click New, and devise a name for your custom show.

2. From the list on the left of every slide in the current file, double-click the ones you want to include in the custom show.

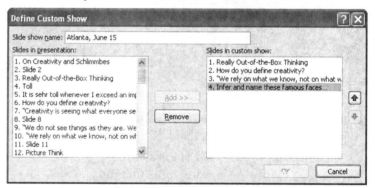

Most of the slides are identified explicitly here, but not all of them. If the slide has a title, this dialog box will show it to you. In this case, Slides 2, 8, and 11 do not; hence the generic identifier for them.

3. Click OK and then Close.

4. To use a custom show, go to Slide Show | Set Up Show.

5. In the Show Slides section, click Custom Show and highlight the name of the show you created in the drop-down list.

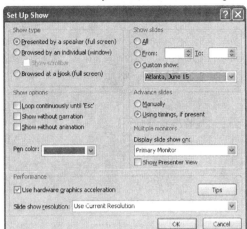

The next time you show this presentation, only the slides in the custom show will display. You can also run a custom show directly from the Custom Show dialog.

Less Flotsam, Better Focus

This beats the heck out of giving a presentation that is full of slides that you know you won't get to, yet that happens thousands of time every day. Nothing like motoring through two dozen slides in five seconds to take your focus away from your core message.

As bad as that sounds, it's better than what *Presentations* magazine recommended several years ago: for each type of presentation you might give, save the PowerPoint file under a different name and then remove the slides you don't want.

Talk about flotsam! What happens when it's time to update the main content? How many versions of the presentation file will you have to open and change? Granted, tailoring a presentation for a particular client or situation is standard procedure, but it should be done from a single slide deck that you clearly recognize as the most current and up-to-date version of your presentation. That can't happen if you have several different versions, each claiming to function as a base presentation or a template.

And let's be clear here that it really doesn't matter if your template is an actual template file, with a .pot(x) extension, or a plain old .ppt(x) file. As we discussed in the last few chapters, there is no real difference between them. The best argument for using a template file is the insurance against inadvertently overwriting the file because you forgot to perform a Save As. The opposing argument is that it is not very easy to make changes to it when you really want to.

But we don't care on which side of that fence you choose to live: having all of your content in one file is the important tonic here, and knowing about custom shows is the straw that stirs that drink.

E=Makeover x Custom Shows[2]

You might know one of my clients: his name is Albert Einstein. Arden Bercovitz does a very good Einstein impersonation and he has been touring the country delivering uplifting and motivating lectures as the brilliant scientist/philosopher.

He appeared at PowerPoint Live a few years ago, but before presenting to a group of presentation pros, he knew that his slides needed an overhaul. He is not a slave to bullets and speaks to his visuals like a pro. But as you can see from his slide master in Figure 12.2, he has not benefited from working with a graphic designer.

De-cluttering his slides and cleaning up his look was not difficult, and Figure 12.3 shows the basic makeover that I performed for him. Just two masters—one for basic content and one for quotes from the good doctor, with an image of him faded into the background. You'll notice that the standard slide master, the first thumbnail, has no bullet—just centered text.

Figure 12.2
Albert Einstein would probably have designed slides like this back in his day, but the modern-day Einstein wanted a more professional look.

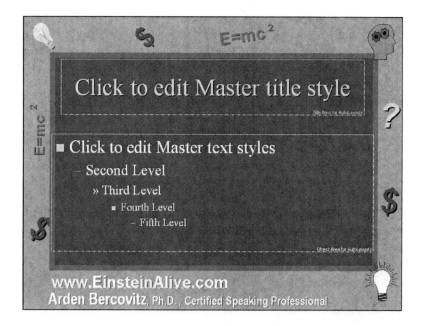

Figure 12.3
No reason Albert shouldn't benefit from a cleaner, more unified look.

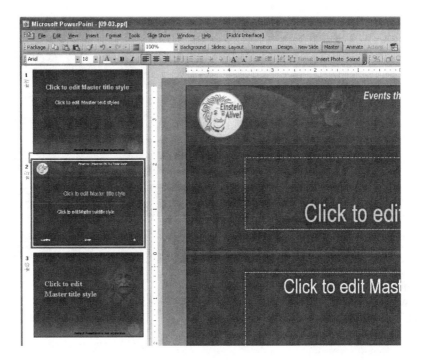

The bigger challenge was accommodating all of his ideas and the creative ways he expressed them. The side-by-side photos of Mona Lisa and Mr. Spock...the coining of "Schlimmbe" (improvements that make things worse), and some great quotes ("The only sure way to avoid mistakes is to have no new ideas").

I recommended to Arden that he prepare for a presentation by acting out the role of Jim Phelps in *Mission: Impossible.* The baby boomers among our readers might remember the classic opening to the television show, right after the tape self-destructed in five seconds. Jim would sit at his coffee table and prepare his IM force. He would browse through the dossiers of several secret agents, figuring out the best match for the specific impossible task ahead. He would invariably pick the same people—television budgets for casting being what they were in the 1960s—but the impression created was that he hand-picked just the right players for the team he needed to have.

Arden liked that analogy but was quick to point out that he might change his mind about which slides to use right up to the morning of a keynote. He didn't want to be locked into a specific set of slides.

This has custom show written all over it. As you can see from Figure 12.4, Arden's slide deck is tremendously vast. Just look at the scroll bar along the right edge for an idea of how many slides are in this deck.

Figure 12.4
One presentation
file...a lifetime of
slides...

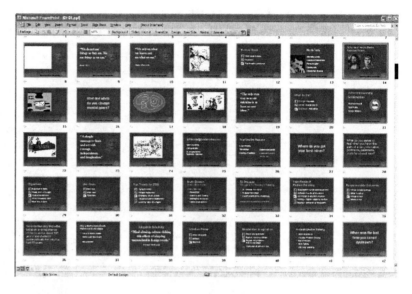

From here, he picks the slides that he chooses to use on a given day. Instead of Jim Phelps' coffee table, he uses the Custom Show dialog box. At any time, according to circumstance or whimsy, he can modify the custom show to add or remove slides.

Arden could go one step further and build standard shows into his template. As Figure 12.5 illustrates, if his lectures fall into general categories, he can build custom shows for those categories that give him an excellent starting point to building a particular presentation.

Just so we're clear, I'm not suggesting that Arden, or you, work off of the same file for every presentation. That is not realistic—you will surely be adding specific content that suits the client or the situation. Hence, you will invariably be saving your template file under a specific name and customizing it from there.

Figure 12.5
If you have a handful
of typical
presentations you
give, you can create
generic custom
shows to jump-start
the process.

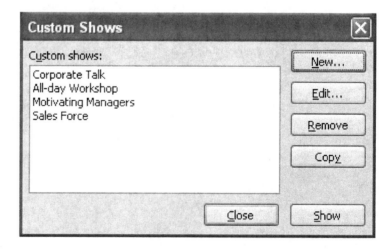

The key is what spawns this custom file, and the more complete your template, the better your starting point. When you get comfortable with custom shows, you can begin to think like Jim Phelps or the head coach or manager of your favorite team (warning, runaway sports analogy ahead). You have your players and for each game, you assemble the best team you can. Your starting players are in your custom show; the rest are on your bench, ready to see action at a moment's notice.

May your players all be all-stars and may your team win the championship. Groan...

◆

The custom show plays a key role in what we consider to be one of the most powerful and advanced maneuvers available to PowerPoint users. Check in with Chapter 27 to read about how custom shows and a few strategically placed hyperlinks can completely transform the way you might choreograph a presentation.

Part Two: The Solution

Chapter 13

The Art of Transparency

The first thing to be said about this topic is that it's a fake. Software programs that can create transparent effects are doing something that is fundamentally impossible in the two-dimensional world of computing. Only in the real world can you see through objects; anytime it happens on a computer screen, it's an illusion.

But oh, what a clever lie these programs tell when they provide the means to create transparent effects. And oh, how useful it can be toward creating dramatic designs and solving problems. In this chapter, we'll explore both the pragmatic and dramatic elements of transparency. And in the process, we'll take a few journeys outside the software.

We will also speak substantively about the increased capabilities that version 2007 brings to this topic. It is nothing short of dramatic, but with that drama comes implications for you.

Through the Looking Glass

PowerPoint versions 2003 and earlier have simple transparency built into the program, as all of its vector shapes (rectangles, ellipses, triangles, etc., but not standard text) can be made to be see-through, provided they are closed shapes. Again, this is just a clever fake: PowerPoint studies the object underneath the transparent shape and whips up an on-the-fly bitmap representation of what the object would look like were there really a shape atop it of a certain color and percentage of transparency.

Unlike with drawing programs, where it's only a worthwhile effect if it can print properly, your burden as a presentation designer is friendlier: if it looks good on screen, you're golden.

Rescuing background images

Figure 13.1 revisits the dilemma we spelled out in Chapter 4, Bitter Backgrounds, of using photos that are too bright, too big, too colorful, too full of contrast. Those are normally good qualities for a photo to have, but not when you are trying to use it as a background. Then you want it to be more subdued.

The simplest of maneuvers can do wonders for this slide. Watch:

1. Draw a rectangle over the entire slide and color it a dark blue.

Figure 13.1
This photo is too strong to serve as a background. It overpowers the text placed on top of it.

2. Using the layering commands, place the rectangle behind the text but in front of the photo. The slide should look like it has white text on a dark blue background.

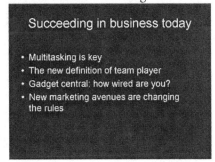

3. Right-click the rectangle and choose Format Shape.

4. Drag the Transparency slider to the right, clicking Preview if necessary to survey various values. At 10-15%, you can just barely see the photo. Here is the V07 dialog box in action:

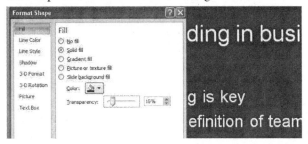

5. Click OK when you have found a satisfactory value. Figure 13.3 shows how a 15% transparency makes the text on the slide perfectly readable.

Figure 13.3

A transparent rectangle draped over the photo reduces its contrast and makes it more suitable as a background.

Download 13-03.ppt to see how this effect is created.

▶ Note from the production team: this is the first chapter that is significantly version-centric and we have done our best to provide instructions in version 2003 and 2007. When the differences are minor, as in the steps on the previous page, we trust that you will figure it out. When the differences are significant, we will offer side-by-side instructions or commentary.

This simple technique of the semi-transparent rectangle has broad implications so I want us to stay here for a couple of paragraphs. Once you know how to tint back a photo, you make it possible to use practically any photo as a background. As we discussed in Chapter 4, overly loud backgrounds are among the most annoying qualities in all of PowerPointdom. With one rectangle, you can completely eliminate this source of annoyance.

In the steps above, I used navy blue for the rectangle's fill because it matched the predominant color of the photo. I could also have used black (dramatic), white (for a washout effect, to be used with dark text), brown (urban), or green (environmental). In each case when you drape a color over the photo you mute all of its colors and reduce its contrast, making it a suitable candidate for a background image.

Version 2007's native solution

With the current version comes dramatically improved graphic support, including many effects previously possible only with the inclusion

Figure 13.4
Version 2007 can tint a photo without needing any help from transparent shapes.

Figure 13.5

A few of the many built-in effects available in version 2007 that can be applied to imported photos. Each of these photos was imported as a conventional rectangular image.

of another shape or an image-editing program like Adobe Photoshop or Corel PhotoPaint or PaintShop Pro.

For instance, instead of draping a photo with a semi-transparent shape, you can apply a tint to the photo itself to create a low-contrast version of it. Figure 13.4 shows the result of 15 seconds spent with the Recolor command within the Format Picture dialog (accessible from the Format ribbon or the right-click menu).

It's worth spending a few minutes with that gallery, as the amount of creative control you can wield over photos is impressive, almost daunting. From soft shadows to glows, bevels to extrusions, you might feel like the kid in the candy store. The Format ribbon offers numerous presets in addition to the more sophisticated Picture Tools dialog.

Witness Figure 13.5—a slide of imported images. The original photos are all rectangular and unadorned; nothing was done to any of them with outside software. All of the perspective shifts, shadows, cropping, and framing are one-click options from the Format ribbon.

◆

As impressive as this is, for basic photo tinting, we actually prefer our transparent rectangle technique. It is extra work, no doubt, but it is more flexible. You have more control over the color and adjusting the transparency slider is easier to understand than playing footsie with Brightness and Contrast. Furthermore, you can set a gradient transparency that changes the degree of transparency across the span of the rectangle. You can't do that with the photo effect controls.

We'll rant on a bit more about this at the end of the chapter, but for now, let's just say that we are rooting for a long career for the transparent rectangle and for a prosperous partnership between PowerPoint and a good graphics package. We will devote the next several pages to strategies and tools that can help you master transparency, as opposed to just applying almost-magical effects in version 2007.

At the end of the day, however, version 2007 provides more choices for creativity, not fewer, and that can only be a good thing.

Half transparent, half opaque

There are times when sinking a photo into the background is exactly what you want and other times when a strong photo needs to remain prominent. In the latter case, you can solve major design challenges by applying a twist to the transparent shape strategy.

Figure 13.6 shows one possible implementation, as the text has been confined to one corner and the transparent rectangle shrunk down to fit in that space. This kind of integration of text and image is usually the domain of design professionals, so be prepared to get lots of props when you roll out slides like this.

All of Figure 13.6 can be programmed into the slide master: the full-screen photo, the transparent rectangle, the title contained within that small space, and the bullets underneath them. You'll need to be heavy-handed with content editing, as many standard-length titles would be too long and you'd be hard-pressed to fit more than four bullets into that space. Hmm, another benefit to this design...

Figure 13.6
This transparency blends well with the photo, creating a unified look.

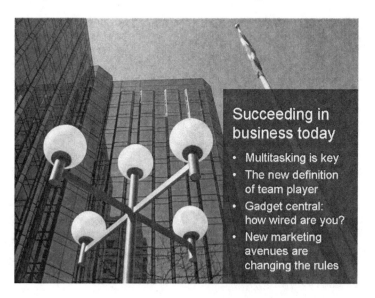

▶ When taking an object all the way to the edge of the slide, as with the rectangle containing the text in Figure 13.6, it pays to actually go one click beyond the slide boundary. Some older projectors and/or video cards might be a pixel off in their display of vector objects and could create an annoying line of color at the edge. This is equivalent to a printer's registration error, and is corrected the same way as with a job for press: by bleeding the object over the edge.

Figure 13.7
A gradient transparency is nice for blending objects into a background.

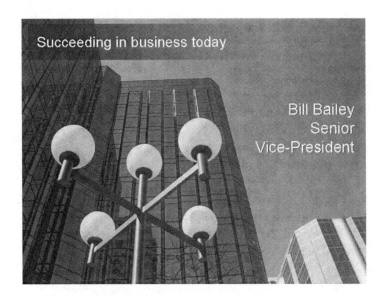

Figure 13.7 shows the use of a gradient transparency, where the level of transparency gradually changes. There are three things worth noting:

- I did not create a rectangle behind the text; instead, I used the text placeholder itself. It can accept a fill pattern and be fitted with transparency, just like any other PowerPoint shape. From the Format Shape dialog, you can set margins for the placeholder and determine where the text is to be situated within the space.

- You create a gradient transparency by choosing to blend from one color to the same color, varying the transparency value for each.

- I could not reconcile the jarring intrusion of the flagpole stretching into the sky, so I removed it. I own the photo and so I enjoy unrestricted usage rights. I am at liberty to modify it any way I deem fit, which in this case was via the Clone tool of my image-editing software. Whether you purchased the photo from a stock house or you took it yourself, you can bring to bear all the tools of your software to make it work for you as best it can.

A Gallery of Transparency

Applying transparency to elements on a PowerPoint slide can serve three important purposes:

1. It helps with contrast issues.

2. It helps integrate photos and images into a single visual message.

3. It softens elements and provides elegance.

At its simplest level, a semi-transparent placeholder for text provides integration with text and photos. Compared with the standard treatment of a solid colored boundary for the text, everything about this simple technique in Figures 1 and 2 says that you gave a moment of thought to how best to drive home the point visually that all forms of travel in this urban center add up to a significant financial investment.

The next two images give away one of our lead author's favorite techniques: the graduated transparency. It can be used to provide a soft border between the text and the photo as in Figure 3 or eliminate the border altogether as in Figure 4. In version 2007 you could create one rectangle that handles the entire transition from solid black to completely transparent with three transparency stops. It's actually easier,

however, to create a thin black rectangle over the transition area that goes from 100% opaque to 100% transparent, and that solution works for both versions.

If the rectangle stops short of 100% opacity, you can see the image underneath. The darkened area creates readability by tinting back the photo behind it. You can either use a uniform transparency (2), or a gradient transparency (3 and 4).

version 2007 supports soft edges to photos which makes easier the task in Figure 5. In order to show only two of the edges as soft, we have to nudge the photo off the right edge of the slide and slip it under the footer below it. In older versions, you could only soften one side, using the gradient rectangle technique.

Figure 6 has a lot going on. The vertical text is tinted deep into the ocean and the text box is set with 50% transparency. The soft shadow behind the text box requires V07 as it is too subtle for V03's controls. Finally, the soft transition between the two photos is too much for either version—that needed the deft virtual hand of a dedicated image-editing program.

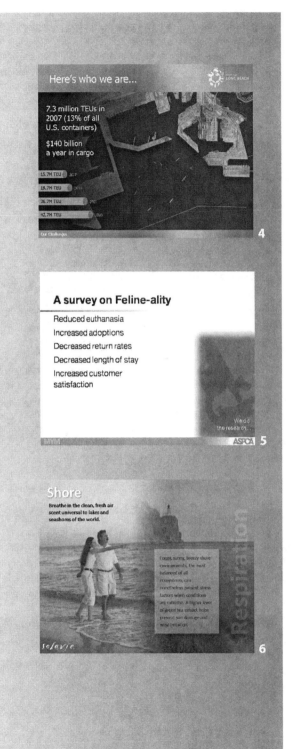

Applying Transparency to Photos

So far, this chapter has focused on applying transparency to simple shapes and placing them atop photos and images. The ante gets upped when we talk about applying transparency directly to the photo. This is not simple stuff, but it's worth the effort as the effects you can create are potentially breathtaking.

If I told you that one of the transparent effects in Figure 13.8 was created outside of PowerPoint, it wouldn't be too difficult for you to guess which one. Between the text at the bottom and the ghost-like image of the golfer, you would be quick to identify the golfer as the one doctored up outside of PowerPoint.

You would be wrong.

In fact, both of these effects are native to PowerPoint. In version 2003, you would have to turn to WordArt to create transparent text, but it can be done. In version 2007, you can apply transparency to any string of text.

But the photo, with its elliptical boundary and semi-transparent quality—the fact that its native address is PowerPoint might be more surprising to you, and it presents an interesting cognitive challenge. Version 2007 can change the shape of an imported photo but it cannot apply transparency to it. You earn brownie points for even trying to solve this puzzle. Let's review a few facts that we know:

■ PowerPoint can apply transparency to vector shapes, provided they are closed.

■ An ellipse is a closed shape.

■ Of the many fill patterns available, one of the options is to fill a shape with a photo.

■ Irrespective of what's inside the ellipse, it can still be made transparent. Here's how you would do it, in both versions of the software:

VERSION 2003	VERSION 2007

1. Create an ellipse large enough so that half of it is hanging off the right side of the slide.

2. In V03, from the Fill Color drop-down in Format AutoShape, choose Fill Effects.	**2.** In V07, from the Home or Format ribbon, click Shape Fill to invoke its drop-down menu.
3. Click the Picture tab, and click Select Picture to find the photo you want inside the shape.	**3.** Choose Picture and find the photo you want inside the shape.

Figure 13.8
This nice effect was created entirely within PowerPoint.

In this case, you are simply instructing PowerPoint to apply transparency to the ellipse. If the ellipse were filled with the color blue, you would see through to the photo underneath, which would be cast in a blue tint. In this case, we suppose you could say that the underneath is cast in a golfer tint. And again, you're only seeing half of the ellipse because the other half is being hung off of the slide. Open the file from the website and you can see this treatment for yourself.

Working with graphics software

As impressive as this is, the real power in these types of effects lies in your intelligent use of an external image-editing or graphic-drawing program. In the age of digital photography, fewer people understand the distinction between the two main types of graphics programs, vector and bitmap. They buy a camera and go on auto-pilot with whatever software is found on the accompanying CD. They tend to gloss over the fundamentals:

- Graphic-drawing software creates high-quality shapes based on mathematics (vectors). The most common programs in this space are Adobe Illustrator and CorelDraw.

- Image-editing software deals in pixels and turns its attention to photos, where you could literally change any one dot of an image. The most common program in this category is Adobe Photoshop, with Corel offering PhotoPaint and Paint Shop Pro.

Part Two: The Solution

Both categories of software have applications capable of creating transparent images that can be understood by PowerPoint. To get technical on you, these advanced programs create an *alpha channel*—an area of data reserved for transparent information.

What, you want more? Okay, computer monitors display color using the RGB model: all color is divided into percentages of red, green, and blue, and any software program that deals even in rudimentary color reserves three 8-bit channels for describing these three colors.

Professional-grade graphics and image-editing applications work with a fourth channel, the so-called alpha channel, which specifies how a pixel's color is to be merged with another pixel when the two are placed one atop the other. This is also referred to as a mask.

Before your eyes roll into the back of your head, know this: however these programs go about creating this type of magic, PowerPoint understands it. There aren't many file formats capable of delivering alpha channel information, and most of them are the formats native to the programs that deal in them:

- Adobe Photoshop (.psd)

- Adobe Illustrator (.ai)

- CorelDraw (.cdr)

- Corel PhotoPaint (.cpt)

- Corel Paint Shop Pro (.psp)

PowerPoint cannot read any of these formats, but it does just fine with the PNG (Portable Network Graphics) format (pronounced *ping*). This is the one generic bitmap format capable of containing alpha channel information and all of the programs listed above can export to this format. PowerPoint will also follow alpha channel instructions in transparent TIFF files, but they are not as easy to create and fewer applications offer that export choice.

▶ There is another format that supports transparency, the GIF format, but we recommend against its use. Its limited color palette (just 256 colors) and inability to make more than one color transparent makes it ill-suited for this type of work. Use it if you want to import an animated GIF file.

Going non-rectangular

When you import a standard image or graphic to PowerPoint, it comes in as a rectangle. A graphic has a *bounding box* that defines its size, and

Figure 13.9
Nothing like a visible bounding box to ruin a perfectly fine design idea.

The most romantic city in the world...

PowerPoint allocates that size and shape for the graphic, irrespective of whether it fills that size. This is why you might have been tripped up by the likes of Figure 13.9, where non-rectangular images import to PowerPoint with white space.

At the core of your challenge is the export of your non-rectangular and/or transparent images with the alpha channel information. This involves telling your software to pay attention to a portion of the photo, not the entire one, and each program will differ in the terminology that it uses:

- In Adobe Photoshop, you use the Marquee tool to define the shape and create a layer from the marquee (right-click | Layer via Cut). Then you use the Save As or Save As Web command, choosing PNG as the format.

■ In Corel PhotoPaint, you use the Mask tools to define the shape and then export to PNG, choosing Masked Area when prompted for Transparency.

■ In CorelDraw, you would either crop the photo to a certain shape or use the PowerClip command to place the photo within a closed shape. Then export to PNG, choosing Masked Area when prompted for Transparency.

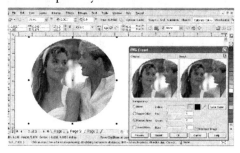

▶ Even though CorelDraw is a graphic drawing (vector) program, it is unusually adept at working with bitmap images, such as these photos.

From any of these programs (and from others), Figure 13.11 shows the happy result of importing that PNG file. All three programs were able to instruct PowerPoint to read the alpha channel information describing the shape of the image. No more bounding box!

This isn't exactly the Holy Grail here—you can produce the same effect by loading a photo into an ellipse or something more creative, as shown in Figure 13.12. Version 2007 performs tricks like this more ably than earlier versions, but you can do this all the way back to XP.

Nonetheless, producing graphics without backgrounds is an important skill to have. Even though it requires a second application to make the PNG file, many veteran users prefer doing that than wrestling with filled autoshapes, where setting the size and dimension can be frustrating.

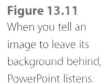

Figure 13.11
When you tell an image to leave its background behind, PowerPoint listens.

Transparency on steroids

Understanding how the alpha channel works is not a requirement for taking advantage of it. In fact, I had to go to Wikipedia for the definition I gave earlier and I've been creating PNG files for over 10 years. But as you get some mileage under your belt, a new horizon of possibilities opens to you.

Programs that manipulate the alpha channel have developed inventive tools for controlling the function. Our favorite is CorelDraw for its

Figure 13.12
Filling shapes with photos is useful to know, but creating PNGs with graphic software will take you further.

Figure 13.13
Complex transparency like this can be accurately described by the alpha channel.

▼ Download couples.zip to see the PNG files created from each program.

▼ Download 13.14.ppt in either version to see the effect.

blended support for both vector graphics and bitmap images and its ease of use. Figure 13.13 shows one of the choices in Draw's suite of interactive transparency tools, which can be applied to any object. This one is called "radial transparency," where a ring is defined from the inside (completely opaque) to the outside (completely transparent).

This is a complicated effect, in which the degree of transparency is constantly changing across the face of the image. Nonetheless, a PNG file can ingest all of it and PowerPoint can digest it. Figure 13.14 shows the potential drama created with these effects. Add a medium-speed fade entrance to it and you really have something extraordinary.

Figure 13.14
When PowerPoint imports a complex PNG file, it figures it all out.

But Will It Print??

Transparent shapes and images are wonderful for slide shows, but they are hell on printers. Many printers freak out with all of that alpha channel hocus pocus, providing results far below any professional standard you would set. Look at the mess that Adobe Acrobat made over our golfer in the top image. And this is the printing standard of the industry!

Reason No. 72b to thank our lucky stars that the presentation medium is so forgiving. No stars, however, will be of any help or solace if you need to get a clean print of a complex slide. You have three viable options:

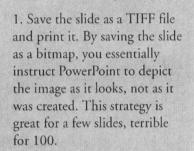

1. Save the slide as a TIFF file and print it. By saving the slide as a bitmap, you essentially instruct PowerPoint to depict the image as it looks, not as it was created. This strategy is great for a few slides, terrible for 100.

2. Select the elements that make up the transparent effect, cut them to the Clipboard, and then use Paste Special | PNG to return them as a static image. This is faster than Option No. 1, but the elements lose their individual identities and properties.

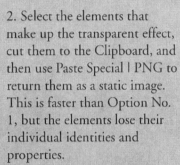

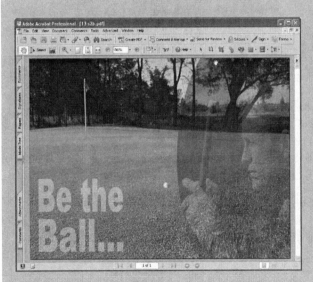

3. Version 2007 users can pick up a copy of Microsoft's free PDF creation tool, which attaches itself to the Save As flyout menu. As you can see at left, this tool does a much better job of handling the vagaries of transparency. Assuming Microsoft has not rearranged its website, you can pick up this tool at http://snipurl.com/make_pdf.

Raising Your Graphic IQ

It's an annual reality check when I ask patrons at PowerPoint Live whether they use graphics software, or for that matter if they know how they are created and with what. One year, we asked for the difference between a vector graphic and a bitmap graphic and the answers were quite eye-opening:

> **"Both are graphics; aren't they the same??"**
>
> **"That's too complicated—just give me something that lets me go Edit | Copy."**
>
> **"When I double-click a photo, some program opens. I just use that."**
>
> **"What's a graphic?"**

Furthermore, we find a startlingly high number of PowerPoint users who settle for the meager tools built into versions 2003 and earlier. To them, a graphic is a star or a triangle. They take this limitation for granted and that stunts their growth as creative professionals.

Vversion 2007 offers dramatic breakthroughs in terms of capability, but not necessarily in terms of understanding. A significant percentage of PowerPoint users are likely to continue clicking buttons to make things happen and go on not understanding the field of graphics.

This phenomenon is not limited to those in the presentation community; we see a world-wide indifference toward creative tools that were once considered *de rigeur*. We note two reasons for this:

- Today, most people associate computer-based graphics with digital photography, where the hardware purchase is seen as tantamount. Cameras usually come with a CD of software and whatever (often meager) programs are present on that CD make up that person's creative suite. People no longer pay attention to the difference between vector and bitmap graphics; they just want something that can work with their digital photos.

- The default choice for bitmap graphics, Adobe Photoshop, is very expensive. Even though the cheaper Elements version is under $200 and would satisfy most users' needs, the $699 for Photoshop CS or the $1,800 for the Creative Suite is what gets their attention in the way of severe sticker shock.

This is why I have been pleased to see Corel make an effort to appeal to the presentation professional with its CorelDraw Suite. For pricing about half of Photoshop CS, you can purchase a bundle that includes vector-drawing and bitmap-editing programs, both offering more power than you'd ever need.

◆

However you get there and with whatever program you choose, becoming proficient with graphic software is key to your development as a presentation designer. Suddenly, you have answers to questions that might have plagued you over the years:

I have a PDF file with text and photos that I want to use; how do I do separate out those elements to import them to PowerPoint?

You open the PDF file in a graphics program like CorelDraw or Adobe Illustrator that knows how to read, recognize, and separate out its parts, and then you export the parts you need as separate files.

I received a logo from a client and it looks terrible. What can I do to improve it?

You can recreate it in a good vector graphic program, possibly using a tool that will automatically trace the logo for you.

The client's logo came to me as an EPS file and my version of Power-Point can't load it.

Open the EPS file in your graphic program and then export it in a different format. (PowerPoint 03 and 07 can read EPS files better than earlier versions, but not as well as graphic software.)

The stock photo I purchased of a race car has a terrible background, full of people working in the pits and cars strewn around. What can I do?

You can remove the race car from the scene and place it in a better scene.

The photo of the girl blowing out her birthday candles has a snot-nosed kid next to her.

Remove him, using the Clone tool of any image-editing program.

The photo is way too dark.

Adjust the exposure.

I want to take the background of my main photo and (pick one) blur it, make it black and white, vignette it, duotone it, recolor it, change its perspective, apply a stained glass to it, add rain, snow, or fog, or do about a thousand other things that I can't yet even imagine.

You get the idea...

Chapter 14

Excelling with Animation

Chapter Six concluded with the following statement:

**When done correctly, animation
can be a beautiful thing.**

Do you recall that? Do you recall reading that and then hurling
epithets in my direction? Did you accuse me of hallucinating?
After all, when is the last time you remember a PowerPoint animation being beautiful? There are two reasons why the answer
might be never:

■ Animation might be single-handedly responsible for more
PowerPoint annoyance than all the other annoyances
combined. Between Edward Tufte and Dilbert creator Scott
Adams, PowerPoint animation is publicly flogged more often
than our politicians are.

■ When done correctly, animation isn't noticed at all.

Good PowerPoint animation is so seamless that you are
unaware of it. It reaches its zenith when it allows audience
members to become lost in the story you are telling. Therefore,
in those rare moments when it is worthy, it rarely gets the credit
it deserves.

I approach this chapter with the same fear and trepidation that I do our seminars on the topic at PowerPoint Live. This chapter, and the one that follows, will probably be the most widely-read in the book, just as our seminars on the subject invariably play to standing-room-only audiences. I know that your appetite for the subject is insatiable, and that your zeal could send you across the bounds of good taste if you are not careful.

And when that happens, it's my fault. I'm helping you commit Death by PowerPoint. Normally, I would refer you back to a chapter to reiterate a point, but this one is too important, so I'm going to repeat it here. Your audience members are completely at your whim with the use of animation, as any movement at all on screen, no matter how subtle, demands their attention. We even go as far as to define it as our Universal Axiom No. 1:

> **When something moves on screen, your audience has no choice but to watch it.**

They often are not aware of this; it is not always a conscious reaction on their part. They just know that they left your presentation with eye fatigue and a general feeling of being yanked around against their will.

Indeed, this is enormous power you have over your audience and the larger issue for us here is how seriously you take that responsibility. If you consider it a sacred covenant, you are on the road to creating trust with them. If you abuse your power, you break trust. So please repeat after me these holy vows of animation:

- I will use animation wisely and appropriately.

- I vow not to offend the sensibilities of my audience.

- I promise not to use an animation technique simply because I just discovered it.

- I swear never to make stuff move on screen just because I like to watch my audience members' heads bob up and down.

Wisely and Appropriately

If you put 10 PowerPoint content creators in a room, you might get 11 opinions about what constitutes "wise and appropriate" animation.

Here is Sandra Johnson's definition: "After you've decided the purpose, then you can determine if and what type of animation is appropriate. Using it in an informative corporate presentation might just help the audience better grasp a complex concept. Bottom line, never use animation just because you can."

Our international editor Chantal Bossé offered the following: "Animate with a purpose...and the purpose is *not* to use all of the bells and whistles. Meaningful animation helps them focus step-by-step when discussing a complex topic."

I have taken these two great comments and created the following prime directive for use of animation:

> **Good animation promotes increased understanding and appreciation of a topic. It calls attention to the topic, not the tool.**

The goal of any animation should be to highlight a slide's story, being careful not to overshadow that story with inappropriate wizbangery.

Can you learn how to play golf from PowerPoint? What could Figure 14.1 teach you about how to hit a golf ball?

I've been playing golf for over 30 years and to this day, a triple-bogey lurks around every grassy knoll. Golf is way too difficult to learn from a slide full of bullets.

How about Figure 14.2 on the next page? This photo triggers your imagination in a way that the plain bullets could never. Yet still, you can't appreciate the mechanics of a good golf swing from a static image.

Figure 14.1
Can you learn golf this way? No chance...

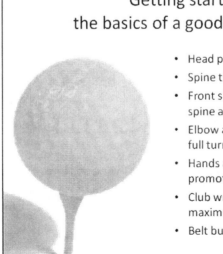

Getting started: the basics of a good golf swing

- Head perfectly level
- Spine tilted beyond vertical
- Front shoulder high to maintain spine angle
- Elbow at 90 degrees to assure full turn
- Hands at or above ear to promote high finish
- Club wrapped around body for maximum torque
- Belt buckle facing target

Figure 14.2
Better, but still not good enough...

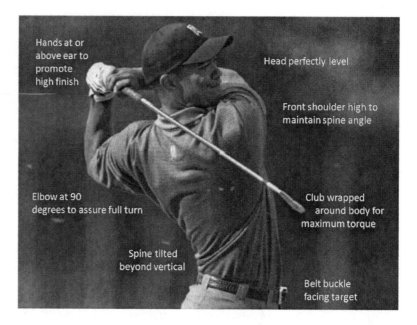

A beginning golfer needs to understand the sequence of events that make up a sound swing, and that cannot come from a single photo.

Figure 14.3 is the ticket. Each of the text strings has been set to appear two seconds after the other, in the order that a student should absorb them (starting with the level head and ending with the belt buckle). Now this is useful!

In many respects, this is one of the finest examples of animation available, even though it is entirely devoid of any of the effects most of us are accustomed to using or seeing. Each point appears, two seconds after the other, that's all. Yet it helps immeasurably in telling the story of a good golf swing.

This is what we should all aspire to: the simplest use of animation that promotes increased understanding among your audience members.

The Sequencing Task Pane?

If you were to ask me, and even if you were to not, I would say that PowerPoint's animation engine was incorrectly named. Too many people equate animation with cartooning or some sort of bringing-to-life experience, and when they expect to apply that to slide elements, the results are often counterproductive.

I wish that the engine were called Sequencing. *Go to the Sequencing task pane to create a build on that slide.* Animation reaches its higher purpose when you use it to strategically display information in the order and the pace most comfortable and inviting to an audience. As we explore specific techniques and strategies for animation, we hope that you continue to ask yourself the all-important question, which bears repeating:

How can I present this information so that I increase understanding and appreciation among my audience?

Three Steps to Better Animation

With our prime directive firmly in mind—animate to promote understanding—here is a basic strategy for determining what to animate, what type of animation to use, and what not to animate. This last point is every bit as important, as the ability to resist use of animation is often the most important quality of all.

1. Define your baseline

Every PowerPoint project has a certain rhythm to it, and the extent to which you identify its meter can help you animate it properly. It begins with the elements that should be regarded as permanent. They would not take any animation, and it is best to define them first.

Figure 14.3
The dynamic of a good swing comes into focus when you see it as part of a sequence.

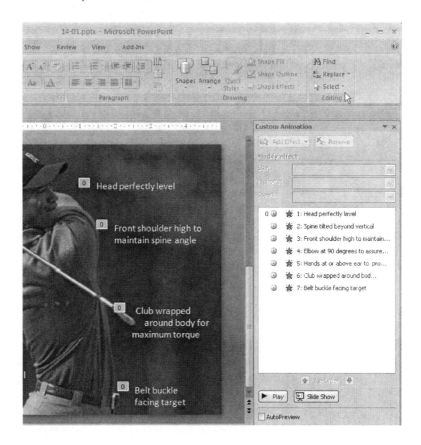

Part Two: The Solution

Figure 14.4
An effective animation strategy starts with identifying those elements that should not be animated.

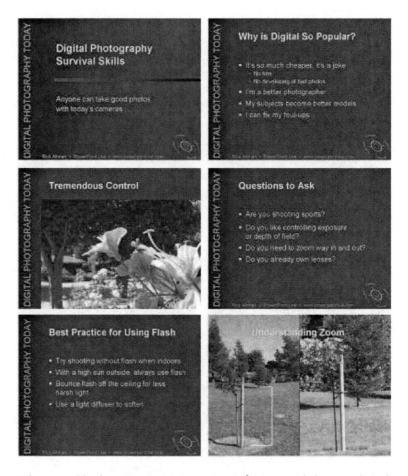

Take a good look at Figure 14.4, a snippet from a workshop on digital photography. On these slides, the running footer, the logo at lower-right, the vertical text, and the background, are constants, appearing on every slide. They are permanent structures, like the walls of the living room you are about to redesign.

Do not animate them. Let them be permanent.

With this decision, you take the first step toward responsible animation by identifying elements that should *not* be animated. Whether they become aware of it or not, your audience members will appreciate having a permanent backdrop that they can count on. Like the walls of their living room.

Moving past the baseline, three of the content slides in this deck are of the conventional title/bullet variety and two others employ photos, not bullets. All five slides have titles and in this case, these titles signal a change in topic. Furthermore, you, as presenter, decide that you want to introduce the topic and say a few words about it before you display the main content for the slide. Therefore, your first animation decision is to stage the entrance of the title. It comes in first, right after the transition, and it is an interesting twist to this exercise that the best way to create this motion is with the Transition engine, not the Animation engine.

VERSION 2003	**VERSION 2007**
1. Open the Slide Transition task pane.	1. Activate the Animation ribbon.
2. Choose Fade Smoothly from the list of choices.	2. From the "transition gallery," choose Fade Smoothly, which is the second one on the list.

3. Set the Speed to Slow, Advance Slide to On Mouse Click, and click Apply to All.

▶ We see anything responsible for sequencing elements and creating motion as part of the animation scheme, regardless of what PowerPoint calls it. Therefore, a slide transition qualifies as animation.

▼ Download 14-04.ppt to see this animation scheme.

The slow fade of the slide transition will have no effect on the baseline elements at all; they will stay put. Content on the exiting slide will fade away while the title on the entering slide will fade in. If you can't visualize this, just download and open the file to see it for yourself.

2. Introduce the stars of the show

Once the title appears and you introduce the topic, then your next click will present the main points of that topic, be they a few bullets or sample photos. This is the heart of the slide, the stars of the slide

Sequence these as you deem most effective, keeping in mind the admonitions of Chapter 6 about using animations that force your audience to track excess motion. If you used Fade to transition the slide, please just continue to use fades for your other builds. If you prefer Wipe, fine, go with that...and stick with it! The only mixing and matching I would recommend is with Fade—it goes with anything.

▶ See Page 47 for our rant against excess clicking when advancing bullets, The War Against "On Click."

If you are trying to simulate real motion, that's different. If you are creating a tutorial on how to, say, mail a product back to a warranty center, a motion path might be just the ticket to show the product heading into the mailbox. Ascend might be just right to simulate stars rising in the dusk sky. And who knows, maybe you really do want to show how a boomerang flies through the air. If you use boomerang on your text, though, that's guaranteed, immediate Death by PowerPoint.

3. Identify the support actors

Are there other elements that need to be part of the slide's story? If so, they should probably be part of the animation sequence, probably set on a click. The sixth slide in Figure 14.4 includes a text string to measure the distance between two objects, and it will be sequenced in when you are ready to reveal that information. It's a perfect example of this type of ancillary animation that many slides require.

It would be rare that support animation like this would ever warrant anything other than the simplest of treatments.

Case Studies

We could fill an entire book just on examples of animation; we'll settle for a chapter and a half. The challenge, of course, is to illustrate and explain dynamic motion using a static medium like a book. As always, downloadable files help.

Three Ways to do X

Creating lists of topics in a style other than a bland bullet list is an ideal opportunity to use animation to best sequence the information and create the best pace for understanding. In the case of the slide here, there are several ways to approach the staging of these elements, dependent entirely upon the pace that you want to set.

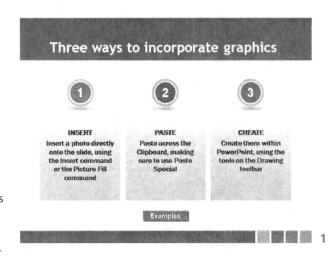

1 This infographic has five elements to it: 1) the title; 2) the three number icons; 3) the gradient shades behind the text; 4) the text; and 5) the Example button.

First question to ask: Does this slide need any builds at all? It wouldn't be the end of the world if this slide were all revealed at once—we've certainly seen more egregious examples of making an audience drink from the fire hose. Nonetheless, this slide presents a good opportunity for smart use of animation.

2 Of the many possible ways to build this slide, one likely way would be to use a fade or wipe transition with the title already in place—part of the baseline. Immediately afterward, the three number icons would appear in sequence (using the cascading fade that I wrote about on Page 49). Optionally, you could use a Wipe from Top on the three text placeholders, without displaying the text. This would create an opportunity for you to tee up the topic, waiting to display the main content until you are ready.

3 You decide whether each of the three strings of text appear on its own click, as shown here, or whether they all would display at once. Either is acceptable here, as the density of text is low. Notice that the text placeholder (set with a gradient fill) can be animated apart from the text inside of it. In this case, all three placeholders appear before any of the text does. Look for the Animate Attached Shape option in the right-click dialog box.

4 Here is the Animation task pane for this slide (shown in V07, so we can give better names to objects). Each text string actually has three animations associated with it—the placeholder, the heading, and the text—and notice that the placeholders are all sequenced first, before their respective text.

▼ Download 14-05.ppt to see this animation in action. It can be opened in either version of PowerPoint.

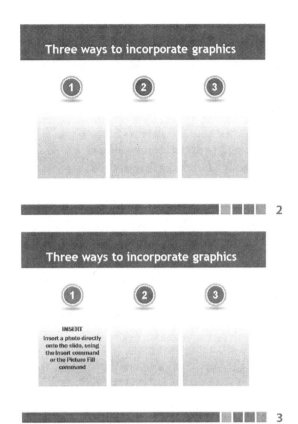

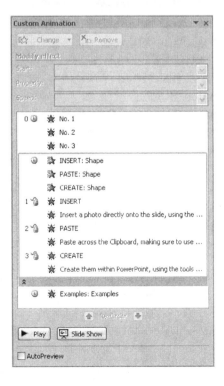

The Off-the-Charts Chart

Few elements benefit more from smart sequencing than data that has to be displayed in the form of a chart or a graph. Audiences are predisposed to tuning out and not absorbing information, especially when they feel as if presenters themselves don't make the effort necessary to describe the comparitive relationship of the data being shown.

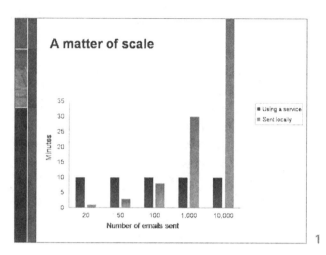

1 At right is a relatively simple chart...with a twist. It tracks the amount of time it takes to send out email two different ways—by yourself using a standard email client, and by contracting with an outside service. The twist here is that the final bar is not part of the graph, but a separate rectangle strategically placed where the final bar would normally be.

There are two critical pieces of information to illustrate: 1) The amount of time to send out email when you use an outside service is the same, no matter the quantity; and 2) The amount of time required to send out email from your office increases exponentially with quantity.

Proper animation of this chart can make all the difference to your audience's appreciation of this point. Most content creators recognize that something should be done to charts like this, but they don't think it through—so instead, they give the entire chart some weird animation, like a box in, or diamond out, or those Venetian blind thingies. Calling attention to the chart is not necessary; it's the only thing on the slide. What is needed here is to *direct* attention, and that requires more thought.

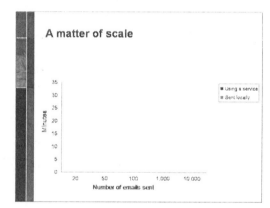

2 I am a big believer in separating the structure of data from the data itself, so whenever possible, I try to show the empty frame of a chart or a table and then place the data onto it. Therefore, I also ungroup charts and tables whenever I can because it then becomes much easier to manipulate them. Allowing, however, for the reality that you will need to keep your data live, this chart will stay a chart throughout this exercise.

The baseline for this chart's animation will be everything you see in the screen image on the previous page: the title, the grid lines, the labels, and the legend. It will all come in on a Wipe from Left slide transition. First, I tried to simply remove the graph's grid and legend from the animation sequence, but PowerPoint removed the animation for the entire chart. So instead, I just applied the generic Appear to it, causing it to appear at the same time as the slide transition. The titles followed right after.

3 After explaining what this experiment was all about, I instructed the chart to build "by series" instead of "by category" and I further asked for each element to get its own build. As soon as I did that, every piece of the graph showed up in the Animation task pane. I then asked for all of the first category, Using a Service, to display at once, each wiping up from the bottom. The idea here is to essentially dispose of this part of the story all at once: "It doesn't matter how many pieces you have; if you use an outside service bureau, it's going to take you about 10 minutes."

4 Then I brought in the second category, stopping after the first three. That showed the pattern and gave audience members a chance to absorb the fact that they are going to start saving time using an outside service once the get past 100.

5 The next click drives that point home with clarity, so I chose to have it be the only element on that click. Sending 1,000 emails takes so much longer than sending out 100 emails; at this point the auience was left to wonder how we could possibly illustrate the time required to send out 10,000. That was the intrigue I was hoping to create...

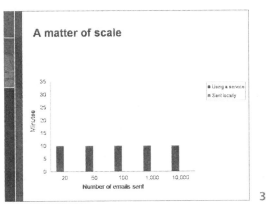

3

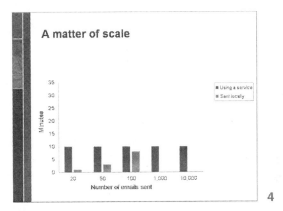

4

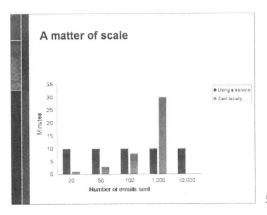

5

6 It became a moment of comic relief when the final bar on the chart slowly moved up from the axis all the way off the chart, and it was worth the effort. In order to accommodate this, I had to zero out the data point for that category.

7 As you can see, creating this animation sequence was no small effort, and if you have never reverse-engineered a finished task pane, this would be a good exercise. We know from studying the task pane that the story is told in five clicks. The first three elements take place on the "zero-th" click—they take place immediately after the slide transition.

The five elements on Click 1 are the entire first category that I chose to introduce all at one time.

Click 2 introduces the first three elements of the second category.

Click 3 is the fourth element, the data point at 1,000 emails. And you will notice that there is a second element, called Item 10, that occurs right afterward. That is the empty data point for 10,000 emails.

Finally, the rectangle that I superimposed atop the graph takes its long journey to the top of the slide.

8 Now for one big caveat to all of this: text quality in animated charts is terrible. Both V03 and V07 display noticeable roughness when rendering chart text during an animation. Knowing how important it is to sequence charts, this is why many content creators choose to ungroup their charts and build the animation from separate objects. See the gory details at right.

▼ Download 14-06.ppt to see this animation in action, in either version of PowerPoint.

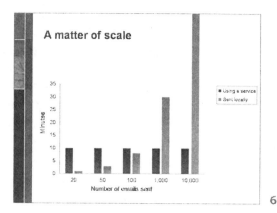

6

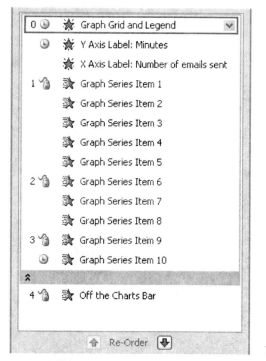

7

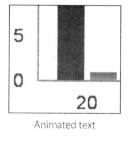

Animated text

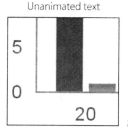

Unanimated text

8

The Case of the Bloated Slide

There comes a time in the life of all consultants when the client makes them do something that makes their skin crawl. With presentation consultants, it is usually a matter of jamming way, way (one more) way too much text on a slide.

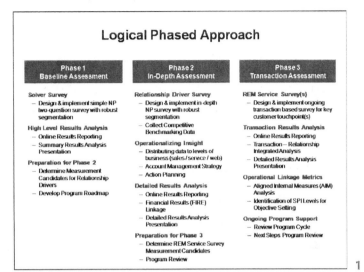

1 At right is a poster child for this malady. No matter what I said about the evils of slides like this, my client told me that it was non-negotiable—he was going to speak to the slide this way no matter what.

I'm sure I would be preaching to the choir to recite everything that is wrong with this approach. The more intriguing discussion is how can we make a bad situation a little bit better. What can we do with this slide to keep the audience from totally tuning out, and at the same time satisfy the client's addiction to the text?

2 The solution that I fashioned was to introduce the slide with all of the text being mostly obscured by three white rectangles, each set with a small fraction of transparency. This tells audience members not to bother trying to read it, and yet it gives them some idea of what they're in for.

3 The baseline for this is the entire slide. The slide transitions on a slow fade, with the title already in place. The three headings then fade in, one after the other, followed by the three semi-transparent rectangles, and finally, the text underneath them. I discovered that it was necessary for the rectangles to appear first, so that when the text faded in, it was already obscured.

This sequencing strategy involves a question of what goes away, not what enters. With each click, a transparent rectangle fades away, bringing clarity to the column of text underneath it.

This insufficient solution at least helps focus the audience a bit and makes the data slightly more digestible.

Our creative editor Sandra Johnson points out that you can use the Transparency emphasis animation to dim this text and then undim it (by changing the transparency value to 0). We applaud Sandy's ingenuity, but not the Transparency function's elegance. It applies the effect in herky-jerk fashion, compromising the value of the effect.

The standard objection to this type of treatment is that the slide cannot function as printed material when there are elements placed on top of the text. Good, I say! Presentation slides should not be made to double as printouts. You should redesign the slide for print purpose, and while you're at it, rotate it to portrait orientation. I'll have much more to say about that in Chapter 17.

▼ Download 14-07.ppt to see this animation in action.
It can be opened in either version of PowerPoint.

The Trouble with Tables

Creating rows and columns of information is a terrific way to show the linear and gridlike relationship of data.

1 As always, the key is in the presentation: how do you get all of the information you see here properly digested without inducing fire-hose syndrome?

The animation capabilities for tables are all but useless, as the only thing you can do is determine how the entire table enters or exits. Unlike with charts, you cannot determine the animation sequence of the elements within. Too bad, because sequencing the rows and columns of a table is the key to this locked door.

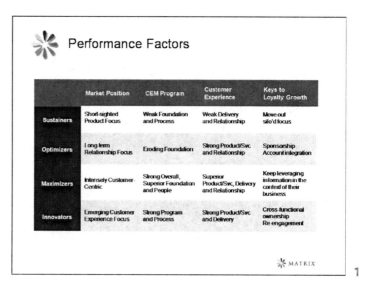

Therefore, the first thing to do with a table is un-table it: use the Ungroup command to turn it into a collection of rows and columns. Now you have complete control over the sequencing of them, and your first editorial decision is to determine whether you want to present the information down or across. Whichever you choose will govern how you regroup the elements.

2 Assuming you are showing this data row by row, select each row of information (but not the left-most category column) and group it. As with the graph, I recommend displaying the header row and the left column first as the baseline. It would be equally legitimate to decide that you want to speak to just the header row first and then bring in the category column on your next click.

3 Tables are a good candiate for the Wipe animation, as text is usually running across or down. The header row would wipe from the left and the category column would wipe down from top.

Then each row would wipe from the left at your discretion.

4 As you can see, the sequencing for this animation is quite simple, with each row (or column) entering as you see fit, in this case each one on its own click. The critical piece of knowledge here is knowing that you can (and must) ungroup the table before you can intelligently sequence it.

Version 2007 devolved with respect to tables, removing the Ungroup command. To work around this, cut the table to the Clipboard and use Paste Special | Picture to bring it back as ungroupable and then selectable objects.

Download 14-07.ppt to see this animation, in either version of PowerPoint. There is one slide showing the animation by row and one by column.

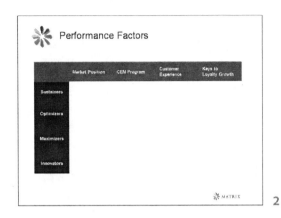

2

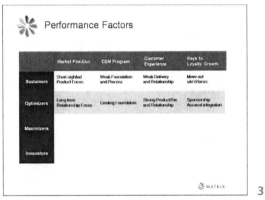

3

4

Part Two: The Solution

The Benefits of Effective Animation

When you use animation in this way, you create a completely different experience for your audience members. They are so used to seeing animation used gratuitously, when they see content that has been prepared with thought and purpose, it speaks well of you. Here are a few of the good things that happen when you use animation properly:

Your audience really gets it

As I said earlier, I'm a proponent of separating form and content to promote understanding. Offering up the empty chart is a great way to prepare your audience for the rest of it. Showing just the topics helps frame the conversation before you give the information within each topic.

You control the pace

Most dense slides are displayed too quickly, leaving audience members with the feeling that they're drinking from a fire hose. If you suspect that members of your audience are not clear on what it is you're about to show them, you can wait until they understand before continuing.

You become more confident

When you prepare a slide with intelligent sequencing, you have control of your audience in the palm of your hand—literally, if you use a wireless remote. Confidence is one of two transferable commodities that can make a presenter more confident. When you are confident about how you handle your technology, you will become more confident about the content of your presentation.

A Word About Pace

Speed kills, as the adage goes. With presentations, so can the lack of speed. Choosing the proper pace for your animation, especially your baseline animation, can often mark the difference between success and failure. When you slow the pace at which your objects appear on screen, you raise the bar of expectation, whether you mean to or not. You send the message to your audience members that this element deserves extra attention. If it doesn't, then you are crying wolf. And if you send it to them too fast, you undermine the very reason you are using animation in the first place.

My rule of thumb, scientifically proven by nobody, is to animate text at twice the speed at which it can be visually scanned.

On the other hand, complex ideas need to be doled out carefully, so as not to short-circuit your audience. The horizontal axis for a

You create trust

This is the second transferable commodity and it's the most important benefit discussed here. PowerPoint audiences are so often on guard in case a presenter does something ridiculous with animation or obnoxious with content, it's amazing that they remember anything. When you take your audience members through a difficult topic with a friendly pace and a well-thought-out plan, you tell them that they can relax, lower their guard, and just take in the information. They can trust that you won't do something stupid and annoying.

And when your audience members begin to trust you with respect to the mechanics of your presentaton, they will become more receptive to your ideas. The trust will transfer; you know what you're doing with the software, maybe you know what you're talking about with respect to the topic of the presentation, too. This is a very real phenomenon.

◆

We spoke in Chapter 8 about the potential insult associated with spoon-feeding bullets. It is an entirely different situation that we are discussing here with dense, chunky data. These slides have to be studied, not just gazed at. Here, you do your audience a service by offering information in a careful and methodical way.

Animation cannot be covered in just one chapter—turn the page and we'll turn up the volume...

complicated graph should be wiped from the left slowly and you should pause before placing the data points onto it. When you slow the pace here, you assure your audience that you will give them the time they need to see both the forest as well as the trees.

It's almost impossible to set slide transitions too slow because the speed settings that the program developers offered are quite blunt. Fast is way too fast, Medium is too fast, and Slow is usually just about right, unless you want to call attention to a transition, in which case Slow is too fast also. When I want to slow down the transition of a slide, I fake it with animation instead: I apply exit animations to the current objects, transition with no visible effect, and then animate the entrance of objects. Wish I didn't have to...wish I had more control over the speed of transitions...wish I could designate it in seconds...oh well.

Chapter 15

More with Animation

We're as bad as everyone we've railed against or poked fun at: we admonish you to use caution when using animation and then we run wild with so much to say about it, we can't fit it all in one chapter. Chapter 14's focus was on the appropriate times to use animation and the best ways to craft it. This chapter focuses on animation choices that are not mainstream, but potentially invaluable in creating emphasis, elegance, realism, or illumination.

Two Animations, One Moment in Time

Once the domain of the experts, the ability to set two objects in motion at the same time has now become commonplace. As with all other matters of animation, that sword cuts two ways, so first, the admonition:

> **If you think that one object moving across the slide is annoying, imagine two objects running amuck at the same time.**

Understanding the With Previous animation event opens many creative doors, and the mechanics are not at all difficult. When you set an animation to start With Previous, you command it to do its thing along with whatever animation was scheduled immediately before it. Standard After Previous animations cannot do this; they won't begin until the previous one is finished. When you use With Previous, you break that barrier. You can still stagger the sequence by adding a delay to one of them, but the fundamental difference is still in place: you can make two or more objects animate at once by employing With Previous.

Figure 15.1
What would happen to this fruit in real life, and can you get PowerPoint to simulate it?

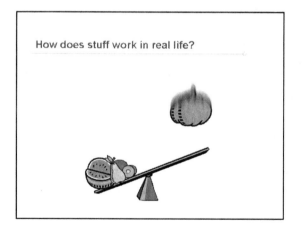

This capability finds its feet when you want to make several objects appear as one system, and I am reminded of the cute demo that we showed at PowerPoint Live a few years ago, courtesy of Julie Terberg, shown in Figure 15.1.

When the pumpkin lands on its end of the teeter-totter, the fruit is going to go flying. "But how will it fly?" I asked rhetorically. "If you're new to animation, it might look something like this..." after which the fruit went flying...one after the other...just as After Previous would do it. People snickered.

Figure 15.2
With Previous is the key to making this fruit fly right.

"So then you get a clue," I continued, "and realized that they need to go flying at once...as a group." The second attempt saw the fruit fly off the slide *literally* as a group. It was hilarious—they became a big clump hurdling off screen.

By now, everyone realized where we were going with this. As each fruit would make its ceremonious exit according to its own weight, mass, shape, and personality, this was a job for With Previous, as you can sort of see in Figure 15.2.

Unlikely that you'll be sending fruit into orbit in any of your upcoming presentations, but the idea is the same: if you want to make something look natural and organic, you're probably talking about using With Previous.

Figure 15.3 shows a menu slide created for a seminar on database management. In order to signal that we are diving down into one of these

Figure 15.3
Animating this slide With Previous integrates all of the parts into a unified action.

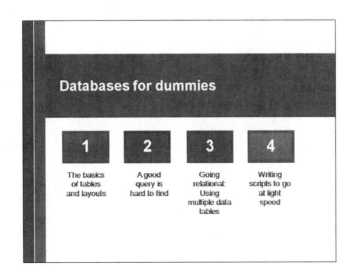

four topics, I faded out the other three. And if you followed the workaround for that hideous three-column slide last chapter, you already know what we're about to do here—we're going to place semi-transparent white rectangles atop the topics not being discused. Here is how I built and animated the slide to introduce the second topic.

1. I used a slow fade transition (and remember, Slow is not very slow), revealing all four of the topics and the title.

2. I drew rectangles over the topics *not* being discussed, two in all, and set them white.

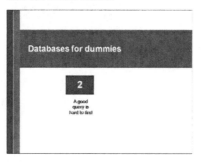

3. I applied a 20% transparency to both rectangles to make it clear that they are subordinate to the current topic.

4. Finally, I applied a fast fade to the rectangles, setting both to With Previous.

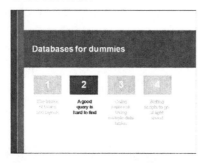

With these elements coming in simultaneously, they create a smooth and refined look, while acting as a roadmap for the presentation.

▼ Download 15-03.ppt to see this animation in action. The file can be opened in either version of PowerPoint.

This example might not rise to the level of usefulness that we saw in the last chapter. In fact, one reader of the first edition took me to task for this example. Guy Everson from Nebraska wrote in, "Sure, you could use fancy fades to highlight the current point, but why not just point to the one you want to emphasize? Or how about just saying 'On to the second point'? Isn't this the very type of gratuituousness that you rail against elsewhere in the book? How about some consistency?"

What do you think, is Mr. Everson right? Is this more fluff than substance? Is this treatment really warranted? Guy's point of view is legitimate and worth airing. And he is absolutely right that the best way to make a point is often to use your own hands or words to direct traffic. I completely agree with that.

The reason that I do not share the criticism of the technique, however, is because the worst that you could say about it is that it is unnecessary. It does not rise to the level of obnoxious or even annoying. It is just a fade. It does not involve wild motion, and it clearly carries the intention of trying to help guide the audience. So we'll leave this technique in and invite further commentary from Guy and all others.

Did PowerPoint Animation Win a Case?

According to notorious PowerPoint critic Edward Tufte, PowerPoint brought down the space shuttle. According to our creative editor Sandra Johnson, it prevailed in litigation. And she ought to know: it was her work that might have earned her client's client millions of dollars. For a recent court case, in which a woman suffered paralysis during childbirth, a law firm hired Johnson to illustrate a complicated medical condition at the core of the dispute.

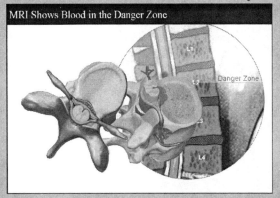

MRI Shows Blood in the Danger Zone

Johnson carefully sequenced the events so that the attorney could explain the situation more easily to the jury. It was effort worth making, as right after Johnson's animations were shown, opposing counsel convinced the defendant to settle. Post-trial jury comments confirmed that they would have likely found for the plaintiff after watching the presentation.

Johnson noted that her clients said they "would never try another case again without PowerPoint."

Figure 15.4
Simultaneous animation helps identify relationships.

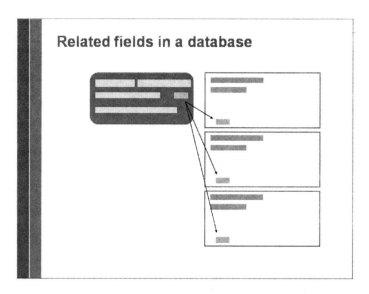

With Previous can certainly do some heavy lifting, also. Witness Figure 15.4, where an intricate relationship needs to be described between elements of a complex database. Relational databases are difficult concepts for many and you cannot just talk your way through a description of the theory behind them; you must create a visual in the minds of your audience members.

Sending several objects onto the slide at one time is key to showing which ones relate to which other ones. First, the main record of the database appears (the one on the left), and soon afterward, the frame for the related records appear, to indicate that *something* else is part of this virtual ecosystem.

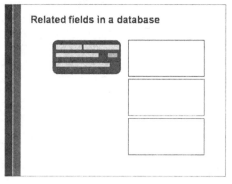

Download 15-04.ppt to see this animation. The file can be opened in PowerPoint 2003 or 2007.

Next, the parallel fields of these related records are displayed, together. Then, the critical field for each related record that pivots around the main record displays, in a different color for emphasis. Finally, simple arrows emanate from the main record, again all using With Previous. The simultaneous quality of this animation is central to its ability to describe the dynamic relationship.

With Previous can be Good P. R.

When the Port of Long Beach engaged me to help one of its executives with an upcoming presentation, I learned first-hand the tightrope that is walked when a heavily-trafficked seaport needs to demonstrate that it also has concern for environmental issues.

In this slide, the environment is identified as merely one of the Port's three challenges, when really, this presentation is about to turn most of its attention to the environment. In effect, the topic is about to be promoted from just another bullet point to a main topic.

So we decided to first make that point visually, with the bullet literally becoming the title. This involved three simultaneous animations: 1) The line of text moves up toward the title; 2) It grows larger to match the size of the title; and 3) The title disappears as the bullet text arrives in its place.

The more significant metamorphosis occurs on the next slide when the photo of the cargo ship at sunset gives way to a peaceful seagull and a montage of photos of birds peacefully taking up residence at the Port. This involves several carefully-choreographed pieces of motion, all working in concert.

This transformation takes about 20 seconds from start to finish, and I cautioned my client to make sure that he had something prepared to say during that time, lest he just start watching the slide morph and the effect would be lost.

▼ Download 15-05.ppt to see this animation. The file can be opened in either version of PowerPoint.

Please Leave by the Exits

I haven't forgotten the first time I saw it. A medal deserves to be awarded for the most elaborate workaround by someone who never knew that an object's departure from a slide could be choreographed as readily as its entrance. Without knowing about exit animations, he went to hell and back to compensate.

Without knowing about exit animations, when it was time to show the next example, he created rectangles the color of the background and faded them atop the old examples. He used rectangles like erasers...except he was not really erasing the examples; he was just covering them up.

He constructed a labrynth of these eraser rectangles, each one entering right when it was time to make an object disappear. This slide involved about 75 objects entering the slide, half intended to simulate the disappearance of objects.

It was a mess.

It was a masterpiece.

And it was largely unnecessary.

As many of our readers know, the better course of action would have been to apply exits to the old objects either right before or at the same time new objects appear.

If you know how to animate, you know how to create exits—you just choose Exit instead of Entrance and do everything else the same. At the risk of oversimplification, there is nothing complicated about applying exits to elements of a slide.

When to exit, when to transition?

To be honest, the biggest hurdle to using exit animations is in knowing when *not* to use them, and Figure 15.6 frames the potential dilemma that content creators face. This slide is part of a promo for a reopening of a downtown restraurant and it starts with a stack of four photos depicting the great food and service offered. Three of these four photos will exit, revealing the text underneath. That text has a few simple builds associated with it.

This is not a terribly complicated animation sequence, but if you create a slide with exits, it will require you to create, format, and animate text while it is underneath the photos. You will probably get adept at using Tab to cycle through the selection of objects and if you are using V07, you will learn to love the Selection Pane (see sidebar, Page 157). But no

Figure 15.6
On this slide, three of the images exit, revealing the text underneath. Working on the text while it is underneath the photos will become tedious. Better to seek an alternate strategy...

matter how facile you get at these tricks, your internal slide plumbing will work against you.

It would be better for your sanity to have the text reside on its own slide, and this suggests a fundamental technique that accomplished content creators turn to regularly. I refer to it as the "stealth transition"—one slide changing to another without the audience noticing it.

▼ Download 15-06.ppt to see the effect created both with exit animations and with a slide transition.

In this case, you would not create any exit animations. Instead, you would use a Fade Smoothly slide transition, but the photo of the server would be present on both slides. This would give the appearance that the three photos have faded away, leaving only the woman. Then you would build the other elements how you see fit, doing so in the comfort of a dedicated slide, not one that has layers upon layers of elements.

The advantage to the transition-instead-of-exit approach is more comfortable content creation. The disadvantage is less control over the action, because your transition choices are much more limited than your animation choices. As I wrote earlier in this chapter, even Slow is too fast in many cases, especially when you are using a transition in place of an animation. Oh well...worse sins have been committed on the audiences of modern-day presentations.

▼ Download 15-07.ppt to see this mosaic of images.

Figure 15.7 offers a situation in which exit animation is the *only* way to achieve the desired effect. In this homage to the sea, the background scene slowly drifts to the right, while other evocative photos appear and disappear in sequence. This must be done on one slide, as there would be no way to cover up the images when it's time for them to leave. It's exits or bust! There are three other things to note about the screen image in Figure 15.7:

- You can't see the Zoom toolbar, but it reads 33%, meaning we are zoomed out quite a bit.

- We have created a temporary dotted white line around the slide to give you a sense of proportion (the background photo is much larger than the slide).

- The Animation task pane shows that three of the elements that fade in then promptly fade right back out (exit animations have lighter-colored icons).

Figure 15.7
This dramatic and sweeping montage of photos can only be created with exits.

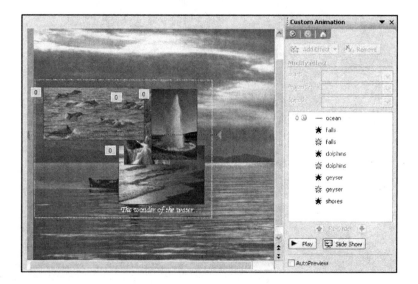

Using the Advanced Timeline

Anyone who has ever used non-linear video editing software such as Adobe Premiere or Microsoft Movie Maker would look upon the Advanced Timeline available in the Animation task pane as something akin to nursery school. Advanced? Hardly.

Be that as it may, sometimes we animators don't need anything more than nursery-school tools, yet a vast majority of PowerPoint users never use the Advanced Timeline, and according to our informal surveys, as many as 70% do not even know that it exists.

Right-click on any of the entries in the Animation task pane and choose Show Advanced Timeline. That brings up a chronological display of the animation sequence for the current slide. Advanced or not, it often beats the stuffing out of having to right-click on every animation and work a dialog box. By sliding those orange bars around, you can

- Set the moment when an object begins its entrance

- Control how long its entrance lasts

- Choose how long it will reside on the slide

- Determine when it will begin to exit

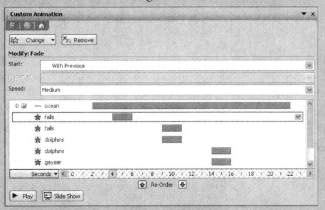

And as you can see here, you can also stretch the task pane to show a much longer duration without scrolling—in this case, we are seeing across 22 seconds, the length of the montage in Figure 15.7.

No element is an island, and that is especially true when a slide has elements set to With Previous or with elements whose exits are tied to the entrances of other elements. Advanced Timeline shows you those relationships with more clarity.

The Path to Motion

Many PowerPoint users overlook the Motion Path option for animation for three reasons: a) they view it as redundant to what Fly can do and they already know how to use Fly; b) working the motion path controls can make even the most accomplished user feel like a moron; and c) isn't all animation motion? Why should you bother with something called Motion Path?

While it's true that some of the animation choices can mimic a motion path, and while it's definitely true that the tools can often make you feel foolish, sometimes you just can't beat a well-executed motion path, especially if you learn a trick or two...

Fly moves in one of four directions, and arcs, ascensions, and some of the other more ridiculous animation choices are similarly limited. But with a motion path, you can move an object from any point and to any point, without restrictions. And combining motion with other animations is exceptionally powerful.

Figure 15.8 is a rudimentary example of motion's value in basic tutorials. Not many people in our user community would need to be taught how to place a CD into a CD drive, but there are plenty of new PC users who would welcome this level of hand-holding. Thanks to a motion path, this CD will literally move directly atop the holder.

If you download and run this animation, you will see that the CD lands right on top of the tray...or does it? Please don't look too closely, okay? We don't really have a clue where it ends up. After about seven or

Figure 15.8
Better hand-holding
through Motion Path.

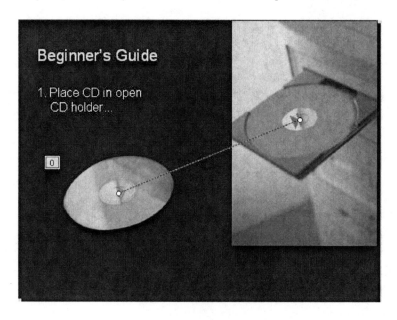

eight tries of tweaking the ending arrow and then playing the slide, we achieved something that perhaps rises to the level of passable.

One of our longer-standing objections with the software is its lack of coordinate points for animations that change the size or position of an element. You can't even eyeball it because while editing the slide, the element is in its starting position, not its ending position.

Throw motion in reverse

Because of this shortcoming, there is a semi-elaborate workaround that is often worth the effort. It involves a little-known ability to ask for a motion to go in the opposite direction. At the Path dropdown on the Animation task pane, choose Reverse Path Direction.

▼ Download 15-8.ppt to see the techniques for using motion paths.

Now when you extend the line out from the element, you are defining its staring point. Now you can use your nudge keys, which, in conjunction with Shift and Ctrl, give you tremendous control over object placement. You can also use the coordinates built into the Format dialog box in V03 or the Size and Position dialog box of V07 to get the ending location of the object just right. Meanwhile, you'll be approximating the object's starting point, but that's okay in this case, as the starting point is not as important as the destination.

But here's the tricky part about this strategy: when you show the slide, the object initially appears at its destination. Then when you begin the motion path, it suddenly jumps to its starting point and moves back to its destination. In the case of the CD and the computer, the CD initially appears in the tray then jumps out into the open space, then moves back to the tray.

This can be solved by one of two techniques that are more easily understood by watching than by reading about them, so we suggest you dissect them in 15-8.ppt. In general

- You add an entrance fade to the CD and you begin its motion simultaneous to that entrance. As long as the motion begins at the same time, the CD will not appear in the tray. This technique is shown in the second slide of the file.

- You make a copy of the computer and place it on top of the CD. As soon as the motion begins and the CD jumps to the starting point, you make the computer disappear. See this effect in the third slide.

This is really geeky, we know. But figuring this stuff out makes you feel on top of your game. As you get more of these geeky little victories under your belt, you'll begin to feel as if there is nothing that you can't simulate or replicate with PowerPoint animation.

Zoom!

For instance, it took a geek to figure out that you could couple the motion path with a Grow emphasis and simulate the feeling of flying over a landscape. Figure 15.9 shows a nice aerial view over a waterway, and if you study the screen image, you will find two clues for what is about to happen:

- The motion line on the photo heads past the lower boundary of the photo, indicating that this photo is going to move a lot.

- According to the Animation task pane, the photo will also grow in size by 500%.

In other words, as the photo is moving down (which is the same as you moving up over it), everything will be getting bigger...just as it would if you were flying toward the bridge in a helicopter.

Download 15-09.ppt to see the effect and to see how we handle the post-zoom issue of finishing with a good-quality image.

There is one important finishing touch necessary: PowerPoint does not actually upsample the photo, so its zoom is going to be heavily pixilated. This does not become objectionable until the zoom stops, so I find it necessary to immediately replace the zoomed image with a static image, sized and positioned to be identical to the final zoom.

Would that PowerPoint provide coordinates for this final location, but I've already belly-ached about that. So once again, you just have to tweak and adjust. Using a round number, like 500%, makes the sizing part easy. Nudging it to the finished location is just trial and error.

Figure 15.9
Add a Grow to a Motion Path and you get a helicopter ride.

▶ Another way to zoom: Insert the picture at the size you want it to be after you zoom in on it. Add an immediate shrink animation to shrink it to the size you want it most of the time. Now, add another grow animation to put it back to full size. The end result: Smoother zooming and less pixilation. You decide which form of elbow grease you want to employ.

Version 2007 and Animation

With few exceptions, the techniques that we have described in this chapter and the previous one have been versionless. And if you were to look at the interface, you might conclude that little has been done in version 2007 to address animation.

Looks can be deceiving.

There are three commands or features in V07 that can make your time with the Animation engine much more efficient and enjoyable.

1. The Selection and Visibility pane

Finally, objects that you create or import can be renamed, and the name that you assign to it displays in the Animation task pane. No more Rectangle 46 or Picture 14. This makes identifying an object's animation settings in the task pane infinitely easier. From the Home ribbon, click Select on the far-right of the ribbon to access the Selection pane. From here, you can not only rename objects, but select them, relayer them, and hide them (more on that one soon).

Here is what the pane looks like for Figure 15.6 and as you can see, you can choose to name elements based on location, content, or source. For the serious animator, this is huge.

2. Hide and seek

The eyeballs to the right of each object in the Selection pane act like a toggle to show or hide it, and this too has major-league implications for those who create complex animations. I will refer you back to the discussion about the relative merits of working with many elements on a slide or creating stealth slide transitions to help you keep everything straight in your mind.

The ability to hide objects on top of others is a game-changer for those who regularly face this decision. It will now be much easier to keep a group of elements that comprise a complex animation sequence all on on slide. Just remember to unhide them before you run the show, okay?

3. The Change Picture command

Animating groups of photos is much easier in V07 thanks to the ability to replace one photo with another and retain the animation qualities of the original image. In earlier versions, this requires a semi-convoluted maneuver in which you create a rectangle and fill it with the photo. Any animation that you apply to the rectangle is maintained, irrespective of what fill color, pattern, or photo is inside.

Version 2007 allows you to employ that same strategy but without the Shape Fill gyration: right-click any photo to see the Change Picture command. See our upcoming case study for a real-world example.

Webinars: Now for Something Completely Different

The ever-growing movement toward delivering virtual presentations on-line, instead of in a room with people, offers a twist to the animation strategy that you might employ after reading these last two chapters. To make a long story short, you will need to forget just about everything we have discussed here!

Most webinar services allow you to show a presentation as if you were delivering it live, but bandwidth limits usually have a profoundly negative impact on animation quality. Fades and motion will stutter, zooms will often fail, and transparency is a roll of the dice. For that reason, many webinar services will require that you simply show slides in Edit mode, as if you were working on them.

Therefore, the safest route to take when preparing for a webinar is to think of yourself as an old-style cartoonist: each frame is a piece of the story. In other words, in order to create a build, just use slide transitions, set to No Transition. Not nearly as creative, but who knows, you might find it a healthy exercise in restraint. See Chapter 19 for more on designing webinars.

Solavie: Environmentally-Aware Care Products

When one of our clients had an opportunity to pitch their product to the QVC shopping net-work, we knew that we had an opportunity to help them tell their story in an engaging and dyamic way. Theirs is the story of hair and skin care products that are specially formulated to work in specific environments—six in all.

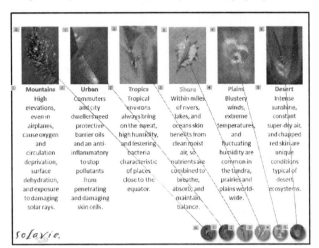

One of the first slides in the deck involves a complex metamorpho-sis of the small round icons that represent the six environments served by the product. In turn, each of the icons moves, grows, and eventually fades into the larger rectangular shape, after which the text for that environ-ment displays.

Fine-tuning the timing, precision, and synchronization was no small effort; it took me over an hour to create the first one, and then I was pondering the specter of having to recreate it all five more times. To be honest, I'm not sure that I would have attempted this in version 2003. I certainly could not have justified spending half a day on this effect, nor in good conscience billed the client for that time.

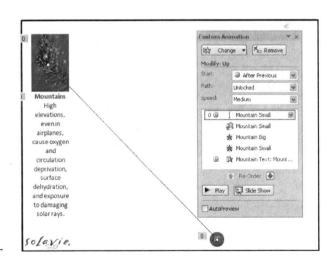

But version 2007 allowed for this slide to be crafted in an entirely different way. I spent the requisite 60 minutes getting the first one perfect, and as the Animation task pane shows, I carefully named each object, in this first case: Mountain Small (the round icon), Mountain Big (the larger square image), and Mountain Text. You can see that there are three anima-tions applied to Mountain Small: a motion, a grow, and a fade out.

In previous versions, I would have to either recreate the elements and their effects for each icon or try my hand at one of several after-market animation-cloning tools. Like I said, I proba-bly would have just given up on the whole idea.

Instead, I made a duplicate of the Mountain Small icon and immediately renamed it to Urban Small. I duped Moutain Big, also. With identical proportions, the only part of the animation that needed to be tweaked was the motion path, and that required no more than about three or four minutes.

Notice how the task pane shows the descriptive object names, allowing you to know immediately what animation goes with what object.

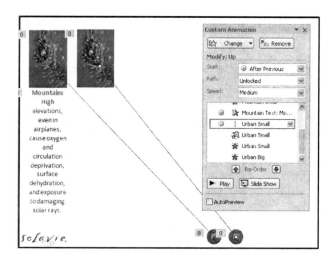

The promised land for this operation, however, is V07's Change Picture command, shown here being used to turn the duplicated mountain image into the urban photo. All animations originally in place remain when one photo is swapped for another. The same will be done for the small round icon, resulting in dramatic savings of time and effort.

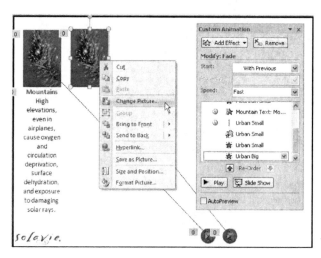

The Selection pane's ability to hide objects came in very handy here, even though there were no overlapping objects. These animations occur in sequential order and that normally makes editing the last few of a sequence quite tedious, as you mindlessly wait for the ones before it to do their thing. But as you can see here, the ones earlier in the sequence have been hidden, making it much easier to test the last few in the sequence.

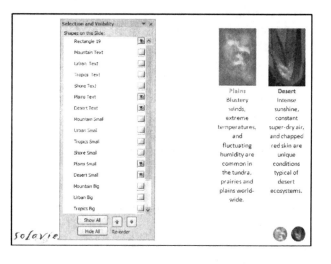

Finally, let's take a look at the Animation task pane for the finished slide. Have you ever seen anything so clean, organized, and approachable? Gone are the arbitrary names that serve only to confuse. When allowed to create a naming scheme that makes sense to you, you guarantee an easier time sifting through the many elements that make up a complex animation.

I particularly appreciate that objects that are hidden with the Selection pane are temporarily removed from the Animation task pane, as you can see in the previous screen image.

These three factors combine to make the creation of complex, multi-object animation a pleasure instead of a chore.

Now if we could just get keystroke commands for adding the animation effects, I'd never ask for another thing as long as I live...

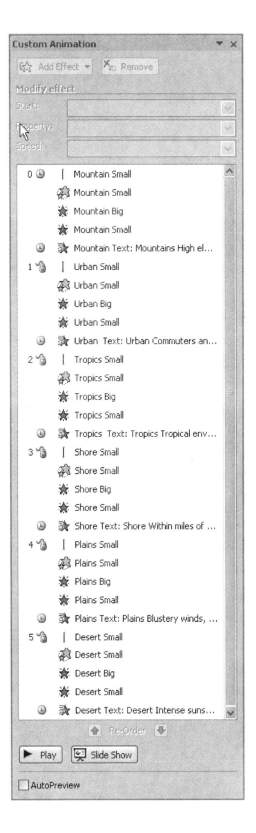

▼ Download 15-11.pptx to see how version 2007 handles the creation of this complex animation effect.

Be Conspicuous in Your Tastefulness

As we arrive at the end of two very long and substantial chapters, I will reiterate what the most important feature is of PowerPoint animation.

Restraint.

Your audiences have seen it all. They've watched the flying bullets, the ridiculous transitions, weird things dissolving into weirder things. Just by standing in front of them and having a slide projecting onto a screen, you have already made a first impression, and through no fault of your own, it might be a negative one, so pervasive is the reputation of a "PowerPoint presentation." Some in your audience will have already concluded that you are probably going to be one of the countless thousands of people who will do stupid things with their slides or put them to sleep with incredibly boring content that provides no insight into the subject at hand.

Why would they think otherwise? They've seen this all before.

Every time you resist the use of a wild animation or some other gratuitous effect, you score sensibility points with your audience. You tell them "I could have done something stupid here—you know because you've seen it a thousand times—but I have consciously chosen not to do that."

You couldn't buy that kind of impact with all the animation in the world.

When they see that you are using animation to help tell a compelling story, they will realize how unusual the presentation is. When your slides illustrate points so cleanly and dynamically that audience members reach a higher level of understanding, you know you've got them.

Every presenter who has ever stood before an audience has some degree of ego on the line, and for most of us, there is some element of showing off that takes place.

Show off your sensibilities. Show off the fact that you understand understatement to be its own form of emphasis. Show that special form of respect for your audiences and they will remember the time they spent with you for years.

Survival Skills for the Non-Designer

In any one of my typical seminars, there are between 35 and 80 people in the room when I ask the question: "How many of you consider yourselves to be professional designers or illustrators?" That question usually evokes between zero and one hand to rise. Of the many bridges that people take to their involvement with presentation content creation, very few of them travel across the arts. Slide creators must rely on their imagination and guile and an often-mysterious sense of what makes good content.

We think it an affront to the profession to imply that graphic design mastery can be achieved by reading five chapters. Nonetheless, there are strategies and perspectives that we think can help you and we will uncover them here.

Chapter 16

The Meaning Of Design

On the topic of design, I would like to start with the most important piece of advice I know. If you were to stop reading after this page, if you were to burn this book, or do something even more violent like give it to a Keynote user, I would be confident that you had received the most important message of all.

Are you ready? Here it is...

You are the presentation.

Did that piece of advice surprise you? Here is my second-most important piece of advice:

It's not about you.

And the third:

Get away from the computer.

This probably sounds like quite a contradiction—you are the presentation, but it can't be about you, and let's talk about PowerPoint but please leave the computer.

And what does any of this have to do with design, anyway?

In fact, it has everything to do with design, and the likelihood that many of our readers might be confused by that underscores the point that most people don't really understand what design means.

To most people, the word *design* refers to how something looks. To most people, these phrases are synonymous:

When people say	They usually mean
That is a well-designed slide.	That slide is pretty.
That is a poorly-designed slide.	That slide is ugly!

When people hear the word *design*, they usually think of *decoration*. But that's different. Design is more fundamental, and I refer you to the Urban Dictionary's definition:

> The process of originating and developing a plan for a product, structure, system, or component with intention.

Structure...plan...intention. These are the essential concepts of something that has been designed. You can have the prettiest slides on

Earth, but if they do not represent purpose and forethought, they cannot perform the heavy lifting of a presentation that moves an audience. The best you could hope for from them would be a sugar high, not a genuine reaction with a lasting impression.

Designing a Presentation

With this definition in mind, the notion of what it means to "design" a presentation takes on an entirely different perspective. It begins far away from any particular slide. Let's return to the three principles that I identified as most important to good design...

1. You are the presentation

Among the tens of millions of presentations delivered since the mid-1980s, do you suppose that, even once, a single member of an audience has ever entered a boardroom or ballroom thinking, "I sure am looking forward to seeing the speaker's slides..."?

Nobody does that. That's not why people attend a presentation, and if you are the one whose presentation they are attending, you need to understand this before you can even have a conversation about what will make you successful.

They are there to hear you. They are there because you have expertise in a subject that interests them. They are there with the hope that you will improve their life in some way.

When new clients begin a conversation with "Here is a printout of my presentation," I immediately correct them.

"This is not your presentation," I reply with noticeable disdain for the pulp that has been placed in front of me. "This is a printout of your slides. Don't insult yourself."

It might be just semantics. It might be a small thing to them, and they might think I am being too anal about it. On the contrary, if you are that new client of mine, it suggests to me that you might have your priorities wrong. It is an immediate red flag that you might be asking your slides to do your work for you. And that never ends well.

You are the presentation, not your slides. No worthwhile discussion about the design of your presentation can take place until you understand, appreciate, and embrace this notion. The job of your slides is to help you tell your story. They must take a subordinate position to you, because none of your audience members cares about them. They care about what you have to say.

▶ As always, this argument presumes that your presentation is to be delivered live. In the case of a webinar, you are the sound track and your slides are the only visual available. Therefore, they become more important. In the case of a presentation file that is delivered electronically, the slides *are* the presentation. That changes everything. See Chapter 19 for more on this subject.

2. It's not about you

The notion that you are the central focus of the presentation does not imply that the presentation is supposed to be about you and about how great your organization is.

We wrote about this in Chapter 4 and it warrants elaboration. You need to find a way to make your presentation about them. Your audience members enter the room because, yes, they want to hear what you have to say, but more to the point, they hope and expect that you address the issues and concerns that matter most to them. They don't enter the room caring about you except in so far as you have something to say about an issue of theirs.

Your quickest path to engagement is to identify, understand, and speak to their issues.

Let's be more direct about this. Your audience members do not start their day caring that your company's mission is to proactively create market opportunities in high-growth sectors. They do not care that you are the leading supplier of distributable commodities when evaluated on a quarterly basis. And they don't care about who your clients are.

No doubt you would like them to care. In fact, it might be your primary objective to make them care. But the burden of caring is yours, not theirs. You have to care first.

This has far-reaching implications for how, here comes that word, how you design your presentation and the slide deck you create for it. If you begin your presentation talking about how wonderful your company is, a combination of four things is likely to happen:

- Audience members will stop listening.

- They will figure out that your focus is not on them and they might become resentful.

- They will be on guard for the rest of the presentation because it already feels like a sales pitch to them.

- They will listen with their ears but not with their hearts or their gut.

And yet, as we have noted numerous times across these pages, most presentations are structured this way. Most presentations are hard-wired to fail at the ultimate objective: reaching out to the hearts and the souls of an audience.

Good design of a presentation begins with the central question: what does your audience care about and how can you connect with their pain and their passion?

If you care about their passion, the chances are much higher that they will care about yours, and that is the best-case scenario. Now, instead of you having to hit them over the head with your mission statement, unique services, history, clients, yadda yadda, as you near the end of your presentation, they just might be asking you about those things. Welcome to the promised land.

3. Get away from the computer

We covered most of this point back in Chapter 7, so we'll be brief here. Your best ideas usually come when you can freely associate them with other ideas and other people and toss them around in an interactive setting. Most people are more creative when they can do that.

As wonderful as computers are, they do not promote that type of creative thinking. They might be unrivaled in their ability to help you express those great ideas, but more often than not, they serve to inhibit you having the ideas in the first place.

So start designing your presentation away from the computer.

- Instead of a keyboard, get a yellow pad and a pencil.

- Instead of Outlook and AIM pinging you every few seconds, put on your favorite music.

- Instead of clutching the mouse, pour yourself a glass of wine.

Okay, so the last point is metaphorical—I think you can see where I'm going with this. Create an environment in which you can freely think about how you want to deliver a message. Don't think about bullet points, slide masters, or fast fades on clicks.

Just you and your ideas. How you can best engage your audience? What do you want them to feel about your message? That's the basis for good presentation design.

Design vs. Décor

Let me share with you a spirited debate that took place last fall between members of the PowerPoint Live conference team. It had to do with the name of one of our seminar tracks, Design and Décor. One of the presenters on our team, Nancy Duarte, familiar to many of you, fired off the first salvo:

> Can you substitue the word décor in the track name "Design and Décor?" There is a huge difference between them and decorating a slide is bad.

Decorating a slide is bad. I didn't know that; I'm still not sure I know that. I wondered if Nancy was reacting to a potential situation that she has probably seen countless times, in which a client or colleague only wants to pretty up a slide, without regard for how the slide deck functions, how it was built, or above all, what message it is trying to communicate. So I pressed on a bit:

> The point of the track name is that designing a presentation and decorating a slide are two very different things. Slide decoration is not an intrinsically bad thing, unless it is done in lieu of design. Décor is necessary; the problem is that many people don't understand what the word "design" means and when they hear the word, they immediately think of décor.

That wasn't good enough for Nancy, who pressed her case a bit, too:

> Décor is simply for visual pleasure. If you look at dictionary.com they even use words like "decorative baubles" to describe it. Whereas the word design has its origins in the word designate. That means there is an intentional way to designate or display things for optimal visual and cognitive intake. Randomly placing baubles in places because you like them there is very different than thinking through hierarchy, purpose, and intentional arrangement of the information.

I thought back to the days when interior designers were called decorators. We had a terrific one who might have taken issue with the suggestion that she dealt in baubles of visual pleasure.

But it was when I spoke with Julie Terberg about this that the issue came into sharper focus. Also a prominent presenter at the conference, when Julie performs makeovers, she often does not have the luxury of being able to scrutinize the message or revisit the foundation of a slide deck. Sometimes, she's just in rescue mode! Yet she too bristles at the idea of being the decorator of slides.

> I never use the word décor. I would use the term embellishment or design element. I like to try to create a cleaner layout, simplify, create consistency, pick up elements that might be pleasant already.

But that's décor, I argued.

> I don't agree. They are graphic design pieces. Décor says that you are fancying it up, sometimes to excess. It has a negative connotation. We don't want to just fancy them up.

Julie put her finger on it: The word has a bad rap. In far too many cases, the only help that a bad slide deck gets is a futile attempt to get prettied up. The quintessential lipstick-on-a-pig situation. So it's no wonder that the mere suggestion of taking into account the aesthetic nature of a slide deck is met with scorn. And you and I know this all too well: the words "PowerPoint," "slides," and "giving a presentation," are often the subject of derision.

Despite the strong opinions of two friends and colleagues whose work I respect and admire enormously, I am going to maintain that attending to the appearance of a slide is not a bad thing; in fact, I think it can be a good thing. But where the three of us agree is that it should never be the only thing.

The next few chapters, in fact, dive into the particulars of slide design (as opposed to presentation design), and I will remind all of us that the underlying foundation to good slide design is that the slide contributes to the tone, direction, and core message that you established when you sat down, away from the computer, to design your presentation.

Part Three: Design

Too Much Text!

My friend and colleague, Dave Paradi, conducts a biennial poll on the aspects of PowerPoint that annoy people. Most people talk with abstraction about their objections with the software; Dave actually finds out and quantifies it (thinkoutsidetheslide.com/survey2007.htm). And since 2005, the issue of text on a slide, too much text, to be specific, has never *not* been ranked in the top three of PowerPoint annoyances.

So this topic strikes me as the ideal place to begin the discussion on slide design (we'll use that phrase instead of decoration out of deference to Nancy and Julie). And because I'm not actually a graphic designer by trade, I will not attempt to create jaw-droppingly beautiful slides that might inspire and intimidate you.

Instead, my goal for everything we do in this chapter and the ones that follow is to make you think *hey, I can do that*.

Why Do We Create So Much Text?

We have identified four legitimate reasons why well-intentioned content creators feel compelled to overload their slides with text. Some are easy to resolve, others not so easy—and in all cases, the text creates one of the most insidious barriers to a presenter being able to connect with his or her audience.

Here, for your reading enjoyment, are The Four Reasons Why Excessive Text Can Ruin Your Day.

1. You do not know any better

We spoke about this way back in Chapter 1 when we sketched one of the typical profiles of the PowerPoint user: the person who comes to the software from other Office apps and has no idea that a quick copy-and-paste from Word could lead to Death by PowerPoint.

If this is you, you're easy. You have not yet formed a multitude of bad habits. You simply followed your instincts and thought that the stuff you wrote in Word would work as well in PowerPoint. You simply need to learn about the foundation of what makes for good presentation content, and with few preconceived notions already in place, that training would likely go quickly and without trauma.

You are the easiest to address. You create slides like the one in Figure 17.1 (repeated from Chapter 2) because that is the only way you have known how to tell a story or deliver a message. You don't have bad habits; you have no habits, and that is a much better thing.

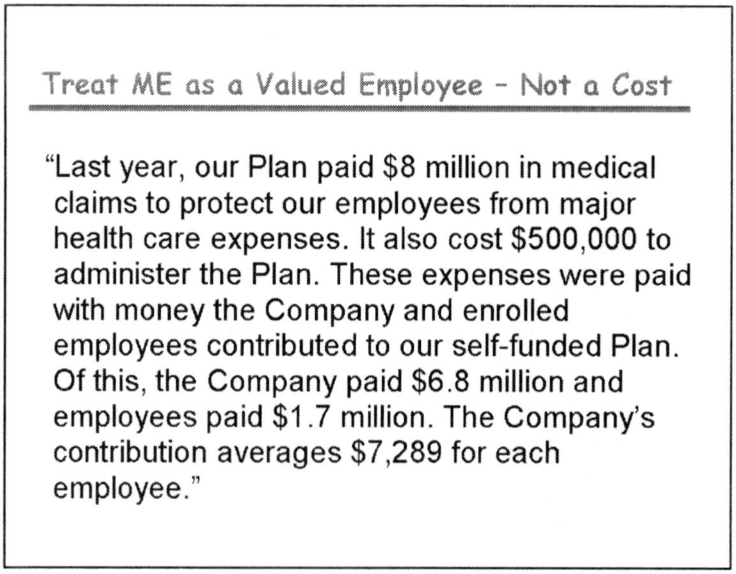

Figure 17.1
A person with no experience whatsoever with presentation design is liable to overcreate his or her slides.

Treat ME as a Valued Employee – Not a Cost

"Last year, our Plan paid $8 million in medical claims to protect our employees from major health care expenses. It also cost $500,000 to administer the Plan. These expenses were paid with money the Company and enrolled employees contributed to our self-funded Plan. Of this, the Company paid $6.8 million and employees paid $1.7 million. The Company's contribution averages $7,289 for each employee."

Figure 17.2

Can one slide sum up everything that is wrong with presentation visuals? Maybe so...

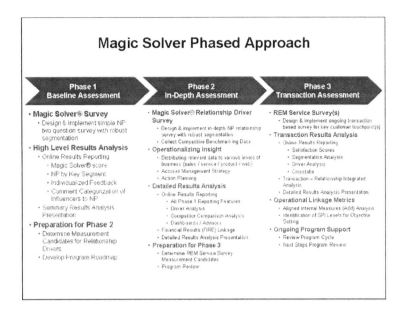

2. You are addicted

Your situation is more complicated than the person who simply doesn't know any better. You might very well know better, but you cannot help yourself. You do not feel comfortable unless everything you want to say is displayed before you. You don't feel as if you can function...you become paralyzed...you feel naked. Without your safety net of a fully-composed script being projected before you, you lose your composure and your poise.

Figure 17.2 will look familiar to those who read Chapter 14. It is the quintessential poster child for the too-much-text syndrome. My conversations with the client who created this slide were, all at once, educational, amusing, exasperating, and telling:

Me: Why do you want all of that text on the screen?

Him: I just feel more comfortable with it.

Me: What if we kept all of the high-level ideas but removed the detail?

Him: That would not be acceptable.

Me: How about if we compromised at two levels of text?

Him: No, I want all of it there. I concentrate better with it there and I'm more comfortable, knowing that even if I forget something, they'll be able to read it.

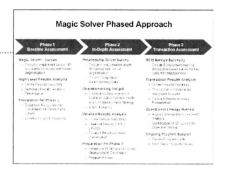

Although I didn't have the heart, it was my obligation as his hired consultant to find a way to tell him that his audience will never be able to read all of it, and worse, they cannot give him the attention he deserves with a backdrop of all of that drek. He listened, nodded, and then said, "Well, that's my style and I'm not going to change it."

It might as well have been crack cocaine we're talking about here—he could not function without it. He was addicted. And I had no opportunity to conduct an intervention—he let me go a few weeks later.

Are you like my former client? Do we need to send you through detox? And what does detox look like with respect to text addiction? I actually have some experience in this matter...lucky me...

1. The first time you, the addict, try to deliver one of your standard presentations without your usual verbose slides, you feel awkward and lost. You don't know what to look at, you have difficulty keeping your train of thought, and you get thrown off by the fact that your audience is (perhaps for the first time) looking at you.

2. The second time is a bit better, as you realize that you must compose your thoughts from what you know, not from what you can read on the screen. It is still scary for you but there are moments when you connect with audience members in a way that you never had before. You want to feel that way again.

3. By your third attempt, you own it. You are more comfortable sharing ideas that come from your heart and your experience and you not only enjoy the better contact with the audience, you begin to crave it. It's like a high.

▶ PowerPoint's Rehearse Timings feature can help as you practice speaking without all that text. It can help you accurately gauge whether you are staying on schedule.

You realize what I'm suggesting here—you have traded one addiction for another. The feeling of true audience engagement is so intoxicating, it is not long before you feel as if you cannot live without it.

This is a good trade!

3. You want your slides to double as handouts

You are not going to like me for this discussion, because while trying to improve the quality of your work, I'm going to hurt the quality of your worklife. I'm both mindful of and sympathetic to of the demands that are placed on presentation designers and creators in today's workforce. Your deadlines are often ridiculous. Nonetheless, I must tell you this:

> **In 15 years as a presentation consultant, I have not once seen a slide deck that successfully functions as both compelling visual content and informative written material. Not once.**

There is just no getting around it: if you create slides for your presentation that follow the ideas laid forth in this book—or the ones authored by Garr Reynolds, Nancy Duarte, Cliff Atkinson, or countless others—those slides will necessarily fail as printouts. And if you create slides that contain fleshed out thoughts for audience members to review afterward, you create instant Death by PowerPoint were you to project them.

These two purposes are hopelessly disparate—the twain shall never meet. And yet you are likely one of tens of thousands who attempt it on a weekly or maybe even daily basis.

My clients and my readers never like to hear it, but it is nonetheless my duty to inform them that they must create two documents in order to do this right. Stay tuned, however, for a creative solution that assuages some of the pain.

4. You are required to

We acknowledge that there are circumstances in which a presenter feels compelled, or is literally required, to read a passage of carefully-composed text and display that same text.

I refer you to Page 9 for the two universal axioms of PowerPoint that describe what happens if you attempt this without special training. There are few things in life more annoying than when a presenter displays fully-formed sentences on screen and then proceeds to read them. And yet, in our travels, we have identified numerous situations in which that very practice is required:

- An annual shareholders meeting, in which the presenter has a feduciary responsibility to report both visually and verbally.

- A pet-adoption clinic that offers an orientation for new pet owners, including lots of DOs and DON'Ts.

- An airline's maintenance training program, in which proper procedure and protocol are of paramount importance.

In all of these cases, ensuring that the message is delivered takes precedence over the elegance of that delivery and we do not fault department heads for erring on the side of over-delivering a message, rather than under-delivering it.

And yet, we know what happens to audience members who get hammered with text—they tune out. Therefore, we refer you back to the sidebar on Page 46 and to the case study upcoming for our recommendation on how to deal with this reality.

Case Studies in Text Reduction

Several significant phenomena take place when you succeed in reducing the amount of text that appears on your slides. Here is a digest of the discussion back on Page 42 where we introduce the Three-Word Challenge:

- Your slides are friendlier.

- Your pace improves.

- You create intrigue.

- You learn your material better.

There is one other important benefit: you become a better slide designer. It is entirely possible that the reason you do not feel confident designing a slide is because you have never had the opportunity. The most accomplished artists wouldn't fare well when faced with slides that contain five and six bullet points, all complete sentences. But when you open up some real estate, you give yourself the opportunity, perhaps for the first time, to think about how an idea could be expressed visually.

That would be a liberation—a deliverance!—for you and for anyone whose PowerPoint career has been defined by excessive text.

The following accounts are proof positive that reducing the amount of words that appear on a slide creates a more rewarding experience for everyone concerned.

Southern California Edison and the Postage Stamp Syndrome

When the largest utility company in the western United States contacted us for presentation help, we knew that we would see some old habits that would die very hard. Edison's "Enterprise Resource Planning" rollout proved to be a difficult initiative to explain.

1 Slides like this one didn't help. I asked why there was a little photo of a man staring off the slide (I was more diplomatic than that), and the answer was telling: "We wanted to break up the text a bit."

My clients' instincts were correct about providing relief from the text, but adding a tiny photo isn't the answer. In fact, a photo like this serves only to add to the visual clutter. I call this the "postage stamp syndrome"—one of several knee-jerk responses that we regularly observe to the problem of too much text.

2 We insisted that the creative team at Edison take the Three-Word Challenge and they were equal to the task. Look at all of that fat that they identified...

3 Immediately upon removing the excess verbiage, one of the team members said, "Wow, look at that poor guy stuck in the middle of nowhere." Indeed, the postage stamp seemed even more out of place when swimming in all of that wonderful white space. It was as if he were now screaming out to be made larger and more prominent.

Leading the Way in Electricity™

Who will ERP Impact?

- ERP impacts different people in different ways, depending on their role
- All Edison employees will directly experience at least some of the changes brought by ERP, including new ways to:
  - Process expense reports
  - Submit vacation requests
  - Register for training
- Even retirees, suppliers and vendors may experience changes
- The ERP program rolls out over several years, so not everyone will be impacted at the same time

Enterprise Resource Planning

1

Leading the Way in Electricity™

Who will **ERP Impact?**

- ERP impacts different people in **different** ways, depending on their role
- All Edison **employees** will directly experience at least some of the changes brought by ERP, including new ways to:
  - Process expense reports
  - Submit vacation requests
  - Register for training
- Even **retirees, suppliers and vendors** may experience changes
- The ERP program **rolls out over several years**, so not everyone will be impacted at the same time

Enterprise Resource Planning

2

Leading the Way in Electricity™

ERP's Impact

- Different people in different ways
- All Edison employees
- Retirees, suppliers, vendors
- Gradual roll-out

4 Once we sized the photo to its full height, it became even more apparent that having him looking off the slide was not such a good idea. When he was just a postage stamp, my clients barely even noticed him. But with the opportunity to actually see elements for what they are, the Edison folks began to think more like designers.

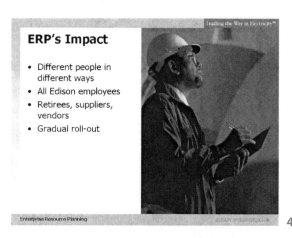

5 Moving him to the other side of the slide was the cognitive leap that had the biggest impact, and I remember well the "a-ha" moment that occurred when that move in turn suggested that the text be shifted to the right. At this point, the slide would have been deemed ready for its debut.

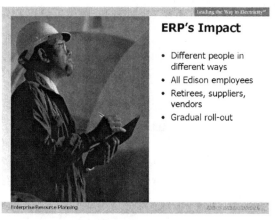

6 I suggested two additional tweaks—moving the headline into the photo and removing the bullet characters from the text. The first serves to integrate the two elements better and the second reflects my general desire to remove bullets when they are not needed. With a short list like this, I believe that the bullet characters serve no real purpose, and the slide looks less "PowerPointish" without them.

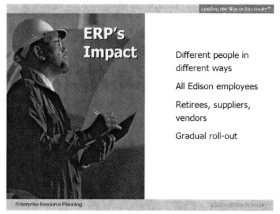

7 It didn't take the design team long to seek other opportunities to create a better visual impact. The very next slide was another paragon of text excess, screaming to be delivered from its purgatory.

What Challenges do ERP Systems Address?

- Many separate systems which cannot share data
- Outdated legacy (existing) systems that cannot support growing business
- Lack of data consistency — multiple entry points and no single "version of the truth"
- Automation – some areas still rely on lots of manual processes
- Strong businesses need to integrate business functions across the enterprise

Enterprise Resource Planning   7

8 Distilling this slide was easier—practice makes perfect—and the presenting team acknowledged that they could do just fine with the key talking points.

Getting buy-in from the presenters to undertake this kind of paradigm shift is vital. We also find it is easier to get their endorsement than you might think. They usually welcome the opportunity to be different and distinctive.

What Challenges do ERP Systems Address?

- No data sharing
- Outdated systems
- Lack of consistency
- Manual processes
- Integration

Enterprise Resource Planning   8

Part Three: Design

9 The new slide design practically presented itself. This photo was purchased from photos.com and the areas of open space were perfect for the remaining text. Using the subtle drop shadows helped readability in areas where there was not high contrast.

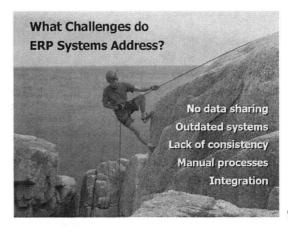

What Challenges do ERP Systems Address?

No data sharing
Outdated systems
Lack of consistency
Manual processes
Integration

9

▼ Download 17-03.ppt to see the progressions of these two redesigned slides.

When is a Bullet Not a Bullet?

US Airways has long felt that its training course curriculum could stand improvement, and this part of the book is peppered with examples of the time that we spent with the maintenance training team.

1 We encountered many slides like this one, in which a subtitle was formatted as a bullet, undoubtedly because that is the default layout for new slides. But a bullet implies a list of points—you cannot have a list of one.

> ⩔ US AIRWAYS
>
> ### Brief Overview of the ETOPS Policy
>
> • The US Airways ETOPS Policies and Procedures are designed to:
>   • Make certain that US Airways aircraft are not dispatched into ETOPS unless the requirements for ETOPS capability have been met.
>   • That all personnel performing maintenance on ETOPS aircraft are properly qualified and authorized.
>   • Ensure that a process for verification of maintenance actions taken on an ETOPS Significant System (s) exists.
>   • Make sure that there is a recurring audit program to ensure compliance with the US Airways ETOPS Policy.
>
> 1

2 As we began "three wording" the text, we realized that the first bullet did not even need to be a subtitle. It was superfluous altogether, so we eliminated it.

> ⩔ US AIRWAYS
>
> ### Brief Overview of the ETOPS Policy
>
> • Aircraft not dispatched until ready
> • Personnel qualified and authorized
> • Verification of maintenance
> • Program to ensure compliance
>
> 2

3 If ever there is an organization that owns compelling visuals, it would be an airline. This was one of countless aircraft-in-the-sky photos at our disposal. With the clouds providing an uneven background, we formatted the text placeholder with a touch of additional white (white fill, transparency of 65%), just enough to ensure readability.

▼ Download 17-04.ppt
   to see these slides.

City Managers Just Want to get to Bed Earlier

When the City of Chino Hills (about 30 miles east of Los Angeles) brought me in to help with presentation design and delivery, I asked a simple question first: "What part of the process provides the most stress?" The answer was quick and unequivocal: "We don't want the city council to always be mad at us."

1 The source of said ire? Slides like this one, often shown after 11:00p during long city council meetings. The slide number at the bottom-right is a clear indicator of the problem: city managers were trying to create a single deck for show and for print. See my earlier rant about how impossible that is. All of the information on this slide, by the way, was already emailed to councilmembers the day before and given to them when they entered the chambers. And now, nearing midnight, they have to look at it again. Imagine their thrill...

2 The makeover began with the ineffective border that did not start at the slide's edge and poached too much space from the content area. I also turned the title into a header. "Heritage Professional Center" is the development in question, but the slide is really about the proposed agreement. That should be the title. Finally, I found the city's logo on their website and integrated it into the running footer. And no slide number!

3 Those changes produced this result, which might be more attractive, but will do nothing to assuage the ire of city council members who want to get to sleep before midnight. So keep reading...

 Download 17-05.ppt to see how this solution was designed and implemented.

Heritage Professional Center

Development Agreement:

- Achieve long-term economic and social goals
- Ensure that the intent of the C-F zone is preserved by prohibiting certain land uses that would otherwise be allowed w/in the C-G zone (i.e. entertainment uses and automobile repair garages).
- Developer shall construct a minimum of 7.5 acres of the property for commercial/retail development (As Revised on the Errata Sheet).
- Phase 3 Retail – Shall be developed w/ at least 80% of the total building s.f. of businesses where 75% of their income is sales tax or transient occupancy tax.
- Tax Exemption Restrictions – Ensures that the City will receive an annual payment of the full property tax value if the tenant or developer receives a property tax exemption.

City of Chino Hills City Council presentation January 22, 2009

1

Heritage Professional Center

City of Chino Hills City Council presentation January 22, 2009

2

Heritage Professional Center

Development Agreement

- Achieve long-term economic and social goals
- Ensure that the intent of the C-F zone is preserved by prohibiting certain land uses that would otherwise be allowed w/in the C-G zone (i.e. entertainment uses and automobile repair garages).
- Developer shall construct a minimum of 7.5 acres of the property for commercial/retail development (As Revised on the Errata Sheet).
- Phase 3 Retail – Shall be developed w/ at least 80% of the total building s.f. of businesses where 75% of their income is sales tax or transient occupancy tax.
- Tax Exemption Restrictions – Ensures that the City will receive an annual payment of the full property tax value if the tenant or developer receives a property tax exemption.

City of Chino Hills City Council presentation January 22, 2009

3

Part Three: Design

My redesign did not stop with a couple of new slide masters—I also made a stop at the Notes master, a part of the program that most users ignore. After all, who cares what the notes look like; they're just for your own purposes, right?

4 I am suggesting here an altogether different use of the Notes page: use it for handouts. You can design the Notes master just as you would the slide master—here you see the graphic element atop, the tree logo and running footer, type set in a serif typeface (this style is for print), and a page number. Normally there is a large slide thumbnail on the Notes page; I shrunk it down to nothing and dragged it off the slide (I learned that if you delete it, it keeps coming back; better to make it invisible).

5 Moving the text from the slide to the Notes page is incredibly easy, thanks to the small notes window normally visible below the slide.

Just copy and paste from the slide to the window...

6 ...And then begin three wording the slide. Now this slide won't offend the sensibilities or strain the tired eyes of city councilmembers.

7 Meanwhile, how's this for a professional-looking handout? Once the master was designed, it took all of 30 seconds to copy and paste the text and set the title in bold.

This is the way that every handout should be done—as a separate document. Using the Notes page to store the printed verbage at least allows you to create both documents in the same PowerPoint file.

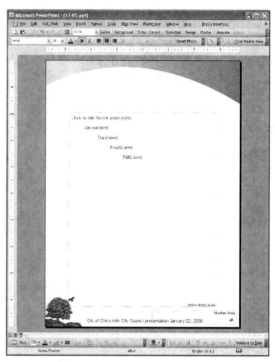

4

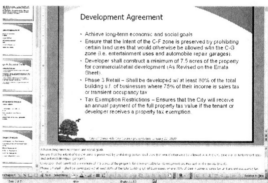

5

6

This became almost cookie-cutter-like for the city managers, as the three images below illustrate: the original slide was given a new design, the text was sent to the Notes page, and then the slide was reduced to key points.

And everyone got to bed on time.

 If you use the Notes master this way, make sure to save the file as a plain PPT or PPTX file, not a template file. The Notes master is not preserved in template files so all of this nice design work would be gone for all of eternity...or until you recreate it...whichever comes first.

Heritage Professional Center

Development Agreement

Achieve long-term economic and social goals

Ensure that the intent of the C-F zone is preserved by prohibiting certain land uses that would otherwise be allowed w/in the C-G zone (i.e. entertainment uses and automobile repair garages).

Developer shall construct a minimum of 7.5 acres of the property for commercial/retail development (As Revised on the Errata Sheet)

Phase 3 Retail – Shall be developed w/ at least 80% of the total building s.f. of businesses where 75% of their income is sales tax or transient occupancy tax

Tax Exemption Restrictions – Ensures that the City will receive an annual payment of the full property tax value if the tenant or developer receives a property tax exemption

City of Chino Hills City Council presentation January 22, 2008   6

7

Planning Commission Actions

The Planning Commission had questions regarding:

1. The economic analysis and the viability of locating two hotels adjacent to one another (one hotel located at Heritage Professional Center and one hotel located on the adjacent project to the northwest, The Golden Triangle).

2. The Planning Commission also had concerns regarding parking due to the adjacent Chino Hills High School. The applicant had stated that they will provide onsite security at the AM and PM peak hours of the high school and any special events. Therefore, the Planning Commission added a Condition of Approval to the project to require that the applicant provide on-site security and signage to restrict High School parking on their property.

The Planning Commission recommended approval of the project to the City Council with a unanimous vote 5-0.

City of Chino Hills City Council presentation January 22, 2008   10

Planning Commission Actions

Questions remain regarding:

- Viability of locating two hotels adjacent to one another
- Concerns about parking due to the adjacent Chino Hills High School.

The Planning Commission recommended approval of the project to the City Council with a unanimous vote 5-0.

Heritage Professional Center

Heritage Professional Center

The Planning Commission had questions regarding:

1. The economic analysis and the viability of locating two hotels adjacent to one another (one hotel located at Heritage Professional Center and one hotel located on the adjacent project to the northwest, The Golden Triangle).

2. The Planning Commission also had concerns regarding parking due to the adjacent Chino Hills High School. The applicant had stated that they will provide onsite security at the AM and PM peak hours of the high school and any special events. Therefore, the Planning Commission added a Condition of Approval to the project to require that the applicant provide on-site security and signage to restrict High School parking on their property.

The Planning Commission recommended approval of the project to the City Council with a unanimous vote 5-0.

City of Chino Hills City Council presentation January 22, 2008   11

Display Every Word...Say Every Word...Just not in that Order

Satmetrix is a client in San Mateo CA, about 15 miles south of San Francisco. Company reps dive deeply into the world of customer experience, feedback, and ongoing relations. They use sophisticated analysis and software, not just warm and fuzzies. They brought me in because their slides reflected that philosophy to excess. (As their work is highly sensitive and competitive, all of the content in these slides has been altered and rendered meaningless.)

1 This slide is a poster child for many of the problems that we discuss in this book. The larger issue, however, is that company officials believe that because this information is so vital to the audience, presenters must say it out loud, as it is displayed here, *and* show it on the slide. We refer you to Page 9 and Universal Axiom No. 2.

2 After the makeover and a bit of organizing of the content, the simple solution was to apply a touch of animation. Here, the slide displays just the three main categories of ideas that these points represent. Now let the presenter recite all of the content. Word for word, if necessary. Of course, now the presenter can't just read the slide; he or she needs to be better prepared than that.

3 When done, one click brings in all of the required content, satisfying the brass. But when you say it all first and *then* display it, it is not nearly as bad as displaying it first and then reciting it. See the sidebar on Page 46 for more on this topic.

 Download 17-06.ppt to see how this simple animation can be so helpful.

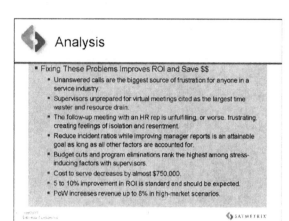

1

2

3

Chapter 18

Practical Strategies for Better Slide Design

We have chosen the order of the chapters in Part 3 with purpose: we think presentation design is more important than slide design. You are the presentation, remember? Your slides are secondary. Your message is more important than your slides, and focusing on the structure of your presentation is a better investment than focusing on how your slides look.

That said, the principles in this chapter are the low-hanging fruit of Part 3: easily understood and easily implemented. You won't need a degree in the arts to follow or recreate any of them and none of the makeovers here will intimidate you. This is written for the non-designer.

Bigger Isn't Better?

There is no shortage of empirical data to indicate when a presentation content creator has created elements that are too small. When people in the back of the room start getting out of their seats and walking forward, that's a pretty good sign that you've blown it with your typesizes. On choosing a correct typesize, I'll defer to my friend Nancy Duarte, who has worked out some way-cool math:

> **Measure the diagonal length of your computer screen. Use a tape measure to place a marker of some sort the number of feet away that corresponds to the size of your screen. (For example, if you use a 21-inch monitor, place a marker 21 feet away.) Start your slide show— whatever you cannot see from behind your marker, probably can't be seen from the back of the room.**

I also like Guy Kawasaki's formula:

> **Determine the age of the oldest person in the audience. Divide that age by two and use that as your minimum typesize.**

Hmm...if my father is in attendance, it means I have to go with 44 pt type for the body of my slides...

In general, if you are in the mid-30s for your headlines and the mid-20s for your text, you're going to be fine in most situations. If you suspect that your meeting room is unconventional in some way, there is no substitute for scoping it out in advance, while you still have time to adjust your slides, if necessary.

I don't mean to be dismissive here, but I am more interested in the opposite condition: type and other elements that are too big. They typically expose a funamental lack of understanding of one of the most important elements in graphic design:

> White space
> Empty space
> Negative space

It goes by several names and it is every bit as important to slide design as the elements that go in the space. Yet many, perhaps most, content creators disregard it.

Figure 18.1
This top-heavy slide suffers from elements that are all too big. There is too much competition for your attention.

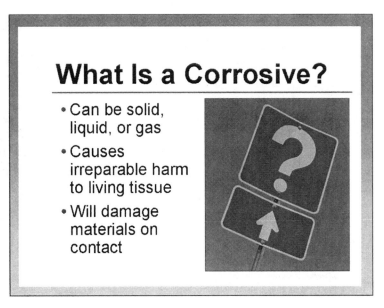

Figure 18.1 has been an example in my Design for the Non-Designer workshop for several years now. What is the first thing that stands out about this slide, other than the fact that corrosive substances sound really yucky? That's right...nothing. This slide lacks focus and loses impact because all of the elements compete for your attention. They are all too large and too shoved up to the top. Your eye does not know where to go. In fact, maybe you didn't conclude that corrosives are yucky, because there was little that invited you in to read the three points of the slide.

We see this more often than we see elements that are too small. To the question, "How did you choose the size of that title?" I regularly encounter the answer, "I picked the point size that would allow it to go all the way from one side of the slide to the other."

◆

Before you turn the page to see the makeover, I want to point out that I am not passing judgment on the slide background, the photo, or the tenor of the words themselves. I will change none of those components.

Instead, I will simply make the title, the text, and the photo a bit smaller. Watch what happens when I do...

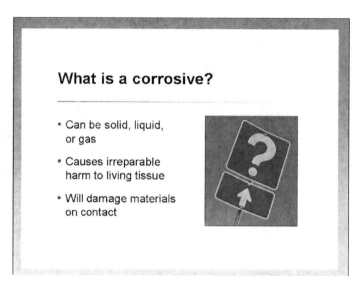

Isn't it amazing how much more prominent the title becomes when reduced in size by almost half (54 pt down to 32) and allowed to swim in all of that space? It's the space around the title that allows it to stand out.

When set smaller and allowed to have its line spacing opened up, the text is more inviting. While the value of the photo is not completely obvious, when set smaller, it balances better with the text. As for the line below the title, I might normally remove it altogether, but my arbitrary rules for this exercise forbid it. So I set it to fade to white as it traverses across.

I suspect that every one of our readers will recognize the second slide as friendlier and easier to digest. Moreover, I didn't do anything magical or complicated (the faded line was as advanced as I got). I just created more white space by making the elements smaller. That's all.

Figure 18.3 is another example of a slide that lacks focus and definition, therefore not inviting the audience in properly. Your eye sees separate disconnected elements on this slide, each one competing for your attention or being overlooked and disregarded. For instance, can you tell us whether the second line of text belongs to the title or to the bullets? We can't either—it's been made into an orphan. Line spacing is not allocated consistently through the main content, and the tagline at the bottom almost runs into the nicely-designed but completely overpowered logo.

In order for it to make a better invitation, we need to "chunk" this slide better. Let's create three distinct chunks of text elements and allocate the space accordingly.

Figure 18.4 shows the value of bringing related elements into proximity and creating space between each chunk of elements. Now it is obvious

Figure 18.3
This text does not do a good job of inviting you in because its elements are scattered down the slide.

North American 'Centric'

How do we grow this business with a dominant region?

- **We leverage Eaton's Electrical Group capabilities:**
  - Project Construction
  - Support and grow into PowerChain solutions
  - Focus on EG's existing market and expand available window into the continuous process industries
- **We differentiate with OEM's:**
  - The right bundle of products
  - Embedded solutions
  - Unique value propositions sold by solutions oriented sales teams

- **We look to non-traditional markets:**
  - Adjacent product markets
  - Acquisitions in related spaces

We are looking at the business differently through segmentation...

Figure 18.4
Better chunking of elements creates a better welcome mat for the audience. And once again, making everything smaller helps.

North American 'Centric'

How do we grow this business with a dominant region?

We leverage Eaton's Electrical Group capabilities
- Project Construction
- Support and grow into PowerChain solutions
- Focus on EG's existing market and expand available window into the continuous process industries

We differentiate with OEM's
- The right bundle of products
- Embedded solutions
- Unique value propositions sold by solutions oriented sales teams

We look to non-traditional markets
- Adjacent product markets
- Acquisitions in related spaces

Looking at business differently through market segmentation...

that the second line is a subhead, the bulleted text has equal space in and around them, and the tagline has been integrated with the logo.

Our international editor Chantal Bossé raises an excellent point here: should this logo appear here at all? Should logos appear on every slide of a deck, or just on title and ending slides? You could make a very strong case for removing logos from interior slides entirely; the question is often whether you can make that case to the brass.

Once again, no rocket science performed here. Nothing that you couldn't do with your own slides. You just need to become more aware of the space around elements and how that space helps define them.

About Face

In most cases, preparing slides for a presentation is easier than creating and printing a color brochure or publication. We slide jockeys don't have to worry about color separations, RGB conversions, trapping, or other vagueries of the print medium.

On the other hand, print designers can choose from thousands of typefaces for a given job, and they can be confident that their readers will see the type as it was intended. If the text is a bit too small, well, that's what reading glasses are for.

Presentation designers have no such comfort zone with their text. Their audiences either sit dozens of feet away from the text, or they are reading it on their own computer screen, in which case it's anyone's guess whether the typeface chosen by the author will appear as intended. Presentation content creators, as with webmasters, are forced to cede a signficant degree of control over their product to their audience. That creates unique challenges for us.

Pick a typeface...as long as it's Arial

The first question that you must address before choosing a presentation typeface is how well-traveled your slide deck might become. Any likelihood that you might distribute your slides electronically will profoundly influence your decisions.

Figure 18.5 is a slide from one of my standard introductions, in which I whine and complain about the topic of the previous chapter. It uses

Figure 18.5
When I can count on the Eras typefaces, this slide looks great...

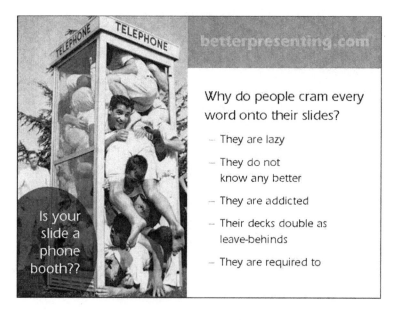

one of my preferred type families, Eras, and when I run the slide show from my own notebook, with all of the Eras faces installed, this slide looks exactly as I intend. In particular

- The URL at the top is both left-aligned to the title and properly centered in its space.

- The title fits comfortably on two lines.

- The bullet copy is well-distributed, with nice line breaks.

If I were to send the slide deck to you, however, what would happen to my meticulous preparation of this slide? Figure 18.6 provides the answer. If you do not own Eras, Windows will substitute another typeface, probably Arial, and that typeface-swapping could be hazardous to my career. Suddenly, the URL at the top is no longer centered, the title breaks over onto three lines, and worse, the care I took on the fourth bullet to create an even break becomes a disaster.

I could try embedding the typeface, assuming I am allowed to, but that creates other potential problems on your end, with nagging dialog boxes about what you can and cannot do with embedded typefaces. These warnings have freaked out enough of my clients that I now know not to go down that road. No, if I have to distribute a slide deck, I revert to a lower common denominator:

I use a typeface that I know everyone owns.

And then my text looks like everyone else's...yawn...but at least I avoid the nasty surprises that you see here.

Figure 18.6
...but on someone else's computer, another face might be used in its place, and that could spell curtains for my design.

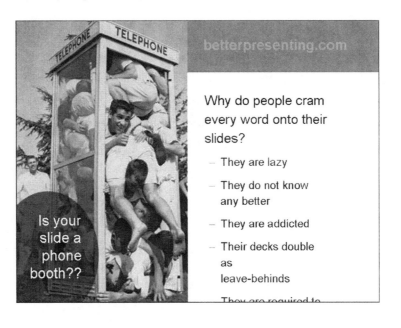

Figure 18.7
How can both of
these statements be
true? It all depends
upon the medium.

> Serif typefaces, like Times New Roman, are better for reading text.
>
> Sans serif typefaces, like Arial, are better for reading text.

Of curlycues and stick figures

Most of our readers understand the difference between serif and sans serif typefaces. Most of you know that the serifs on a typeface, like the ones in the first string of text in Figure 18.7, are the cute little feet and hats on many of the letters.

Serifs guide the eye from one letter to the next, increasing readability in newspapers and magazines. That is why the first of the two statements above is true.

The exact opposite is true with text that is displayed or projected onto a screen. Text on a computer or projection screen is of a much lower resolution than the fine ink or toner used for print. At lower resolutions and with less-than-optimal lighting, the serifs get in the way and actually decrease readability. For screen work, sans serif typefaces ("sans" means without) are easier to read...and that is why the second statement above is also true.

The other quality of sans serif typefaces is their uniformity of width. Type purists would argue that they are less distinctive and interesting, and they might very well be right:

Garamond (serif)   Arial (sans serif)

The first five letters above certainly have more character. But those uniform widths of the sans serif letters ensure that they will project prominently. While you won't see it at sizes like this, in smaller sizes and with older projectors, the thin strokes of the "w" and the "e" above might disappear altogether. That won't happen with a sans serif face.

Experienced designers could successfully mix and match—using sans serf for all main content and a serif face for larger headlines—but most of us would just get into trouble if we tried. Better to pick one typeface and stick with it throughout.

- Consider a serif face if you know that all of your copy will be above 24 pt and you have good contrast between text and background.

- Otherwise, pick a sans serif face.

Here are ones that you can count on to be present on most computers:

Arial	We expect strong fourth quarter results
Tahoma	We expect strong fourth quarter results
Century Gothic	We expect strong fourth quarter results
Lucida Sans	We expect strong fourth quarter results
Trebuchet	We expect strong fourth quarter results
Verdana	We expect strong fourth quarter results
Calibri	We expect strong fourth quarter results

Users of Windows Vista or Office 2007 will all have Calibri, but you can't count on it with Windows XP and Office 2003 users. And because it sets much tighter than the rest, typeface swapping that might occur could affect your layouts. Too bad...it's the nicest one of the bunch. Most Mac computers will have the first six.

To review, if you are designing a slide show to be played on just one computer, you can pick any typeface that it has. If you are designing a slide show for distribution, then you would be well-advised to choose a face that you can confidently predict a majority of your recipients will own.

Here is one last piece of advice about type:

Don't say don't when you mean don't.

Any questions...?

No Chart is an Island

I need to confess to a bias before we go any further in this section. It threatens to undermine any integrity I might have on this subject:

I do not like charts and graphs.

They are usually misused, abused, and elevated in importance beyond all reason. The software engine for them is terrible, and one last thing, they're ugly. *Tell us what you really think* comes to mind as an appropriate response to all of that.

As long as I'm indulging in full disclosure, I'll also tell you that I have no real interest in teaching anyone how to create a chart or a graph. The world doesn't need any more of them and I can offer no real insight into how to use Microsoft's charting engine. The one in Office 2007 is much improved, but it doesn't particularly inspire me any more than the terrible one that plagued previous versions.

To those who must create charts on a daily basis, I feel your pain. And the best way I know how to help assuage some of that pain is to help you recognize instances when you can avoid using them.

The problem with most charts is that they usually end up being isolated from the rest of the slide. You enter some weird chart-engine mode in order to work on them and that usually leaves them seemingly disconnected from the other slide elements. Therefore, most charts create the impression that they are separate entities onto themselves, often relegated to their own slides, apart from the content that relates to them.

Figure 18.8 represents this syndrome quite well. An otherwise well-designed and clean slide completely lost its way when its creators at the Port of Long Beach felt compelled to create a chart to show the annual traffic patterns, projected out 20 years.

The first thing I noticed about the chart when I was brought in to work on this slide deck was the chronology running opposite to intuition: the year 2030 at the top and 2007 at the bottom. I'm sure you could make some argument for doing it that way, but I really appreciated the response of my client when I asked why they did.

"We wanted to change it, but it was so much trouble, we just decided to leave it this way."

Now there's an answer I can relate to! It also explains why so many charts are created with opaque backgrounds and unncecessary lines and tick marks. It's just too much $%&#@ trouble figuring out how to get rid of them.

Figure 18.8
All too often, charts become isolated little bubbles onto themselves.

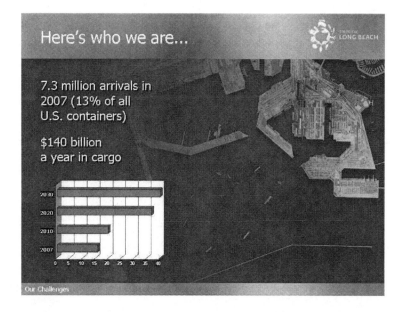

Much of the time—I would argue most of the time—the only real value of a chart is to show relative values of a particular commodity. You are trying to show how one thing measures against another. Do you really need a full-blown chart to show you that? Turning to the chart engine is a knee-jerk reaction...*sales are up over last year—let's create a graph to show that...*

Resist! There are better ways to show relative values than an ugly chart! Figure 18.9 shows a very simple grouping of text, rectangles, and ellipses that anyone reading these pages could create. Just the fact that it has

Figure 18.9
These rectangles and ellipses do just as good of a job, are easier to create, easier to animate, and easier on the eyes.

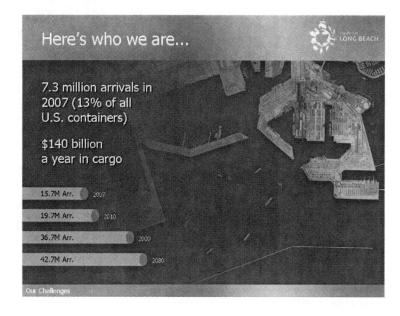

no backround serves to integrate it better with its surrounding environment, and it is so much easier to color coordinate and to animate.

▼ Download 18-08.ppt to see how simple a chart can really be.

I concede that it does not contain live data; you can't link this back to an Excel worksheet; they're just a bunch of shapes. But that is the only concession I am willing to make—a non-chart chart enjoys myriad of advantages over a Microsoft-style chart. Your audience won't care if one of them is off by a few pixels; everyone will grasp the impact of the relative values that you are intending to show.

While I try to avoid them whenever I can, when I do have to create an actual chart of some sort, I will turn first to my library of charts, graphs, and other graphic elements from smartdraw.com. The charting engine is friendlier and more sophisticated, and it integrates nicely with PowerPoint. Figure 18.10 was created in a fraction of the time that it would have required of me had I used just PowerPoint. When you buy the product, you get an almost-dizzying collection of templates, primitives, and starter elements.

Most of the time, however, I am nothing more than a one-trick pony when it comes to charts: I just create rectangles and drop ellipses on top of them when I want to visually show comparative data. A professional designer could create something wonderful with opportunities. I am content to create something that does not look so "charty," and you should be, too.

Figure 18.10
Creating this whimsical chart was made simple by smartdraw.com's ability to import chart elements into PowerPoint.

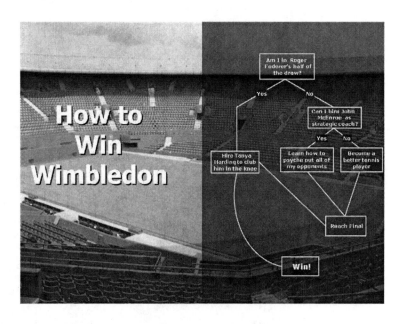

Measuring the Pain of Traffic

When the Southern California Association of Governments sent us the slides for its 2008 Regional Transportation Plan, we recognized several important and impactful points to be made, not the least of which is the forecast of population increase in the region.

1 In order to punctuate the point, the creators had the vertical text and its yellow arrowed background all fly in from off the screen.

2 This slide uses the same photo, cropped differently, and draws the important conclusion: you will be driving slower.

I really liked where the Association was was going with this, but I wanted to see if we could integrate these two thoughts a bit better. Do we really need two slides to tell this story? Shouldn't the number of people and the speed be shown together? I also wanted to shift more of the job of telling this story to the presenter.

3 This slide requires 40 seconds of narration and is best understood by downloading it and running it. It starts with a very tight shot and, thanks to a shrink and a pan, gradually zooms out to reveal a huge, ugly snarl of traffic. Atop that scene fades in the essential data—more traffic, slower speeds. These shapes wipe from the right to simulate meters calculating their values. Once again, the graphing of these values is utterly simple and unadorned. The key is the telling of this story all at once: an ugly rush-hour scene, the forecast of increased population, and the specter of slower drive times.

1

2

3

▼ Download 18-11.ppt to see this slide in action.

This is Important...So Is That...and That Other Thing!

I remember the first time I saw it. In fact, I did it. It was 1985 and the term "desktop publishing" had just been coined. Until that time, a bunch of us editors were playing footsie with our typesetters, trying to figure out how to practice desktop publishing before it had a name. (Did I ever tell you that I actually invented desktop publishing? Well, that's for another book...)

I was at a CopyMat, renting time on an HP LaserJet IID, a 300-dpi printer with four typefaces built in (Dutch, Swiss, Courier, and Symbol) that was too expensive to buy (about $7,000). There were four computers connected to it: three Apple IIs that looked like toys and one lowly PC clone stuffed in the corner with no applications on it.

Nobody there had ever heard of the software I was using (Ventura Publisher...nobody still knows about it...and that too is for another book), so I would create PCL files by sending my output to a 5 1/4-inch floppy disk (which really was floppy), driving it to the CopyMat (yes, we had cars back then), and sending it to the printer by issuing a Copy command from the DOS prompt.

To any of you still wondering, I'm not exactly Gen X or Y.

It was incredible that I could set type in boldface without having to mark it up on paper for our typesetters. I could also drop a screen behind type, create boxes around headlines, round the corners of rectangles, and underline. This was nothing short of a miracle for a young man who had cut his teeth on X-acto knives (sorry, bad visual) and wax machines.

Unfortunately, I had no capability for color, gray tones looked horrible, and we only had about six typesizes available. So how did I create emphasis? With a deft combination of boldface, underline, all caps, and rounded rectangles, illustrated exquisitely by one of my restaurant ads in Figure 18.12. All of the type is bold except for the address and phone; if you want to emphasize the fact that all ingredients are fresh and you've already played your bold card, what do you do? And after underlining and enboldening, how do you make the tagline stand out? Of course, all caps and an exclamation mark—what else was there to do with the equipment at the time and the design sense of its user?

Fast forward 24 years. We now have incredibly sophisticated software and instant output to the medium of our choice. We have unprecedented capability to deliver a message to one person or one million people. And so how do we create emphasis today?

Figure 18.12
How clueless was our lead author back in 1985? This clueless.

The Green Shutter

Homemade breads
Hot breakfasts
Fresh juices
<u>All fresh ingredients</u>

Nothing but THE BEST!

22650 Main St • 510.555.5555

In many cases, we create it as badly as I did back in 1985. I was pretty good at centering—you'd have to give me that.

Theory of relativity

Emphasis is a question not only of degree, but of relativity. Something is only prominent by comparison to its surroundings. In short,

**If you make everything bold,
you have made nothing bold.**

That notion was completely lost on me in 1985, and it remains a lost concept to many who create slides today.

This phenomenon is not far removed from the one that we have already spoken about—when you make everything big, you make it difficult to call attention to particular chunks of content. The make-everything-bold compulsion is a first cousin, and together they conspire to send an audience a stupefying collection of jumbled messages.

I also want to remind you about the most important piece of advice that Part 3 offers, which I outlined on Page 163: you are the presentation. The role of your slides is subordinate to your role. That will be an important undercurrent as we begin this part of the conversation.

ADVANCE RESPONSIBILITIES
PPQ 55-05

The *__maintenance supervisor,__* *__manager__* or *__Quality Assurance__*
__manager__ must ensure the following are completed prior to
departure from maintenance stations:

Quality Check – recorded in logbook and **manager notified**

Service as appropriate – May be accomplished when practical but **final
walkaround must occur within four hours**

Review and/or document any verification requirements

Approve outstanding reports to assure applicable effectivity

Return all log pages to manager on duty

Figure 18.13 is a generic version of an actual client slide with all of its
design elements removed. As we survey this slide quickly we see

- Bold and upper-case title

- Bold regulation number

- Bold introductory sentence with several job titles set in italic and
underlined

- Bold copy

With all of that bold, how ironic it is that the part that stands out to
me are the few words set in normal weight. Everything else is just
noise—boldface has been so abused here as to become utterly meaningless. The creator of this slide has made everything bold and so therefore nothing is bold.

Figure 18.14 is the result of a 10-minute makeover which includes very
little text-editing. Half of the intro sentence has been relocated at the
bottom of the slide, the regulation number moved to the top-right, and
all bold removed from the main copy. Set in bold instead are the key
action words associated with each requirement. The people responsible
for compliance are listed at the bottom; they do not need to be set bold
as they are prominent by their positioning on the slide.

I want to be clear that we are not challenging the importance of the
phrase that you might want to set bold. In Figure 18.15, for instance,
the phrases that are set in bold might be critically important. Our
point is that if it is truly important, it deserves better treatment than

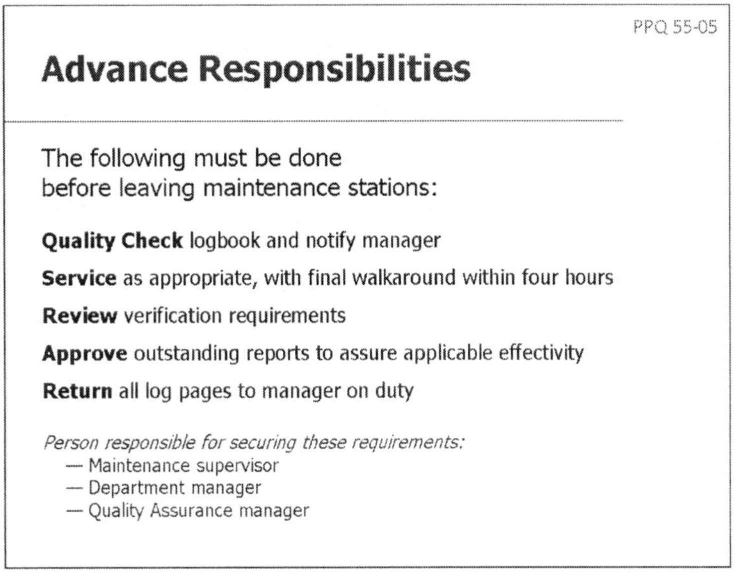

Figure 18.14
The bold on this slide is used judiciously and therefore has much more impact.

PPQ 55-05

Advance Responsibilities

The following must be done
before leaving maintenance stations:

Quality Check logbook and notify manager

Service as appropriate, with final walkaround within four hours

Review verification requirements

Approve outstanding reports to assure applicable effectivity

Return all log pages to manager on duty

Person responsible for securing these requirements:
— Maintenance supervisor
— Department manager
— Quality Assurance manager

merely being set bold on the slide. By virtue of the fact that you are the most important part of the presentation, it is your responsibility to distinguish relative importance and deliver emphasis when warranted. Don't pawn off that critical assignment onto your slides; that's your job! Create emphasis with your voice inflection. Walk to the screen and touch the part of it that merits emphasis. There is no better way to highlight a passage of text than for you, the presenter, to reference it directly, visually and/or verbally.

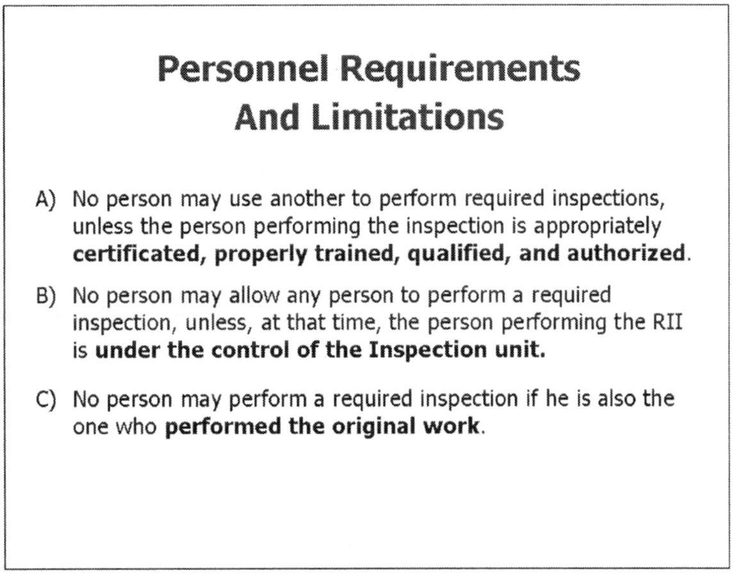

Part Three: Design

Figure 18.15
If certain words are worthy of highlighting, you should do it with your voice and with your gestures. That will carry more weight than a bit of bold on the slide.

Personnel Requirements And Limitations

A) No person may use another to perform required inspections, unless the person performing the inspection is appropriately **certificated, properly trained, qualified, and authorized**.

B) No person may allow any person to perform a required inspection, unless, at that time, the person performing the RII is **under the control of the Inspection unit.**

C) No person may perform a required inspection if he is also the one who **performed the original work**.

Figure 18.16
With text that is to
be emphasized, try
setting it bold but in
a softer color.

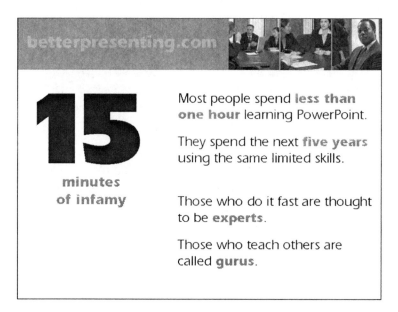

Emphasize with understatement

Recalling the discussion about eye fatigue and its insidious and negative effect on a presentation (see Page 44), if there is a time when you feel that a passage of projected text truly warrants highlighting, consider using a color that is softer, not louder. With black text against a white background, try setting the passage in bold and with a sky blue fill or a soft gray. The lighter color provides a softer contrast, but the text still stands out. I find that audiences respond better to it.

Case in point—Figure 18.16, a slide for a webinar bemoaning the lack of training time that most people get with PowerPoint. The central element of the slide is undoubtedly the gigantic "15"—beyond that, there are a few key words in each of the four statements, and while you can't see the soft blue on these pages, those words clearly stand out from the rest, even in gray, but they are not as potentially jarring as black bold might be.

Too Much Attention, not Enough Focus

At a recent workshop, an attendee sent in this slide for critique and it acutely reminded me of this issue of emphasis.

1 Between the red title, the ornate arrows, the rule around the bullets, and the yellow box, there is entirely too many elements competing for attention. Nice logo at the bottom and attractive strip at the top...neither of which gets noticed in this slide's current state.

This is not just a workplace safety issue

➢ In fact office ergonomic injuries can require major surgery.
➢ Early detection = $3,500
➢ Delay in responding = $80,000

Taking it to the next level
requires a change in the culture of JBSV

◇ **JBSV**

1

2 First step in our remodel is to move the title up to that strip where it belonged in the first place. And by removing the rule and the yellow box, you can now actually see the white space on this slide. As soon as that was done, it becomes immediately apparent that the first bullet should not be a bullet. And yes, those bullets are ugly...

Not just a workplace safety issue

➢ In fact office ergonomic injuries can require major surgery.
➢ Early detection = $3,500
➢ Delay in responding = $80,000

Taking it to the next level
requires a change in the culture of JBSV

◇ **JBSV**

2

3 That first bullet functions much better as a subtitle and, with the title, forms a nice intregrated unit.

The two remaining items in the list look better without their bullets, but they appear a bit isolated. And with everything left-aligned, the concluding text sticks out sorely.

Not just a workplace safety issue

Ergonomic injuries can require major surgery

Early intervention = $3,500
Delayed response = $80,000

Taking it to the next level
requires a change in the culture of JBSV

◇ **JBSV**

3

Part Three: Design

4 At a minimum, the arrows are more active and energetic than the equal sign, and arguably, they represent the relationship better. Opening up the space between them helps, too.

Not just a workplace safety issue

Ergonomic injuries can require major surgery

Early intervention ➡ $3,500

If you delay ➡ $80,000

Taking it to the next level
requires a change in the culture of JBSV

◇ **JBSV** 4

5 Finally, by punching up the text and using the bold-yet-softer technique, the concluding text has much more impact. I recommended to the author that it be set on a click and faded in toward the end of the discussion.

▼ Download 18-17.ppt to see
the progression of this redesign.

Not just a workplace safety issue

Ergonomic injuries can require major surgery

Early intervention ➡ $3,500

If you delay ➡ $80,000

We need a cultural change!

◇ **JBSV** 5

Chapter 19

Designing Presentations for Remote Delivery

The last time I felt like this was in 1999. We asked at the CorelWorld User Conference who in the audience owned a digital camera. Just three years after its introduction to consumer markets in the United States, over three dozen hands rose in a room of about 250.

"This is going to be huge," I said to a friend from Corel Corp., begging the real question as to why I couldn't leverage that prescience into a home with a Beverly Hills or Central Park address. Irrespective of my own lack of investment acumen, indeed, digital photography became THE killer app of the 1990 and early-2000s.

There is another killer app on its way for the presentation community—so new, I barely know how to write about it. Presentations are slowly freeing themselves from the traditional constraint of notebook/projector/screen/person. Leading this charge are webinars, portable devices, and social networking sites. This chapter examines (and speculates) on the unique demands of designing for these emerging presentation destinations.

We Try Harder...

For the better part of 18 chapters, you have had to read my badgerings about getting out from under your slides, not letting them derail you, reducing the amount of text they contain, and practicing restraint with animation.

Well, not so fast.

As we define and discuss alternate ways to deliver a presentation, the common characteristic that these alternatives share is their nomadic quality. One way or another, they deliver a message without a warm body in the room. The most important component to all great presentations is being removed from the formula. You. You are missing!

Your slides will now have to represent you in a way that has heretofore been regarded as impossible or unacceptable. Your slides are going to have to be smarter and they are going to have to try harder.

They are going to have to become the presentation. That changes everything.

Delivering a Presentation File Electronically

The simplest incarnation of the remotely-delivered presentation is the PowerPoint file that you send via email or make available as a download. In this case, we will retreat from none of our admonitions about gratuitous animation or stupid transitions—that's still a one-way ticket to amateur land.

There are a handful of considerations that must be addressed with the self-running PowerPoint file:

Typefaces
Your slide deck will run on someone else's computer and will be at the mercy of that person's typeface collection. Best to play it safe and use a sans serif face that is universally distributed, like Arial or Tahoma.

Security
You will be doing more than showing your slides; you will be giving them away. Make sure that your Notes pages do not contain confidential, compromising, or embarrassing information. My mind invariably drifts to the pharmeceutical conference I once worked. A slide deck was being delivered to the organizer for queueing on the presentation computer. The file opened in Notes view (files remember the view settings present during the last save) and there on the title slide was the

following directive: "Make sure to use all of the proactive verbs that PinHead demands." We're not sure who was represented by this less-than-flattering moniker, but we're pretty sure that the salary of the presenter suddenly became dependent on the sense of humor of he whose hatsize came under scrutiny.

More at issue here is the fact that all of your presentation content is available to be looked at, extracted, and distributed. Yes, you can password-protect the file and disallow saving, exporting, and printing, but it's better for your peace of mind to just build a bridge and get over it. The more restrictions you place on the file, the more unfriendly you make it, and someone hellbent on getting at your content will do so anyway. Our advice? Scrub the file of anything sensitive and send it out without restrictions. If you're squeamish about your audience being able to get a cursor on your text or graphics, send them a PDF file instead. The tech savvy will still be able to extract what they want to, but most won't bother.

Version

Version 2003 enjoys wide-spread saturation in the businessworld, but the same cannot yet be said about version 2007. And because V03 files are reliably read by V07, the safest file format choice for delivery is PowerPoint 2003.

Voice

Here you must address the most fundamental question of all: how will the slides be narrated? The fact that you won't be there alongside them does not absolve you of the responsibility of determining what type of voice to offer. This is usually done one of three ways:

1. Allow the titles of each slide to lead the way. This is the easiest approach, technically speaking, but requires that your titles be descriptive, clear, and inviting.

2. Apply a "textover" (I might have just made up that word). Integrated with the slide's build is text that is clearly recognizable as the narration of the slide. This requires an additional element beyond using the title, but I nonetheless find it easier to create and better received by the audience.

3. Adding a voiceover. By integrating audio clips, you bring back the idea that a human presenter is leading the way. This is obviously the most labor-intensive. Is it worth the effort? You tell me...keep reading...

A Case Study in Choosing Narration

A primer on digital photography provided the perfect backdrop to experiment with adding narration to a slide deck that was to be delivered electronically.

1 When shown, this slide deck begins with a menu offering the three choices outlined on the previous page. Each of the three numbers is a link to a custom show set to show and then return to this menu. All slides past the menu are hidden and the setup calls for an infinite loop, so if you were to try to advance to the next slide, you would stay right here. In other words, the only way to proceed with this presentation is to click one of the numbers.

2 This slide relies on the title and the animation to describe the value of framing your subject(s). After the title appears, when the viewer follows the <space> prompt, the black rectangle appears and the photo crops to it. After that, the story of this slide is over and the "Press <space>..." line at the bottom appears.

3 This next slide employs "textovers"—strings of text that appear in the animation sequence along with the crop. It is more dynamic than just using a title, as it simulates a narration, but without the overhead and effort of creating and embedding audio clips.

▼ With most of the topics in this book, downloading the examples is optional. This one is different: in order to appreciate this case study, you will need to download cropping.ppt from whypptsucks.com.

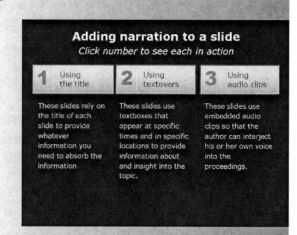

1

2

3

4 This slide uses embedded audio clips to tell its story. It is the most engaging, and the most arduous. There are two clips on this slide, along with a title (which, as you can see, can afford to be more coy and less descriptive) and a text string that accompanies the narration.

5 The build for the narrated slides is more involved, as the audio clips need to be blended with the text, with the cues, and with the crop animation.

The file is bigger, also, and it took more time to create. I created the audio for all six slides using Audacity, the free audio editor. I did it in one take, even though I messed up several times. After a mistake, I paused for one second and repeated that segment. Then I cleaned up and exported each segment into its own WAV file (22Khz sample rate, 16bit sample size, mono), and integrated each one into the slides.

6 I ensured that all WAV files were embedded in the presentation file by setting the Link Sounds threshold very high. As a result, the file is not small: 10MB.

Recording the audio clips only took about 10 minutes. Editing and exporting them to individual WAV files (15 in all) was about a 30-minute job, and then sequencing them with the existing animations required about an hour.

▶ The technique of presenting all three methods to you in cropping.ppt will be of interest to advanced users, and it will be the subject of discussion in Chapter 27.

4

5

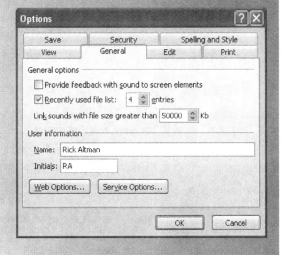

6

Part Three: Design

Navigation

There are two approaches that most presentation designers take to creating a self-running presentation: 1) Establish the timing automatically and have each segment build and each transition occur according to a timed sequence; and 2) Have them occur manually and prompt the viewer to advance when ready.

Doesn't this call into question the very definition of a "self-running" presentation? Does it not imply that you, the viewer, can just sit back and watch? Perhaps it does, so you'll forgive the entire industry for using inexact terminology: a self-running presentation is one which is not delivered live by a presenter but is instead run, controlled, and/or watched by the viewer. This can be a video at a trade show in "kiosk" mode (where it runs on an indefinite loop), a slide deck that has pre-established sequences and timed transitions, or one that cues the viewer to advance.

I am a proponent of getting the viewer involved and an even bigger advocate of being consistent with whatever choice you make. Little is more frustrating to a viewer than not knowing if and when to advance. Either do it all for your viewer or do none of it.

And again, consider doing none of it. This will be a very passive experience for your audience members as they watch their screen without a live person. Involving them in even the smallest way, pressing Space, will help engage them. More important, if you establish the timing for the show, you imply that you know better than they a myriad of factors that you probably don't—like the pace at which a person prefers to read text, process information, and ponder ideas.

I think empowering the viewer to control the pace is a sign of courtesy and respect.

Mechanically speaking, it does not require much to create on-screen navigation—download cropping.ppt to see the simple <space> cues that appear on the slide. An arrow would suffice, as would the word <advance>. You can even create a hyperlink back to a menu slide and build an entire web-like construct.

If you do consider such an approach, it is helpful to consider which elements belong on the slide master and which ones should not go there. Figure 19.2 is an example of a slide that has been converted into an electronic presentation, with clear links along the bottom to aid in navigation. The table builds row by row, and when it is done, the Press Space for next cue appears in the lower-left.

Figure 19.2
This slide is made friendlier and more navigable by the links along the bottom. But not all links should be created equal...

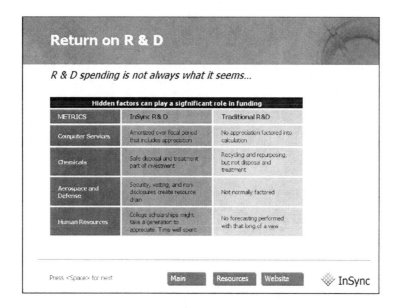

Part Three: Design

You might be tempted to build all four elements that appear along the bottom into the slide master, but that might be inadvisable in all but the simplest of slide designs. Placing the three links along the right on the slide master is a fine idea, as you want them to always be visible, always available, always clickable.

If you place the Next slide cue on the slide master, it too will always be visible...whether you want that or not. There will be many times, we predict, that you will create a more involved build that will involve intermediate clicking. It would be vital for the viewer to know not to press Space until he or she were ready. Yes, you could make it part of the animation sequence of slide master elements, but that dooms it to appearing before any animation performed on the slide itself. Better to build the Press Space cue on the slide itself, where you can better control when it appears.

On the other hand, if you just want a persistent button that, when clicked, advances, go ahead and build that on the master slide. But then, most users know how to advance a slide deck, so how much value is it really bringing to the experience?

Our conclusion is that the most helpful on-screen cue is one that tells you, the viewer: the current idea on display is over, and when you are ready, press a key or click the mouse to move to the next idea.

Verbosity
All that stuff I told you about the three-word challenge and putting your slides on a diet? Well, you can forget about that when your slides

are called upon to do the heavy lifting. When the text on a slide is the only way to communicate a verbal message, a whole new set of design principles assume command. It is more critical than ever that your slides engage the viewer and that you control the flow of elements. You are capable of being brilliant; I don't think your slides can be. There's a limit to how good presenterless slides can be. So in a way, you work from a disadvantage when you design and create self-running presentations. How best can you overcome that disadvantage?

Figure 19.3
Viewers of this slide will need to read this text for themselves. Can its readability be improved?

Richmond Rescue

Personalized Adoption Appointment Program

We know that life is busy, so we have introduced an innovative way for you to adopt your pet. In addition to our regular adoption hours, our Personalized Adoption Appointment Program enables you to set up a convenient time to visit pre-selected pets that fit your lifestyle, wants and needs. Please call our Adoption Center at (804) 555-1307 and let us know you'd like to set up an appointment to visit with our pets. It is that easy! Please note that appointments are not required to visit with our pets.

PETRESCUE

Figure 19.4
Opening up the line spacing and dividing the text into three chunks certainly helps.

Richmond Rescue

Personalized Adoption Appointment Program

We know that life is busy, so we have introduced an innovative way for you to adopt your pet.

Our Personalized Adoption Appointment Program enables you to set up a convenient time to visit pre-selected pets that fit your lifestyle, wants, and needs.

Please call our Adoption Center at (804) 555-1307 to set up a visit with our pets.

Press <Space> to advance

PETRESCUE

Figure 19.3 is a slide about a municipal pet adoption program. As a self-running presentation, it has a lot of work to do—it must explain the program, generate interest, and include a call to action.

If this were a live presentation, this block of text would define the worst kind of Death by PowerPoint. Is it any better as a self-running presentation?

Only marginally.

Just because it is now acceptable to include more text on a slide does not mean that a solid block of text is going to be welcome. Just the opposite; it is even more vital to make the text as inviting as possible.

Figure 19.4 is much better, with the copy in three distinct sections, the margins narrower, and the line spacing opened up. And if the corporate brass allows something so unique, Figure 19.5 is even better. Two things:

■ Note that Figures 19.4 and 5 both have navigation control. Even something as simple as the one word in 19.5 is sufficient.

■ Including a lot of white text on a black background is risky, however dramatic it looks here. Readability suffers with reversed-out text and it would be hell to print. A slide like this one is near the threshold of tolerance for white text. Anything more dense, and I would argue against its use.

Figure 19.5
There is no reason why you still can't look for a big evocative photo to blend with your text-based message.

Preparing Webinars

The notion of delivering a seminar from your own home or office, attended by people in their own homes or offices, was gaining traction before the bottom fell out of our economy. As travel budgets are getting sliced into smithereens, the webinar is becoming even more popular.

In most cases, preparing a webinar does not require that you learn new software, only that you use PowerPoint in different ways. As with the remotely-delivered presentation, the different medium suggests several shifts in strategy and this section of the chapter will define and discuss those strategies.

The bandwidth variable

The single biggest influence on your experience as content creator and/or presenter of a webinar is the performance drag created by your Internet connection. Little is more frustrating than watching your carefully-crafted fades and morphs become reduced to pathetic spasms of pixelation by the rush-hour traffic that we refer to as "latency."

For this reason, you should forego every form of animation except for the basic Appear. Wipes are likely to become herky-jerky, fades become stutter steps, and the more ornate choices promise to embarrass you to your core.

Furthermore, some of the online services will request that you not even run your slides in Show mode; you will be asked to simply step through them in Edit mode. In that case, the only way to create a build is from one slide to the next. Experienced webinar creators often choose that route to begin with so they are prepared for any scenario.

Even with your slides stripped of all forms of excess motion, the very act of advancing from one slide to the next will take place for your audience more slowly than what you will see on your own computer. This is why we always recommend that you request two nodes into the webinar from your location—as host and as guest. If you have a notebook PC at your disposal, log on from it as a guest and have it next to you as you deliver your content. You will then see exactly when a latency storm hits so you can adjust your cadence and pace accordingly.

One last admonition: Unless you have carefully tested them, avoid using transparent objects on your webinar slides. They could go from looking beautiful to looking awful before your eyes.

Strong voice, strong visuals

Listening to a disembodied voice is never as engaging and as vital as when watching a live presenter. No eye contact, no watching lips move, no absorption of gestures—these all suggest that your voice has to carry the day. You need to find occasions to raise your voice, opportunities to create emphasis, and times to stage dramatic pauses.

And whatever you do, don't read your slides. It's even more irritating for an online audience than it is for a live one. At the same time, it's much easier for your webinar audience to give up on you if you commit Death by PowerPoint. They're just one new email or text message away from tuning you out if you become a drone.

Figure 19.6 is a run-of-the-mill slide for a webinar discussing strategies for better workplace performance. If this slide appears like this, Universal Axiom No. 2 immediately rears its ugly head, as you feel the overwhelming compulsion to read the slide.

Say goodbye to half of your audience in 10 seconds. The only thing worse than watching a presenter read this slide after you have already read it is listening to a disembodied voice read it after you. Your audience would tune out, determine that you are an inane drone, and you would deserve it.

Audience engagement is a much more fragile commodity on a webinar, so the stakes are higher.

This is the best opportunity ever for you to substitute big, strong visuals for your text. Even if you are addicted to reading text word for word, you can get away with it on a webinar—nobody sees your script.

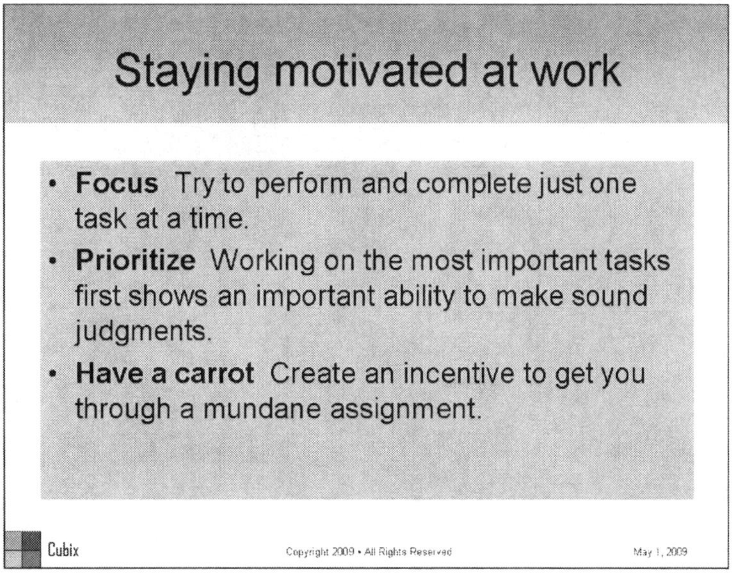

Figure 19.6
Nobody on a webinar will want to read this slide and then hear you say it. They'll be off checking email in a flash.

Staying motivated at work

- **Focus** Try to perform and complete just one task at a time.
- **Prioritize** Working on the most important tasks first shows an important ability to make sound judgments.
- **Have a carrot** Create an incentive to get you through a mundane assignment.

Cubix   Copyright 2009 • All Rights Reserved   May 1, 2009

These slides will prove much more effective to the fleeting attention span of a webinar audience. This first image is one that even non-golfers can relate to—who would not rather be anywhere than at work?

The next slide introduces the three key objectives that you want them to focus on, and it is here where you make your case. If you have to, read your script word for word.

And when you're done, then reveal the rest of the copy. As we discussed in Chapter 8, saying it before displaying it is a much better experience for your viewers.

If the webinar organizers intend to create PDF files from your slides and send them as handouts, try to persuade them to let you create them instead. A progression like this one is great for visuals, but tedious and annoying as three separate pages of a handout. Better to use the strategies discussed in Chapter 17 and craft a dedicated set of handouts.

They're going to multitask...get over it

It is the dream of every webinar leader that he or she is so captivating and engaging that every member of the audience is riveted to the browser window, hanging on every word.

Emphasis on dream.

It is not necessarily a reflection on you or commentary on your webinar skills if the attention of your audience members wanes. They are in their cube or home with their Blackberrys, not in an environment in which it is rude to check their emails and texts. Not to put too fine a point on it, but during a webinar that you host, you are not a speaker so much as you are just another application window.

Sorry if the truth hurts.

You have two choices: fight it or accept it. If you try to compete with the distractions, you will find yourself just pumping up your volume to the point where, as we discussed last chapter, in your attempt to emphasize everything, you will be emphasizing nothing.

Accepting this situation does not mean conceding; just the opposite. Understand that while you are talking, audience members might be listening to you while watching something else. Or as you have moved to a topic that doesn't interest them, they are waiting for the next topic.

So give them easy-to-follow cues that tell them that they should regroup and return their attention to you and the webinar screen.

- State prominently: "Okay, for our next topic..."

- Transition between starkly-different photos.

- Ask a rhetorical question or make a controversial statement.

If you try to make everything important, you cry wolf. If you reserve this type of emphasis for transitions, your audience members will appreciate the cue and will indeed stop what they are doing and pay attention to the new topic.

If only for a moment...sigh...

A Brave New World of Social Networking

We are wholly unqualified to speak to this final topic of the chapter, but that's okay—so is the rest of the world. Nobody really knows what is about to happen at the intersection between presentation theory and FaceBook, Twitter, SlideShare, YouTube, and others.

At its core, presentation is a form of communication, and these new technologies are redefining the way we communicate. Twelve months ago, few of us were writing on anyone's walls and nobody was following anyone's tweets. Likewise, it wouldn't surprise me if, 12 months from now, we are uploading slide decks to the cloud and burning feeds for them.

Just about any content you create today can be shared in multiple forms, and if the next version of PowerPoint doesn't sport a wide and robust Export command, Microsoft will have swung and missed in that department.

I suspect—no, actually, I am certain—that these four paragraphs on this topic will be an entire chapter in our next edition.

Working Your Back Channel

Today, we look with scorn at audience members who are playing with their mobile devices during a presentation. Those days might be numbered, though. Many of those who seem to be disconnected from the presentation content are actually anything but—they are busy disseminating the ideas they are hearing in real time.

Twitter has created the ultimate back channel for modern-day presentations, and instead of measuring the success of your talk by how attentive people look, you might soon be counting how many heads are pointing lapward at mobile devices. The more tweets a seminar gets, the wider its reach becomes.

What's more, presenters can tune in to their own Twitter tags during a presentation and take the pulse of the audience, gauge feedback, and adjust on the fly.

I'll get back to you when I decide if my prevailing reaction to that idea is excitement or fear. Either way, never a dull moment these days in the presentation community...

Chapter 20

Real-World Makeovers

I am never entirely comfortable with the idea of presenting makeovers that I perform for clients, and this is for two specific reasons, both of which I need to learn to deal with:

- **It feels like showing off.** This is completely stupid of me, because I operate in a community in which just about everything I do is showing off. I present in front of large audiences, I host an internationally-known conference, and I write books like this one. Why is showing my work any different? Maybe, it's because of the second reason...

- **I'm no designer.** What business do I have performing a makeover when I barely know what I'm doing??

It's true, I have no formal background in the arts. I describe myself as a serviceable craftsman of clean business graphics. Your jaw is not going to hit the floor when you see my work (which you've already seen plenty of times already across these pages). More important, I don't want you to be intimidated, as you might if you saw some of the wonderful work done by the truly brilliant people who design presentation graphics.

I want you to say to yourself, "I could do that." I want you to be able to relate to the work. I want you to be able to visualize how you could do the same things in your own work.

US Airways: A New Look from the Trainers

Most people think of PowerPoint as the tool used to persuade or move audiences. In fact, some estimates suggest that it is used more for training than in sales, marketing, and entertainment environments combined. The Maintenance Training department at US Airways conducts regular training classes for its team of mechanics and relies heavily on PowerPoint slides to guide the instructors through the curriculum. When the supervisor called me in for assistance, it became immediately clear to me that the slides created for instructors were usually working against them, not for them.

1 This title slide, typical of all title slides across the curriculum, is created without regard for audience connectedness. (We have greeked potentially sensitive passages of text.) All-caps titles are difficult to read, line breaks are haphazard, the US Air logo is too small, and the vertical swoosh not balanced with the text. The one nice visual element might be invisible to you: a nice photo of an aircraft is tinted so far into the back that you probably cannot even see it here in print.

Do you watch "The Office"? This title slide appears to have been created with all the personal warmth of Dwight Schrute. Maintenance training is serious business, no doubt, but there needs to be the sense that there are human beings behind it, and this first impression misses that mark.

2 & 3 These slides exhibit many of the tendencies that we have described here in Part 3: bullets of one; too much emphasis, resulting in no emphasis; titles set all in upper case; poor spacing resulting in no visible relief. For the

1

2

3

"serious flight hazard" warning, the slide creator ran out of emphasis options (the bullet is already set bold), so he needed to resort to underlining. The swoosh has moved to the bottom, where it collides with the text, and the watermarked aircraft remains on these pages. I kept thinking about what a nice image it is...if only people could see it.

4

4 When untinted, the aircraft in the background creates a stunning image. It's clear and sharp, and is set against a beautiful sky-blue background. It was crying out to be used in a more promi-nent way.

5 Dropping the plane down a bit on the slide accomplishes two things: 1) It depicts a stronger sense of motion, as the plane is now flying up into the slide; and 2) It creates great usable white space (blue space?) along the top half of the slide.

5

6 With a more prominent logo, and sensibly-sized titles, this creates a much stronger identity for the curriculum. And with so many new hires coming through these courses, this becomes a first impression of the entire airline.

Trainers expressed concern over titles that would be too long to fit that space, and you can probably guess what my response was. Shorten them! Who needs titles that long?

As it turns out, they do, as much of the wording for this curriculum must follow FAA requirements. However, when we removed the upper-case lettering, every title fit. For any that require more words, the subtitle is set smaller and could accommodate that.

Our technical editor Geetesh Bajaj insisted on his own commentary here: "These slides look so much happier!"

6

The Registered
Maintenance Item

MPPM 555-55

U S AIRWAYS

7 Interior slide designs were kept very clean and simple, because heaven knows there will be enough content asking to be used. The curvy line was replaced with two straight ones, using the US Airways colors, and the fading rule below the title matches the accent color below.

The title is formatted to be bottom-aligned and the main text top-aligned. That ensures, as you can see here, that the space above and below the fading rule will always be the same.

8 This second master represents only a subtle change, but it has proved crucial to the content creators, who kept getting into trouble with bullets of one, or with attempts to remove the bullet, causing funky indents. This master accommodates complete sentences (a fact of life, due to the FAA regulations) that should not be formatted as bullets.

9 The concept of a transition slide was foreign to the department—content creators simply reused the title layout. This design is similar to the title, but with the aircraft tinted deep into the background.

The more challenging part of my time spent with US Airways involved my admonitions about reducing the amount of verbage on slides (see the facing page for a couple of doosies).

This involves much more effort and forethought than the creators probably anticipated. Many harbor the belief that they can bring in someone like me to make their lives easier and reduce their workload. In fact, many of my suggestions to them involved putting forth more effort, not less. Creating the appearance that your slides are not working so hard is only accomplished by you working hard.

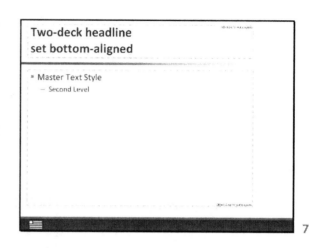

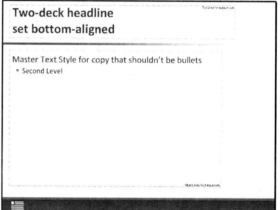

Before

After

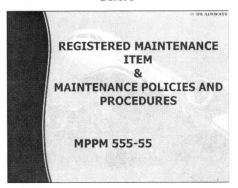

21 CXR Part 555.555 Requirements

ALL ETOPS approved part carriers must have:

1. Αν ΕΤΟΠΣ Μαιντενανχε προγραμ δφινιν ρεσπονσιβιλιτιεσ ανδ προχεδυρεσ ινχλυδινγ:
   * Α λιστ οφ ΕΤΟΠΣ Σψστεμ
   * Δεφινεδ ΕΤΟΠΣ μαιντενανχε ρεθυιρεμεντσ
   * ΕΤΟΠΣ συππορτ προγραμ ανδ προχεδυρεσ
   * Δυτιεσ ανδ ρεσπονσιβιλιτιεσ φορ εσερψονε ινωολωεδ ωιτη τηε φλιγητσ
   * Α λιστ ρεφερενχιν λοχατιον οφ ματεριαλ ρεγαρδιν ΕΤΟΠΣ
2. Α Ρεθυιρεμεντ φορ Δαιλψ ορ ΕΤΟΠΣ Σερωιχε χηεχκ

21 CFR Part 555.555 Requirements

All ETOPS-approved Part carriers must have:

1. Αν ΕΤΟΠΣ Μαιντενανχε προγραμ δφινιν ρεσπονσιβιλιτιεσ ανδ προχεδυρεσ ινχλυδινγ:
   - Α λιστ οφ ΕΤΟΠΣ Σψστεμ
   - Δεφινεδ ΕΤΟΠΣ μαιντενανχε ρεθυιρεμεντ
   - ΕΤΟΠΣ συππορτ προγραμ ανδ προχεδυρεσ
   - Δυτιεσ ανδ ρεσπονσιβιλιτιεσ φορ εσερψονε ινωολωεδ ωιτη τηε φλιγητσ
   - Α λιστ ρεφερενχιν λοχατιον οφ ματεριαλ ρεγαρδιν ΕΤΟΠΣ
2. Α Ρεθυιρεμεντ φορ Δαιλψ ορ ΕΤΟΠΣ Σερωιχε χηεχκ

ETOPS Significant System Maintenance Verification

MPPM 555-55

Three Types of Verification:
* Α γρουνδ οπερατιοναλ χηεχκ
* Αν ιν-φλιγητ σεριφιχατιον
   * ΕΤΟΠΣ ρεσενυε φλιγητ πριορ το ΕΤΟΠΣ εντρψ ποιντ (ΕΕΠ)
   * Νον-ΕΤΟΠΣ ρεσενυε φλιγητ
* Α τεστ φλιγητ

NOTE: *Ground Operational Checks*

* Τηε Γρουνδ Οπερατιοναλ Χηεχκ ωιλλ βε περφορμεδ ΙΑΩ τηε αππλιχαβλε ΑΜΜ
* Αλλ Γρουνδ Οπο Χηεχκσ ρεσυιρεδ φορ περφιχατιον οφ μαιντενανχε αχτιονσ ον ΕΤΟΠΣ αιρχραφτ αρε ΡΙΙ

Maintenance Operations Control (MOC) will make the determination as to which type of verification will be required based upon the criteria outlined in the MPPM 555-55

ETOPS Significant System Maintenance Verification

MPPM 555-55

Three Types of Verification:
* Α γρουνδ οπερατιοναλ χηεχκ
   – Περφορμεδ ΙΑΩ της αππλιχαβλε ΑΜΜ
   – Χηεχκσ ρεθυιρεδ φορ μαιντενανχε περιοιχατιον αρε ΡΙΙ
* Αν ιν-φλιγητ σεριφιχατιον
   – Ρεωενυε φλιγητ πριορ το ΕΤΟΠΣ εντρψ ποιντ (ΕΕΠ)
   – Νον-ΕΤΟΠΣ ρεσενυε φλιγητ
* Α τεστ φλιγητ

Maintenance Operations Control (MOC) will make the determination as to which type of verification will be required based upon the criteria outlined in the MPPM 555-55

Brief Overview of the ETOPS Policy

* The US Airways ETOPS Policies and Procedures are designed to:
   * Μακε χερταιν τηατ ΥΣ Αιρωαψσ αιρχραφτ αρε νοτ δισπατχηεδ ιντο ΕΤΟΠΣ υνλεσσ τηε ρεθυιρεμεντο φορ ΕΤΟΠΣ χαπαβιλιτψ ηαωε βεεν μετ.
   * Τηατ αλλ περσοννελ περφορμιν μαιντενανχε ον ΕΤΟΠΣ αιρχραφτ αρε προπερλψ θυαλιφιεδ ανδ αυτηοριζεδ.
   * Ενσυρε τηατ α προχεσσ φορ ωεριφιχατιον οφ μαιντενανχε αχτιονσ τακεν ον αν ΕΤΟΠΣ Σιγνιφιχαντ Σψστεμ (σ) εξιστσ.
   * Μακε συρε τηατ τηερε ισ α ρεχυρρινγ αυδιτ προγραμ το ενσυρε χομπλιανχε ωιτη τηε ΥΣ Αιρωαψσ ΕΤΟΠΣ Πολιχψ.

Brief Overview of the ETOPS Policy

* Aircraft not dispatched until ready
* Personnel qualified and authorized
* Verification of maintenance
* Program to ensure compliance

Solavie: Giving a Facelift to a Face Product

Proof that Facebook can be good for business, I reconnected with Pam, a high school friend from about 175 years ago. As we wrote on each other's walls, she told me about Solavie, her line of skin and face care products that feature specific formulations based on the climate in which you live.

Most health and care products focus on your skin-type, not your environment, and that not only caught my interest, but also the interest of the QVC shopping network. QVC editors asked her to visit with them so they could determine whether to carry her product line.

The graphic work done to this point was elaborate—in fact, too elaborate for a presentation that needed to feature the woman as much as the product. Pam is an energetic and passionate advocate for her ideas, and I felt it critical that she shine during the QVC visit.

Therefore, a few things bothered me about the slides that Pam showed me. First, the watery background, while clever and on message, displayed as a drab gray and only served to reduce contrast and readability. Second, the first two content slides in the deck, **2 & 3**, would put Pam on defense. All of those data points and all of those paragraphs would derail even the most experienced presenter, which Pam was not. We had to find a way to brighten up the imagery and ensure that Pam could get out from under the slides.

On the positive, the logo is beautiful and the six enviroment icons are clean and descriptive. I wanted to create visual memory around them.

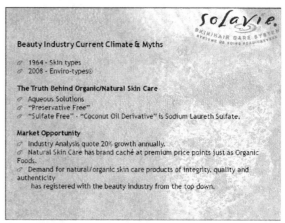

1

2

3

4 As far as I was concerned, if Pam just wanted to put up this one slide and talk, she'd likely succeed. The longer this title slide stays up, the more those six icons become ingrained and the more that Pam just talks, sharing her expertise and her zeal for the product.

5 I normally resist such a strong and intrusive running footer, but not in this case. I loved the logo along the bottom left and wanted every opportunity to tie in those icons with the six enviro-types that form the basis for Pam's innovation. (See Page 157 for a discussion on the animation technique we devised for introducing each of the six types.)

6 The icons also served as gateways to information on demand—content that would be too dense, unless specifically asked for by the QVC staff. For instance, clicking the Shore icon from any slide whisks you to this slide here, after which you are returned to your previous location.

Pam had never heard of a wireless remote and I insisted that she purchase one. The last thing I wanted was to have her tethered to a notebook—we didn't know the type of room she would be in, but I wanted her free to roam it.

She suffered the type of withdrawal typical whenever I take away slides full of text, as her entire experience with giving presentations was limited to displaying documents on the screen and then repreating them. As always, though, when you find someone who has something compelling to say and you give her a chance to say it, good things happen. Meanwhile, we're still waiting to hear back from QVC...

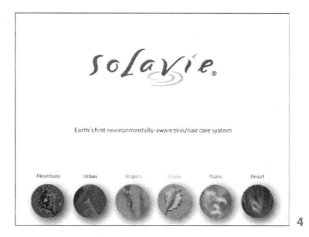

4

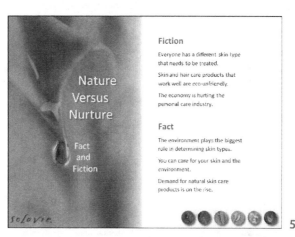

5

6

Part Three: Design

Before

After

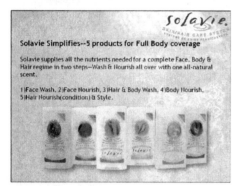

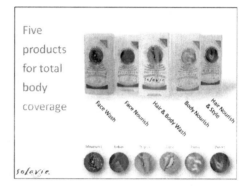

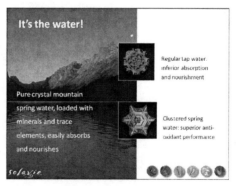

Hillary Clinton Commits Death by PowerPoint

As part of her narrative on being the more electable candidate for the hotly-contested 2008 Democratic nomination, the campaign for Senator Hillary Clinton distributed a PowerPoint slide deck to Democratic members of the House of Representatives on May 9, 2008. It was her hope that it would be viewed by many uncommitted superdelegates who might decide to commit support to her.

1 Not to suggest that she lost because of this, but the slides that the campaign sent up to Capitol Hill that night did nothing to help Clinton's chances. If the Clinton campaign had sought my advice, I would have pushed, at a minimum, for an entirely different approach to the design and execution of this self-running presentation. But if I'm being completely honest, I would have advised them against sending out the slide deck at all.

Those of us not in and around the Capitol did not get to see the actual slides, just low-resolution representations like the ones at right. But there were enough pixels for us to conclude that Senator Clinton did indeed succumb to Death by PowerPoint.

The slides contained a weak attempt at branding, via a slide header that contained the campaign logo. Beyond that, however, the slides exhibited a near-total lack of cohesion and design. Let us count the ways...

1. Headlines shout in all caps and all have underlines (**2** and **3**). I can only wonder how many congressional aides clicked on them, thinking they were hyperlinks.

2. The headline isn't even a headline—it's more like a running header. The slides do not actually contain true headlines.

3. Photo use is haphazard with one of the senator stuffed into the lower-left corner on two different slides and then a non-descript

1

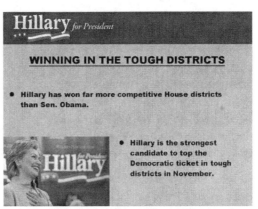

2

3

and incongruous photo of the capitol building dropped onto another slide.

4. The table (**4**) is too much for any busy professional to deal with and the PacMan chart next to it does nothing to illuminate the message.

5. We're not sure where the bar graph (**5**) came from, or the pie chart (**6**), but they are clearly static images, not live charts. How do we know this? Because on both slides, the images were pasted on top of the text! It is particularly egregious and embarrassing on Slide 6, where it appears that someone tried to cover up a legend with an opaque rectangle, and in the process, concealed much of the final paragraph.

6. The last slide (**7**) lacks any sort of punch befitting a concluding slide. It repeats the photo from Slide 2, repeats the running header, and offers a concluding sentence that appears to have been massacred by a committee on political correctness. This slide also displays the line "Paid for by Hillary Clinton for President." We hope they didn't pay much for it.

As I said, we did not see the actual slide deck, so we cannot say for sure whether the Clinton team attempted to create builds to sequence some of the chunkier data, like the charts and graphs. If we give her content creators the benefit of the doubt and assume that they did create builds for the more dense slides, then they are guilty of creating no navigational assistance whatsoever for the viewers working through the slides. In other words, if they did click through a build, they would have no way of knowing when that slide's sequenced information had concluded.

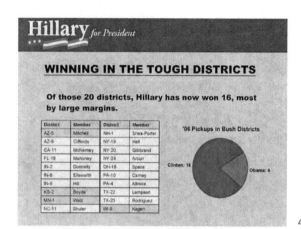

4

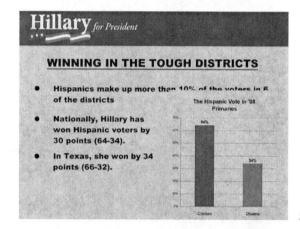

5

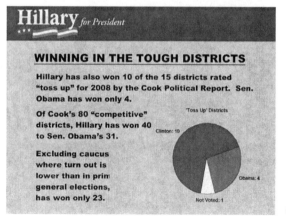

6

The Makeover

This should not have been a slide deck in the first place; it should have been a document (elaboration coming).

Be that as it may, as we ponder how we would go about recreating these slides (pretending that we were hired to redesign them; we were not), we note that there is nothing in the original slide deck to move someone to take action. There is only an appeal to the intellectual component of the argument and that is rarely enough to compel someone to action.

8 The irony in all of this is that this visually unappealing and unemotional slide deck was put together by the same campaign that created a killer website, replete with thousands of excellent photos. In about 90 minutes, I was able to produce an entire makeover of the slides, relying just on low-res screen grabs of website photos.

9 I did not concern myself much with a slide master or a color scheme, as I knew the layout of each slide would be determined by the photo I chose for it. But I did set a standard for typeface (Verdana) and size (28 for titles, 20 for text).

10 The other common element I employed is a favorite technique for helping blend text with a photo—the gradually-changing transparent fill. Over areas that need less contrast and a darker background, I create a black rectangle and set its transparency to go from 0 (solid black) to 100% (completely transparent). I then set the text over the less transparent part.

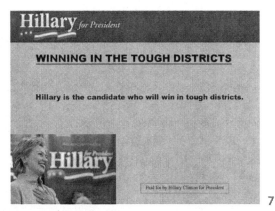

7

8

9

10

11 The remake of the table slide was the most arduous, requiring first a photo with sufficient open space and then a trip into my image-editing software to blur out the background. Perhaps I should have gone a different way with this slide, instead of trying to burn the table into a photo, but I only allowed myself 90 minutes. So this is as good as it got.

Again, it was remakable how easy it was to get good imagery of Senator Clinton and equally unfathomable why the campaign itself ignored all of it.

Still Not Good Enough

While I think that the makeover is much better than the original effort (if you can even call it an "effort"), there is still a fundamental disconnect that is taking place here with the campaign's appeal to superdelegates.

In short, this message should not have been created as slideware; it should have been a PDF document. Without a live person advocating these positions, the bulleted content is insufficient for fleshing out the argument, in the original slide deck or the improved one.

11

12

Clinton's arguments are too nuanced to be made by static bullet slides, especially poorly-designed ones. They require deeper discussion and development, and if that is not going to be made by a live presenter, it needs to be made by printed words.

This deliverable should have been a completely-formatted document, created in InDesign or Xpress, or at a minimum, Publisher, with evocative photos, fully-formulated paragraphs, and integrated data charts. The whole thing should have been RIPed to a PDF file with relevant links to URLs for yet deeper analysis.

The data and the argument were potentially compelling, but I score this as a missed opportunity for the New York Senator…

Part Four

Death, Taxes, and Public Speaking

We would like to start by telling you what this part of the book will *not* do. These four chapters will not teach you the art of public speaking. I couldn't do that if we were in the same room together—to suggest that the pages of a book could do it would be mere pulp fiction. There are some who believe that outstanding public speakers were born with their talents and all the training in the world couldn't equal that. We won't participate in that debate, because we're not interested in whether you were preordained to be a great speaker—we care only about making you better than you are right now. And on that score, there is only good news: there are real, tangible, physical behaviors that you can perform to make you a more effective presenter. And that is our focus here.

Better than Bullets

What if we told you about a visual aid that is more effective than PowerPoint, less abused than bullet points, and does not require the rental or purchase of a projector?

The lights can be completely up while you use this particular aid and a screen is not required. You do not need extensive training to use it, and you don't have to buy a book like this one. You do need to read a short chapter in said book, Chapter 21 to be precise, but that's all.

Best of all, you do not need to buy this visual aid. You already own it. In fact, you own two of them, and that's good, because they work best in pairs.

We refer, of course, to your hands—the best sidekick a good storyteller could possibly have. Your hands are how you direct attention, how you bring nuance to an idea, how you provide color commentary to complement your slides' play by play.

Communicating With Your Hands

Here is the most important piece of advice that we can give you about your hands:

Show them!

When you offer the palm of your hand to your audience members, you do the public equivalent of baring your soul. It is an important component of the trust-building process, and trust is the first ingredient of a good presenter-audience relationship. This doesn't change with the size of your audience: one or one hundred, your hands might say more about you than anything else.

You might be a natural at this and not need any direction. Most aren't. Most need to make conscious efforts to work their hands into a presentation in a way that feels natural and genuine. And I can write about this until my hands fall off from writer's cramp and it won't be as effective as your seeing it in action. All of the following photos are still images taken from low-resolution video, but they capture moments in time when various speakers have become one with their hands.

One of the most polished presenters in our community is Jim Endicott, who authored the foreword for this book. No stranger to anyone who has attended PowerPoint Live, Jim describes himself as introverted, almost shy, when he is not speaking; put him in front of an audience, though, and he comes alive.

Figure 21.1 has captured one of Jim's trademark gestures, as he asks his audience "who among us wants their presenters to be perfect?" He doesn't have to verbally ask for a show of hands; by raising his own hand, he invites audience members to raise theirs. And with the "who among us," phrase, he removes potential barriers between himself and his audience. In these five seconds, and with this one gesture, he creates a connection with the room that he will be able to cultivate over the next hour.

Even with an audience of presentation professionals, most in the room are unaware of this complex dynamic. They just know that they're interested and engaged in what their seminar leader has to say, and our evaluations confirm this.

Jim concluded the point by sharing a personal experience and Figure 21.2 shows a body in perfect synch with the words. If he were actress Sally Field, the caption might read "You like me!" Kidding aside, arms out and palms open says to the group "I'm hiding nothing...this is the real me...I'm willing to be vulnerable." These messages resonate loudly

Figure 21.1
This show of the hand is how Jim Endicott asks his audience members for a show of their own hands.

on many levels, most of them subconscious. You probably don't know Jim Endicott, but don't you feel as if you could place your trust in him from seeing this photo? His hands help to give you that impression.

▶ Jim is quite deft at making gestures while holding a wireless remote. Believe me when I say that this takes practice. The first time I tried to count to one in public, while my index finger was on the slide advance button, I used my second finger. That didn't go over too well...

Figure 21.2
Jim invites trust with gestures that open him up.

Better gestures while seated: the instructor's challenge

Half of the work that I do with PowerPoint is instructional. Therefore, I often find myself seated at a table behind a computer, actively working with a software application. While the audience accepts this physical barrier between us, I must still work to overcome it.

Figure 21.3 shows two such moments. No subtle gesture at my sides or even in front of my chest will be absorbed by others in the room. All of my gestures must be wide and/or high. Most of the time, my audience members are not even looking at me—they're watching the screen. And when they watch the screen, I'm not just asking them to view a PowerPoint slide; I'm insisting that they follow my cursor as it drives software.

When I have a point to make, I have to bring their attention back to me, and I am not comfortable blanking the screen (my point might only take 10 seconds, yet many in the room will prefer to continue to study the screen). From that seated position, I am going to have to make an emphatic gesture, requiring good posture and good computer screen clearance.

I have a simple measure for a good day leading a seminar: if my shoulders are sore and my back hurts, it means I've done well...

Figure 21.3
Seated presenters must work their bodies and hands even more.

Julie Terberg is a brilliant designer who has chosen PowerPoint as her medium. We hired her to speak at the conference without knowing her aptitude as a presenter. We frankly didn't care—she can design such incredible slides, we figured, we'd find a way to get the knowledge out of her, even if she didn't speak English.

Figure 21.4
For her design makeover clinic, Julie Terberg was in the zone.

Julie uses personal warmth and her design instincts to tell stories about her work. She looks back on her debut year at PowerPoint Live and describes herself as having been stiff. We're not sure that's true, but in any event, by her third year, she had come into her own. Figure 21.4 shows her describing a continuum from one idea to another: "With a good color scheme, all of your decisions become easier, from simple slides [left palm] all the way to complex charts, timelines, and infographics [right hand]."

She made several references to those complex elements made easier with a well-crafted color scheme, and she was able to do so merely by holding her right hand out to the side. She had already defined that space to be "all that complicated stuff," and a wave of the hand was all that was required to refer to it later.

I suspect that she did this without awareness. When you get on a roll, you experience the best kind of intelligence, where your body knows instinctually what to do without your brain having to get involved. We athletes call it being "in the zone"—that all-too-fleeting experience where everything is working right with minimal effort.

Let's not assume——let's ask her...

[sixty minutes later]

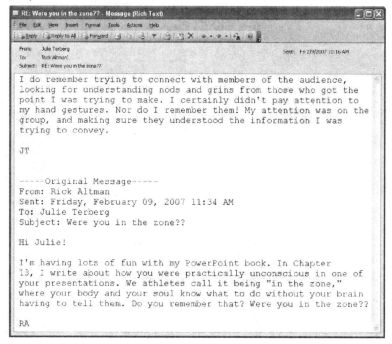

I do remember trying to connect with members of the audience, looking for understanding nods and grins from those who got the point I was trying to make. I certainly didn't pay attention to my hand gestures. Nor do I remember them! My attention was on the group, and making sure they understood the information I was trying to convey.

JT

-----Original Message-----
From: Rick Altman
Sent: Friday, February 09, 2007 11:34 AM
To: Julie Terberg
Subject: Were you in the zone??

Hi Julie!

I'm having lots of fun with my PowerPoint book. In Chapter 13, I write about how you were practically unconscious in one of your presentations. We athletes call it being "in the zone," where your body and your soul know what to do without your brain having to tell them. Do you remember that? Were you in the zone??

RA

Active Hands, Quiet Body

Ask anyone who knows me——I'm a hand-talker. My hands are in constant motion while I speak. My clients, my audience members, my friends, and the seventh and eighth grade girls on the softball team I coach——they will all readily attest to this.

While I was once concerned about my hands being too active, I have since come to realize the value of channeling that energy, and it has caused me to reevaluate advice I used to give on this subject. In the first edition of this book, I wrote about the so-called neutral position, and its importance as a base from which to start gestures. "In order for a gesture to have impact," I wrote, "it must come from a position of rest. Just like bold type, it is the contrast that makes it work."

Figure 21.6 is a photo of me trying to practice what I preach. While audience members tell me that this neutral position looks natural, it feels anything but, and I grew self-conscious trying to make peace with it. Trying to quell the continual motion that my hands craved led to a litany of compensations:

Hands behind my back This looks relaxed, but if I hide my hands, I look shifty. Remember, showing the palm of your hand is an important gesture of trust.

Hands clasped in front of navel I don't feel like such a dork in this position, but gestures end up getting clipped at the forearms. Before long, I look like I'm praying.

Hands together and down This is fine for about five minutes. Then I get lazy and out comes the "flashing fig leaf"? That's when a speaker speaks so quickly, the hands can't keep up. They remain cupped in front of the private parts, except for the occasional flip of the wrists.

Hands in pocket Too surfer dude.

One arm resting on side of lectern This is a comfortable position, but it is not sustainable and therefore isn't neutral. After five minutes, I begin to fidget, shift my weight, cross one leg over the other, and generally act like I don't belong up there.

Holding a microphone This I can do—during the expo at the conference, I routinely walk around with a wireless hand-held all day. But that's just it: it's great for being a strolling host, not as good for being an impassioned speaker. Inevitably, the combined requirement of holding a microphone and a wireless remote becomes too much.

Trying to find a neutral position created more problems for me than it purported to solve. I became too fidgety with my lower body, shifting my weight between my feet, crossing one leg over another,

Figure 21.6
Sometimes the hardest thing to do is just stand there.

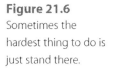

Part Four: Public Speaking

foot-tapping, you name it—all of my nervous energy would come through my lower body.

I have since abandoned that entire line of thinking and I now let my hands do whatever they want to. Setting them free has also liberated my lower body and I can now stand much more comfortably and quietly. The more I channel energy through my hands, the less I fidget with my legs and feet, and that is more comfortable for everyone in the room. Figure 21.7 illustrates that.

Using a Lectern

While I normally choose not to, it's no crime to stand behind a lectern, and there are some occasions where the extra formality is appropriate. For situations where you are speaking from freshly-written notes, a lectern is tremendously convenient.

Figure 21.7
I am more comfortable with active hands and quiet feet.

Figure 21.8
While comfortable for many presenters, using a lectern creates a few challenges that need to be addressed.

But you must understand that a large hollow box of usually-fake wood between you and your audience members will not help you in connecting with them. You will need to work harder to compensate:

- You should pause more often, making sure to look up from your notes for several seconds at a time. Ideally, you would begin your next thought while still looking out before having to refuel and take in more notes.

- Stand as upright as you can. In fact, lean over the lectern—audiences will feel it.

- Above all, make sure your gestures are up and out in front of the lectern.

Figure 21.8 depicts a typical challenge for not only using a lectern, and making sure that gestures are sufficiently emphatic, but also for managing furniture traffic. We'll return to that subject in Chapter 23.

Chapter 22

Fighting Nerves

I remember the first time I came face-to-face with paralyzing nervousness, and all I was doing was sitting on a couch. It was 1978 and I was 19 years old. Six years prior, I stood up in front of 200 people and chanted in Hebrew for my bar mitzvah. But that was nothing compared to this scene.

It was the ninth inning of Game Two of the 1978 World Series between the Dodgers and Yankees, and L.A. rookie Bob Welch struck out Reggie Jackson to win the game. I was sweating vicariously for Welch, who looked like he was about to walk into a gas chamber. He faced Mr. October, the man with more post-season home runs than anyone, and he struck him out.

I've never seen anyone so nervous and I've never been so nervous for someone else. What I didn't consider, however, is whether Jackson was nervous. Years later, he addressed the question.

> **"If I'm not nervous, then there is something wrong. If I don't feel those butterflies, it means maybe I don't care as much as I should."**

I always feel better about my own anxiety when I think of that quote, and so should you. It is neither realistic nor helpful to believe that you can quell your nerves; it would be better to learn to live with them. If the greatest World Series performer in history was nervous, it's okay for you to be, too. Here are a few strategies to help you become one with your nervous half.

The Lowdown on Laughing

This might be the oldest advice on record: start with a joke. Laughter relaxes you, it makes you feel more comfortable, and it allows you to loosen up. It is the classic icebreaker.

Well, what if you're not funny? What if your joke bombs? As Jerry Seinfeld said to George Castanza one afternoon, that's a pretty big matzah ball hanging out there.

Unless you have a joke that is guaranteed to be funny and is relevant to the topic of your presentation, the risk is too great. Besides, there is a better idea than trying to make your audience laugh...

Make yourself laugh.

I'm very serious about this (ha ha). If the audience laughs at your joke, it *might* make you feel better. If you laugh, it is virtually guaranteed to make you feel better. And the stakes are much lower.

This talk today on warehouse efficiency, it seems kind of funny that I should be the one leading it...[chuckle]...and if you ask my mother about this, she'll agree...[snicker]...because you've never seen a kid growing up with a messier room than mine. How I got to this point where I am expected to act as an authority on this subject is...[laugh]...well, that's just beyond me...

Audience members might laugh along with you or they might not, but it doesn't matter either way. You're not trying to be comically funny, and so this isn't a joke that can bomb. It's funny to you in a reminiscent way and therefore it is appropriate for you to see the humor in it.

You know that story about "If it's Tuesday, this must be Belgium?" I now know what they mean. This is my fourth city in four days, and yesterday I woke up and literally forgot where I was...I [laugh], I thought I was already here in Austin, about to speak to all of you. I left the hotel and immediately got lost, until I realized that I was in San Antonio. So...[laugh] to say that it's good to be here takes on a whole new meaning.

This anecdote might not be funny to your audience but anyone can see why it might be funny to you, so again, it doesn't seem like forced humor. It almost doesn't matter what kind of story you share—*make it up if you have to.*

Laughing uses good muscles, not bad ones (more on this soon) and it's easier to make yourself laugh than it is to make a roomful of strangers laugh. So all around it's a better strategy to employ.

How Slow Can You Go?

It's been over 100 pages since we introduced one of our universal axioms, so here goes—Universal Axiom No. 4:

> **However quickly you think you're speaking, it will seem even quicker to your audience.**

And Universal Axiom No. 5:

> **However slowly you are speaking, you can always slow down even more.**

When you speak quickly, you do more than just make yourself nervous; you make your audience nervous. You make the whole room nervous. The projector and screen probably get nervous. The quicker you go, the more fidgety you get. You don't give yourself any time to make large gestures, so all of your gestures are small ones involving small body parts. Small, fast, fidgety little gestures. And out comes the dreaded fig leaf once again.

The whole thing spirals, as your fidgety gestures make you speak even quicker, which in turn makes your body try to keep up, and so your gestures become even more halting and spastic, because that's all you have time for, and the quicker you speak, the higher your voice gets, and that raises the frequency of the entire room, and through it all, *you drive your audience nuts!*

But if you slow down your speech...

...you'll slow down your entire body...

...and that will calm everyone down.

So why do we do speak so quickly? It's not enough to just say we're nervous and that's why we speed up. What is making us speed up?

Much of the time, it's a fear of the unknown: you don't remember what's next or you're just not confident about your next transition. You have stopped living in the moment as you fret about what you are to say next. Very few people forget about what they are talking about now; it's always that they forget what comes next.

When you know what your next idea is, it's uncanny how much easier it is to discuss your current idea. Absent of panic or dread, you can practically luxuriate in your words. And then, you can indulge in the holiest of all moments before an audience:

You can pause.

No, I mean a long pause.

Longer.

Longer still, and look at people while you pause.

This is not an awkward pause; it's a commanding pause. You have complete control of the room and everyone knows it. And how have you won the room? Why have you become so confident? Because you know where you're going. You know what you want to say next, so you can live in the moment, without panic, fear, or fig leaves.

▶ See the discussion in Chapter 8 (Page 47) about displaying all bullets at once vs. having them appear one by one. We are staunch advocates of the all-at-once practice, precisely for the reasons discussed here: it gives you context, makes it easier to focus on the current topic, and eliminates an opportunity for you to forget what you are to say next.

For my money, this is one of the most wonderful feelings when speaking before an audience—when I know my material so well that I can completely control the pace. I can linger on points, make extended eye contact, take questions, invite debate. Once I have established this level of control, no reasonable pause feels uncomfortable. Even if I am 30 feet away from my notes and I do completely forget what I want to say next. If I control the room, nobody will think it odd if I silently walk the 30 feet back to the lectern, spend five seconds looking at my notes, and then five more collecting my thoughts.

Anyone who has ever gone to Toastmasters or taken a course in public speaking has had to perform the exercise where you must make five seconds of eye contact with an audience member before shifting your gaze. I would argue that five seconds of silence is a better drill.

It's all made possible by knowing your transitions. Practicing them is more important than rehearsing the flow of a particular idea.

Air Under the Pits

The symbiosis between the voice, the body, and the nervous system makes for a fascinating study. Unless it's *your* body we're talking about, whose byproduct of this relationship is usually profuse perspiration. Then it's not fascinating; it's frustrating. Each one of these parts of the system is responsible for changes in the other:

- If you are nervous, it will show in how you move your body and how you speak.

- Changes to your vocal pattern create change in body motion, which affects pulse and heart rate.

- Command over your body can create command over your speech and your nerves.

We have already discussed the syndrome whereby a nervous speaker accelerates his or her speaking pattern, which in turn causes the entire body to speed up. Whether fidgets are the cause or the byproduct of your nerves, they are not your friend, as they perpetuate the cycle and they affect your audience.

So think big.

Think about making big gestures, not little ones. Create a reason to raise both arms above your head or out to the sides. Get some air under your armpits!

Working gross motor skills is the equivalent to slowing down your vocal pattern. Your body responds more positively to a big action than to a little one. A big gesture can actually help relax you. At a minimum, it takes longer to make a big gesture than a fidget, and that alone creates a better pace for you. Our advice about making yourself laugh has relevance here: laughing uses your diaphram, a big muscle.

I've found that raising both arms over my head, can be interpreted many ways and audience members are generally willing to view the gesture in context.

CONTEXT: Question from an audience member about a situation that troubles her.

ME: That frustrates me too [gesture]. It's like whatever you do, it comes back to bite you. Try doing this...

CONTEXT: We solved a problem or addressed a difficult issue.

ME: [gesture] Thank the heavens, we figured this out.

CONTEXT: I ask a question and an audience member answers it correctly.

ME: [gesture] (Nothing needs to be said—the gesture serves as a "Eureka!")

Now if you feel like an idiot doing this, don't do it. The gesture has to be a part of you, but it's worth the effort to find one you are comfortable with. One colleague likes to cup his hand to the side of his head and then move it away, as if he has just had an epiphany and all this amazing stuff is flowing out of his brain. He uses that to great effect in many scenarios.

I know a woman who likes to hold one finger up, but she really goes for it, raising it well above her head. She uses it to mean "Listen up," "wait a minute," or "here's the beef."

Another uses her hands very effectively to create relationships in time, distance, or some other set of variables (just as we saw Julie Terberg do in the previous chapter). "Over here, you have the question of cost," she might say with her left palm outstretched all the way out to one side, "and over here is the issue of resources," as she stretches out her right hand. Having created those two spaces, now anytime during that conversation, she can stretch out her left palm and the audience knows she is talking about the cost factors. She has created a terrific cerebral connection with her audience...and she gets to air out her pits.

Find your own big gestures and use them to engage your audience, to improve your pace and vocal pattern, and to help quiet your nerves.

◆

As I look back on this chapter, I have to laugh. It seems as if we are advising you to become a phony:

- Fabricate a story to laugh about.

- Conjure up situations in which you can make long pauses.

- Make up a gesture and fake your way into using it.

But let's face it, speaking in public might always feel like an artificial situation to you, so it makes sense that a few artificial devices can help you with it. Anything that helps get you to a place where you can speak naturally and share ideas freely is a good thing.

Natural speaking through fabrication...what a concept.

Chapter 23

Working the Room

In social or political situations, the phrase "working the room" takes on a wholly different meaning than the one we have in store for you here.

A good host for a party works the room by meeting everyone, introducing people who don't know each other, and ensuring that no glasses go empty.

If you are running for office, you work the room to gather campaign contributions and win votes.

Our definition is not nearly so captivating. It examines the physical confines of your speaking space and offers strategies for good performance. In preparing my thoughts for this chapter, I'm reminded of a golf cliché that we duffers find maddening:

The course never has a bad day.

In golf, your only real opponents are the golf course and yourself. The course will never chunk a drive or skull an approach shot, while meanwhile your own mental machinations could drive you bonkers.

It's the same with your seminar room: whatever challenges the room creates for you become your burden to solve.

To solve this for you, we thought of creating diagrams of every seminar ballroom in the United States, along with instructions on how to set them up, but our team of elves was busy in December. Instead, we'll just tell you this: unless you get to set the room up yourself, there will always be something wrong with it. Your flexibility is the most important asset you can have.

Home Base

This concept of home is one that most presenters and most members of an audience understand but rarely think about. We want you to think about it. Home not only creates comfort for you, it creates comfort for your audience. Home is where you would go to

- Take questions.

- Drink.

- Regroup.

- Check your notes if you have them. And when in doubt, have them. Unless you have been delivering the same speech for years, don't rely on your memory and don't rely on your bullets to guide you through a presentation.

The best home base is one that is raised up from table level and off to one side, preferably the left side when looking out into the room. If you enter a room to find a single head table in the middle of the room, ask if you can move it and ask for a table-top lectern or a rolling podium. In either case, place them on the outside of the table.

This advice assumes a standard setup with a projector displaying to a screen placed in the middle of the room. If the room is set with rear-screen projection, the middle of the room becomes available to you, however we still recommend you create home base to the left of the screen.

▶ As with the question of hand gestures two chapters ago, this is another instance where my advice has changed between the first and second editions of the book. I used to advise people to set up home base on the right side of the screen when facing the room. I have reconsidered that point of view and will discuss this more soon.

If your only possibility for home base is a standard table that you stand behind, your notes will be further away from you than normal and the risk is higher of them creating psychological distance between you and your audience. At a lectern, you only need to look down a short distance to see your notes—you can probably do it just by moving your eyes. But if your notes are on a table, the geometry worsens. The angle and the distance from your head to your notes both increase. At a minimum, you'll wish you had printed them in a larger typesize. Here are some tips:

- Spread your notes across the table so every page is visible. Don't leave them in one stack.

- Make prominent marks at your transition points. You need to be able to see where they are at a glance.

- Take questions often, and every time you call for questions, do it from home base and use that as an opportunity to check your notes.

- Be mobile. It's a long way down to your notes from a standing position, and the more stationary you are, the more you call attention to that distance. But if you can sneak a peak while you are walking up to the table, walking away from it, or even just turning to one side of the room or the other, it is less conspicuous. This is not easy to do—it's like walking, talking, chewing gum, patting your head, and rubbing your tummy all at the same time. If that becomes too much to think about, forget it.

The head table dilemma is why many colleagues of mine travel with folding lecterns that can be placed on a table. Getting your home base raised up a bit is always more comfortable.

The downside of this is if you become a prisoner to it. As discussed in Chapter 21, a lectern or podium can become a barrier, and we are not suggesting that you spend 60 minutes behind it. Home base is not where you live; it's where you retreat to at various intervals.

Going Out into the Deep End

I know that we're mixing our analogies something awful in this chapter, but here comes another one: home base is like the shallow end of the pool, where it's safe and comfortable. Your notes are nearby and you can rest your hands on the lectern.

And if home base is the shallow end, venturing forth from it is like treading water in the deep end of the pool. It can be a bit scary out there, but most really good audience connections happen when you are out there.

Going into the deep end is important—your audience needs to see you front and center, away from your notes, away from lecterns and tables, without barriers. Just you, them, and your hands. But if you get stuck out there, you could drown. This usually happens when you run out of things to say and forget what you want to say next. It's okay if you don't remember every topic to discuss—that's what your notes are for. But if it happens when you're in the deep end—it could make you feel uncomfortable.

So look over your notes and find a time when one topic moves so naturally into another topic that you will never forget. That's the time to head to the deep end. We discussed this in the last chapter (Page 246): when

Johnny, It's Time to Come Home...

Your notes can tell you when it's time to head to the deep end, but they won't be as helpful in bringing you back. In Chapter 8, we discussed a strategy that you can implement to ensure you know when the last bullet on a slide has displayed (on Page 50, involving an inconspicuous rectangle or other object that automatically appears after the last bullet). You can use this same strategy to notify you when you should return home.

1. Identify the parts of your presentation that you know really well and the places where you would be more comfortable working from your notes.

2. Create a thin rectangle, fill it with a color close to your background, and place it on the edge of the slide or in some other place where it can be inconspicuous.

3. Animate it to Appear, After Previous.

4. In the Animation task pane, move it up or down until it is in the desired place in the sequence of animated events. If necessary, move it in between a set of bullets.

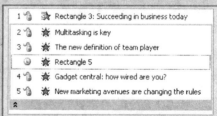

When the rectangle appears, it means it is time to return home to consult your notes.

Figure 23.1
Good notes should tell you not only what to do but when to do it.

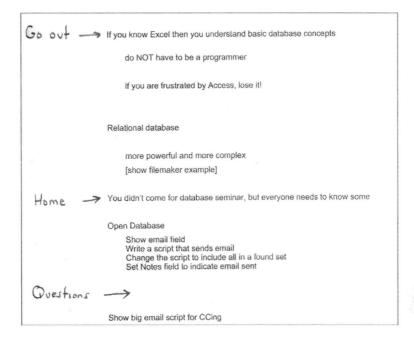

you know your next transition, that's the time to lose yourself in the presentation, without worry or fear of losing your place.

Get out there in front of your audience, make lots of eye contact, pause often, vary the pace of your delivery, take questions, ask if anyone needs you to repeat the last point, or don't ask, just do it, to emphasize its importance. And then pause some more.

You know that you can stay out in the deep end all the way through to the middle of the next topic, before you have to swim back to shallower waters and consult your notes.

These are the times when you could be at the top of your game—when you are in command of your content and the pace with which you deliver it. Look for places in your notes where you know your content and your transitions well and get out there right in front of your audience. In Figure 23.1, I have identified in my notes when I intend to swim in the deep end and when I need to come home.

Why return home?

The simplest reason to return to your home base is if you know there is a passage of your presentation that you will not be able to remember. We're not talking about remembering a passage word-for-word, which you should never try to do. We're referring to a passage that you forget to even bring up. The one where, 10 minutes later, you realize that you skipped entirely. Your best defense against forgetting these passages is to not even try to remember them—just schedule regular trips back home where your notes will remind you.

Here are a few other times to return home:

- If you intend to quote somebody or read a short passage from another work. Don't try to do this by heart—it's fake. If you are reading a quote or passage that somebody else wrote, read it!

- If you want to relate an anecdote that has a fair level of detail. Trying to remember those details could sprain your brain.

- When it's time to change the pace of the presentation. Being in the deep end can be tiring for you. Returning home is like taking a moment to rest.

Where does your notebook computer belong?

Many presenters place their notebooks at home base and simply use the internal display as their notes. Some configure PowerPoint to show the notes page on the internal display.

These strategies are fine...as long as you can take your eyes off the damn thing. Remember Universal Axiom No. 1:

> **When stuff moves on screen, your audience has no choice but to watch it.**

With your notebook on the lectern right in front of you, you become a member of the audience in this regard: every time there is an animation or a transition, your eyes are going to go to it. This argues for you removing all unnecessary animation and you spending more time in the deep end...both good things.

Many presenters prefer to place their notebooks closer to their audiences. I know several who reserve the middle seat in the front row, right next to the projector, for their notebooks. This way, they can easily keep tabs on what their audience members are seeing behind them without having to change the angle of their gaze much at all.

This can be an effective strategy (and an efficient one—cuts down on VGA extension cables), but it takes practice to not become imprisoned by it. If you become fixated on your monitor, the audience will feel it and bust you for it.

I'd much rather you refer to the screen than stare at your monitor—see Myth No. 3 coming up soon.

Trainers have an additional challenge, as they will often have to sit at their notebooks and actively use the software. We'll address that soon.

When not to go into the deep end

The smaller the room, the less opportunity there is to swim in the deep end. In the smallest of rooms, going out into the deep end will feel stupid. In a conference room, for instance, where a dozen or so people are watching you from around a table, you can make eye contact with everyone from your lectern and your gestures will be received by all with no problem.

In a room of that size, the geometry changes. I predict you would feel awkward, maybe even foolish, if you went parading around the table, and even a journey of 10 feet or so would require that the others in the room pivot in their seats in order to watch you.

In this situation, just getting out from behind the lectern so everyone can see all of you would be entirely sufficient.

Rule of thumb: if your journey to the deep end requires that audience members turn their chairs or their bodies in order to see you, you're out too deep.

Becoming One with Your Bullets

I'm already on record, emphatically, about my belief that bullets are better displayed all at once than one by one (Chapter 8, Page 47). The advice offered here reinforces that opinion: there is nothing more comforting when you're in the deep end than knowing that all of the points you intend to make about a particular topic are displayed on screen.

There are other strategies that you can adopt to help you work more seamlessly with a set of points that you have displayed for your audience, and they all come down to physical positioning.

We have alluded several times in this chapter to how it's better for you to be to the left of the screen (when facing it) than to the right. Granted, working the room effectively implies connecting with all of your audience members, and you do that best when you visit every corner of the stage (keeping in mind our qualification above, when not to go into the deep end). However, when you are speaking directly to a series of bulleted points, your position in the room can go a long way toward helping the audience absorb them.

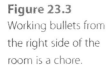

Figure 23.3
Working bullets from
the right side of the
room is a chore.

Figure 23.3 is a pretty bad photo of me speaking to a slide, but it's a good visual of this issue. As I discuss each of these points, I am referring my audience members to the screen, either implicitly, or as is the case here, explicitly.

This is a 10-foot screen that I am working with, so each bullet point spans a distance of about seven feet. If I want them to look at me, and I also want them to read the bullets, I'm asking them to play visual ping-pong: look at me over on the right, and then head all the way over to the left side of the screen to read the bullet.

It is better for you to work a bullet slide from the other side, as I am doing in Figure 23.4. Now your audience members can flow more smoothly from me straight through the bullets. For cultures that read from left to right, it is better for you to position yourself this way.

This might never register on a conscious level, but in an environment where you are trying to create an emotional connection as well as an intellectual one, it is simply one more opportunity to make your audience feel more comfortable during the time they spend with you.

The Presenter's Triangle

This suggests an entire strategy for positioning that is worth your consideration, even if you ultimately reject it for being too confining, too restrictive, too anal, too whatever. It goes something like this:

Figure 23.4
From the left side, you become the first component of each bullet, exactly as it should be.

1. On the left side of the room (when facing the screen), draw an imaginary line from the left-most audience member to the left edge of the screen.

2. That line helps define a triangle, in which you can comfortably circulate, without fear of being in anyone's view of the screen.

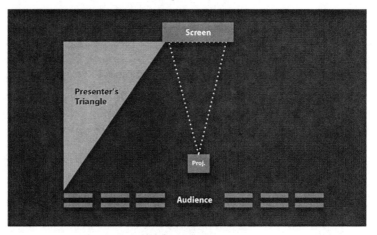

3. When you want to speak to points on the screen, you would move to the back of the triangle, near the screen.

4. When you want to make a strong point, you would move to the front of the triangle.

5. When you want to just talk, you would find a point in the middle of the triangle.

Indeed, this is quite anal, and following it to the letter could reduce you to a robotic drone, to say nothing of ignoring those on the other side of the room. Many good presenters define triangles on both sides of the screen:

- For bullets, they use the back of the left triangle.

- For less specific imagery, like photos or charts, they know they could use the right triangle.

- They head out to the tips of either triangle for emphasis.

- And they define mid-points on both sides for neutral speaking.

Positioning lecterns and tables in the triangle

I have changed my thinking about this point. I used to advise that your lectern should go in the middle of your triangle, on the left side of the screen when facing it.

Having gotten more experience using my triangle, I now advise against that. (I could never run for office—too many flip flops.) Unless you intend to spend all of your time behind the lectern (and we hope you don't), it's better to keep your triangle free of obstacles so you can command that space. I have found that placing the lectern on the other side (the right side when facing the screen) defines all of the space better.

If you need a head table with a computer, the decision about where to place it depends upon how much time you expect to spend at it. If your presentation is predominated by active demo time, where you have hand to mouse and your audience is watching your screen in action, it is not as important from which side of the room you operate. We simply recommend that you position yourself close enough to the screen so your audience members don't have to pan across the room too much to change their attention from your screen to you.

If your computer work is more occasional, we recommend two things:

- Place it on the right side so it will not interfere with your triangle work, where you will spend most of your time.

- Consider using a square table, not the more standard six-foot table. Unless you have an elaborate setup or are teaming up with another, you probably don't need to consume that much space.

Figure 23.6 defines my preferred room setup. I remove the podium altogether and keep my triangle completely clear. I expect to spend about 75% of the time on my feet so I only need a small table for my PC. I place it close to the audience so it is out of the way when I work

Figure 23.6

My preferred room setup: uncluttered triangle, no lectern, small PC table on the opposite side, close to the audience.

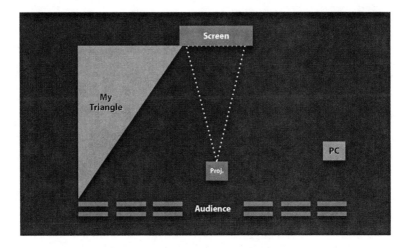

the room and so I can more easily make eye contact from a seated position should I need to.

I don't use notes for the times that I am sharing ideas and discussing the key points of my topic, but I keep fastidiuos notes for when I have to work the software. Those notes, of course, live at my small PC table.

Without a lectern, it means that I really don't have a home base—I am out in the deep end all the time except when seated at the PC. This was a bit daunting at first—nowhere to hide, nowhere to retreat—but I find it much easier to engage the audience this way. It's almost as if I am showing my audience members my willingness to be exposed and vulnerable to them. I think this helps make a stronger connection.

The Magical B Key

We've spent a fair amount of toner in this chapter discussing how you can create the best possible relationship with your projected content. We would be remiss if we didn't mention the best way of all to do this.

Turn off the projector

Axiom No. 1 is more powerful than you think. Stuff doesn't have to move on screen to compel an audience to look at it—it just has to project. If it's there, people are going to look at it. And if it's been there for awhile, and you're not speaking to it any longer, it's now just digital flotsam.

There is no better way to refocus attention than to blank the screen. And you can do that with one click:

■ Press B to turn the screen black.

- Press W to turn the screen white.

- Press the Blank button on your wireless remote.

If available, that third choice is the best, but even if you have to retreat home or head to wherever your notebook is to do it, it's worth doing when a slide has gone stale and/or you want all eyes on you.

In all three cases, the key or button is a toggle: press it again to redisplay the screen.

I wondered out loud in the first edition whether it is better to blank the screen with black or with white. In this decade, with projectors becoming so bright, it is common for us to present in rooms with the lights all the way up. I wondered if a white screen might allow the screen to more smoothly sink into the background. Having become aware of this since then, I have concluded that even with bright rooms, black screens are better than white, the latter just being too bright.

White or black, the screen should only go blank when you want it to, so please turn off your screen saver...

Mythbusting

Let's end this chapter by challenging a few of the conventional points often made about presenting to an audience.

Myth No. 1: Don't cross in front of the screen

If you never cross in front of the screen, how do you get to the other side of the room? I've seen presenters go to inordinate lengths to avoid committing this unpardonable sin, including walking down the aisle to walk around the projector and (true story) walking behind the screen.

Please.

If you need to move to the other side of the room, please just walk in front of the screen! Don't look into the projector and don't stop or dilly-dally. If you can keep your train of thought and continue speaking, it will seem perfectly natural. Trying somehow to avoid the screen will appear contrived, unnatural, and ultimately far worse than whatever perceived transgression is associated with casting a shadow on the screen.

Myth No. 2: Never turn your back to your audience

I once saw somebody trip over a chair trying to walk backwards, so obsessed was he with heeding this advice. Once again, common sense must be allowed to prevail, otherwise you're going to do yourself far more harm than this supposedly bad thing could possibly do to you.

I turn my back to the audience every time I venture out into the audience. I walk out there and then I walk back. If I walk back while continuing to speak, nobody even notices it.

Myth No. 3: Don't look at the screen

This is a younger cousin to the never-turn-your-back myth, and it's pure crap. How come everyone else gets to look at the screen and you don't? That's not fair!

Looking at the screen is more than perfectly appropriate; it's an essential device to direct attention. If you look at the screen, it is virtually guaranteed that every member of your audience will, too. You don't need to completely turn around—a simple rotation of the hips will get the job done. When I do this to look at the screen, I know that my entire audience is looking at it, too.

And really, what's the alternative? If you look at your notebook computer screen instead, it's a disconnect on several levels. Now you're looking down at something that they don't get to see.

Everyone is looking at the screen; it is completely natural for you to do so, also. Busting this myth became truly liberating for me as I now interact with the screen in a much more effective and natural way.

Myth No. 4: Laser pointers are rude

Now this one has some truth to it. Most people who use laser pointers haven't practiced enough, so the little dot jumps all over the place and drives people nuts. The worst is when a presenter is done pointing at something but forgets that he or she still has the laser on, sending the little dot careening all over the screen.

You really don't need a laser pointer to point at the second bullet of a four-bullet slide. If you want to talk about the second bullet, refer to it by name—the "second bullet" or "second idea." Better still, and this harkens back to the previous myth, walk over to the screen and touch it. There is nothing more direct and compelling than using your hand to direct traffic.

A laser pointer becomes effective when you have to call attention to an element on screen that is not so easily identified. The part of a photograph where the sun meets the horizon...the part of a clamp that failed on a forklift...the fifth icon from the left on the second toolbar down...these are all good opportunities to use a laser pointer.

To use a laser pointer correctly, tuck in your elbow to anchor your arm to your side; don't let it float in open space. Once it is anchored, then activate the laser. Try to hover it for about two seconds, then turn it off.

Myth No. 5: Silence is bad

_____.

Chapter 24

Thoughts From The Experts

Here I sit, with the notebook on my lap, my daughter up past her bedtime, the dog sneezing on my feet, and my wife asleep in front of a book. Shouldn't I be writing a novel or something??

The closest I may get to novel-writing is to suggest that this chapter might be a work of fiction. Now, I have critics who claim that everything I write is fiction, so this doesn't faze me too much. But in truth, as I prepare the final chapter of this part of the book, I'm honestly not sure if it will contradict the previous three or complement them. When I'm done with it, I'm not sure if I'll be sure then, either. I'm not sure of anything. Are you sure you want to read it...?

As I look over the last three chapters, I am reminded of an episode of I Love Lucy from 1954. Ricky and Fred take up golf and turn Lucy and Ethyl into golf widows. They decide to take up the game, too, and during a lesson, Lucy hears 15 individual pointers (knees bent, elbow straight, wrist firm, back slightly tilted...that kind of stuff) and attempts to incorporate all of them at the same time. The resultant swing that she perpetrates is physical comedy at its finest.

I wonder what would happen if you took all of the advice over the last three chapters and tried to incorporate them at once. Would you end up like Lucy? Maybe I have done nothing more than ensure paralysis by analysis. If I were you, I would get my money back for this shoddy excuse for journalism right now.

If I have turned you into knots trying to keep up with all of the points made here in Part Four, read this chapter instead. It takes a big step back and offers quotes from noted presenters and commentators on the presentation community. In the process, you just might find some common principles essential to being a good presenter.

Know Your Audience

When asked, dozens of public speakers waste not a moment to turn the equation 180 degrees. It has less to do with you, they say, and more to do with your audience, as we declare emphatically in Chapter 16 and several other places along the way. Stand on the left...stand on the right...turn here, don't turn there—none of that matters if you don't have a firm grasp of what your audience is looking for, why they chose to show up, and with what they hope to walk away.

Emma Crosby
Anchor for Sky News

"You have got to imagine that you are talking to just one person who is in their living room or in their office. You have to think about them constantly, inform them as much as you can, and more importantly ask the questions that they want the answers to."

Anthony Frangi
Author, Successful Business Presentations

"What makes a good presenter? Someone who can stand up and gain the respect of an audience, no matter what size.

"Good presenters know their subject matter inside out and it shows. When a person is passionate about the topic, their eyes light up, body language is positive and their voice excitable.

"Becoming a good speaker means you must learn to work or connect with your audience. A presentation is for the benefit of an audience. Effective communication skills are essential for anyone in business. Standing up to make a presentation is not just about opening your mouth."

Be Yourself

Experienced presenters learn something that inexperienced presenters do not, simply because it takes years upon years to learn this: audiences do not want perfect presenters. They want presenters who are more or less like them. They want to be able to relate to them, and nobody can relate to perfection.

Jim Endicott
Presentations Coach
President of Distinction Communication

"Several years ago I found myself watching a television show called the Actor's Guild. Every week they bring in Hollywood stars who are interviewed about their careers and asked questions from an audience of young acting students. One particular week they had Keifer Sutherland from Fox's hit series *24* on the show. One of the acting students asked him what piece of advice has most shaped his very successful career. Without hesitation he said it was something that his dad Donald Sutherland told him when he first got into acting. He said, 'Keifer, never let them catch you acting.'

"With just slight adaptation of the concept, there's an important principle here for today's business communicators

   Never let them catch you presenting.

"There's something that fundamentally changes in the nature of human beings when they go into 'presentation mode.' Some rise above the moment and maintain a critical authenticity while most get caught up in their remote pointing devices, PowerPoint and electronic projectors. Their warm smiles get replaced with emotionless faces. Meaningful eye contact is exchanged for impersonal scanning of crowds and screen watching. Methodical delivery of content is substituted for passionate and conversational speech.

"Here's the point: the art of presenting is first and foremost a relational skill. The best presenters are those who have resisted the idea that being a good presenter has anything to do with presenting in the first place."

Geetesh Bajaj
Microsoft PowerPoint MVP,
Editor, indezine.com

"Sincerity starts it all since that ensures that the presenter believes in every word contained in the presentation, slides, notes, concept, etc. Then that sincerity brings forth some amount of confidence, but this amount of confidence should not venture into the area of over-confidence."

Guy Kawasaki

Chief Evangelist for Apple in the 1980s and now a venture capitalist

The 10-20-30 rule

I hear pitches from entrepreneurs every day. Sixty slides in their pitch: they only need 1% of the market, patent pending, unique this, proven that. Every one of them says how terrific they are.

Because I have to listen to this crap, I came up with the 10-20-30 rule.

10 slides or less, not 60.

I don't care if you have a curve-jumping, paradigm shifting, google-adword-optimized, SQL-based way to sell dog food online.

20 minutes or less

You might have an hour window for the meeting, but if you have a Windows laptop, it might take you 40 minutes to connect it to the projector. Everything you have to say to me you should be able to say in 20 minutes or less.

30 point type

Never use a type size less than 30 point. That way, you'll put a lot less text on your slides, and that will force you to actually know your presentation, to just put the core of the text on your slide.

If you need 10pt, it's because you don't know your material so you're going to have to read it from the slide. If you start reading your material because you don't know it, your audience will figure out that you are a bozo. They're going to say to themselves, "This bozo is reading his slides. I can read faster than this bozo can speak. I will just read ahead."

If you don't buy that 30 points is the right size, I'll give you an algorithm. Find out who the oldest person in the audience is, divide his or her age by two. That's your optimal font size.

Anthony Frangi

"Becoming a good presenter is about being yourself. Don't ever try to mimic another speaker. Letting your personality take over allows the audience to see the real you. In return, they will respect any comments you might make and adopt any advice given.

"A good speaker must be able to appeal to an audience on various levels—political, emotional, etc."

Aristotle

"Think as wise men do, but speak as the common people do."

Being Prepared

The Boy Scouts' credo certainly has its place in the presentation community, and it is most conspicuous in its absence: ill-prepared presenters tend to rely on their slides and this turns them into drones. But well-prepared presenters rise well above their slides by the simple fact that they don't need them.

Tom Bunzel
Author, Solving the PowerPoint Predicament

"The major criterion for a good presenter is someone who really knows his sh*t—or in kinder language, is thoroughly familiar with his or her subject matter and knows how to deliver it effectively.

"This means that the audience members are getting their money's worth, whether they paid or not, in terms of receiving value for their time spent. Even in a sales presentation, a presenter who is there to provide real value is more likely to succeed than one who is there just to sell. And again, the basis for success will be knowledge of the issues facing the prospect and the ability to solve those problems."

Julie Terberg
Microsoft MVP
Presentation Designer

"A good presenter never reads from the screen and does not rely on bullet point after bullet point. The words that do appear in the presentation are minimal, perhaps key phrases or topics. A good presenter ensures that all projected text is legible to everyone in the audience. A good presenter respects the audience and tests the presentation—in the actual meeting room with all of the equipment—prior to the event."

Part Four: Public Speaking

Geetesh Bajaj

"Since the presenter is blessed with the right amount of confidence, he or she is bound to be a little nervous. This helps because then the presenter does not leave anything to chance and that butterflies-in-the-stomach feeling makes him or her walk that extra mile to keep the audience happy, convinced, and contended."

TJ Walker

President, Media Training Worldwide

Perfection: The Speaker's Enemy

It has been said that the enemy of the great is the good, but when it comes to public speaking, the enemy of great speaking is that quest to be great at everything. I work with business people, politicians and celebrities at every level of speaking skill, and the one problem that cuts through all classes of communication is the desire for some form of perfection in speaking.

Guess what—perfect speaking doesn't exist. There is no such thing as a perfect speech or a perfect speaker. Something could always be better.

I have found the single best way to improve speaking skills is to stand up and give a speech or interview while being videotaped. Then look at the tape and focus on what you like and don't like about your presentation. The problem for some of my clients is that they only see what they don't like. If they do 99 things well and botch one word, the only thing they do is criticize themselves and beat themselves up over that one word. They needlessly compare themselves to some image of perfection that doesn't exist even in their own imagination.

I believe in having high goals for yourself and doing everything you can to reach them. But if you obsess over every single negative to the exclusion of your strengths, assets and accomplishments, you end up paralyzed and depressed.

So my challenge to speakers who overindulge in self-criticism is this: watch a video of yourself and write down one thing you like about your presentation for everything you didn't like. That means if you can't find anything you like, you don't get to criticize the things you don't like.

Until the cycle of negativity is broken, it's nearly impossible for any speaker to improve.

Storytelling

It's difficult to articulate the difference between a presentation and a story, but when you hear a good storyteller, you just know. A good storyteller touches all your senses and triggers your imagination. When you supply your own imagination, you add to the story and make the presenter that much more effective.

Julie Terberg

"A good presenter pulls you in, makes you want to stand up and say 'Aha! I understand.' and 'Yes, I agree!' A good presenter tells a great story, making connections from personal experience. A good presenter is well-rehearsed, rarely referring to notes or script. A good presenter makes a speech seem effortless and conversational. A good presenter is compelling, thought-provoking, and articulate.

"A good presenter uses many memorable visuals to help you grasp ideas and concepts. Later on, those images are easy to recall as you replay the presentation highlights in your mind.

"A good presenter leaves a lasting impression."

And Finally...

"All the great speakers were bad speakers at first"

Ralph Waldo Emerson

"If you have an important point to make, don't try to be subtle or clever. Use a pile driver. Hit the point once. Then come back and hit it again. Then hit it the third time—a tremendous whack."

Winston Churchill

Make sure you have finished speaking before your audience has finished listening."

Dorothy Sarnoff, Broadway singer and author

They may forget what you said, but they will never forget how you made them feel.

Carl W. Buechner
Author and Presbyterian Minister

"Today's public figures can no longer write their own speeches or books, and there is some evidence that they can't read them either."

Gore Vidal, 1952

"According to most studies, people's number one fear is public speaking. Number two is death. This means to the average person, if you go to a funeral, you're better off in the casket than doing the eulogy."

Jerry Seinfeld

"Is sloppiness in speech caused by ignorance or apathy? I don't know and I don't care."

William Safire

"There are always three speeches, for every one you actually give. The one you practice, the one you give, and the one you wish you gave."

Dale Carnegie

Working Smarter, Presenting Better

"I'd like to cover a few advanced topics, too," I wrote to one of several interested publishers of this book. "If there's time," came the response, "and if the page count allows it."

Reason No. 34B to publish this book myself: there is never enough time and the page count never allows it. Yet as we enter the home stretch, we suspect that a great many of our readers will see this set of chapters as the most useful of all.

If you've made it this far, you deserve to sink your teeth into some truly advanced material, which the next five chapters seek to offer. Then we'll degenerate into an anarchy of tips and tricks in our final chapter, Junk and Miscellany, without which few books bearing my name are ever published.

Chapter 25

Building a
Better Interface

This chapter will not teach you about any new special effects or nifty animation techniques, and it won't show you how to create a cool drop shadow or a transparency mask. In fact, this chapter does not contain any tips or tricks at all, at least in the conventional sense. We'll even go so far as to suggest that if you are satisfied with the way PowerPoint displays itself to you and with the overall design of the interface, you can skip this chapter altogether.

But if you have longed for better access to PowerPoint's commands and tools, you'll want to read every word of this chapter. Microsoft offers a robust (and largely hidden) capacity to customize the interface, and it takes center stage here.

This chapter includes step-by-step instructions, and we start with the basics. But the ramp is short and steep, because we presume that most of you who want to customize the interface are already familiar with it in the first place.

This chapter is specific to version 2003 and earlier; the subsequent chapter will speak to the customization opportunities in version 2007.

Tool Terminology 101

This chapter will be easier to digest if you start by learning a few terms and definitions.

Microsoft's definition of a *tool* within Windows is quite specific. At the top of the interface lives the *Menu*, and right below it is the *Standard toolbar*—although you'll discover in this chapter that it's not so standard after all. Below the Standard toolbar (or to its right if you ask for it to be there instead) lives the *Formatting toolbar*, and at the bottom of the screen resides the *Drawing toolbar*. These are default locations, from which you can change their locations. You can also hide them altogether using the View | Toolbars | [ToolbarName] toggle.

If you right-click an object, the *Context menu* appears at your cursor position. Unlike the other toolbars, this set of commands changes to suit the occasion: right-click a rectangle and you'll see commands for arranging and ordering; right-click a subhead and you'll see a Font choice; right-click a misspelled word and you'll see a list of corrections.

If you've been working with the program for a few years, you have probably taken for granted where certain commands reside and the path you take to get there. But in this chapter, we will take nothing for granted and we will hold sacred none of the established defaults and conditions that are thought to be standard.

Required Options

If you consider yourself a proficient user, there is a set of options that should not be thought of as optional. Let's start with the factory settings that are in place when you first start the program. Figure 25.1 shows how PowerPoint greets the user of a freshly-installed copy of version 2003.

In this screen image, we have just pulled down the Insert menu, and so all of the commands relevant to inserting, adding, importing, etc. are visible. I'm sorry, did I say "all"? I meant to say "most." Actually, make that "some." Okay...a few.

What was going on in Mountain View CA on the day they decided to create menus that do not show all of the choices available to the user? What a great way to learn an application: create menus that intentionally leave off 75% of the items that belong there. Yes, I know about the dumb little chevron thing that points downward and shows the entire menu when you click it. That's just what I need in my life—a second click just to open a lousy menu.

Figure 25.1
When you first bring
it home, PowerPoint
is like an untrained
puppy.

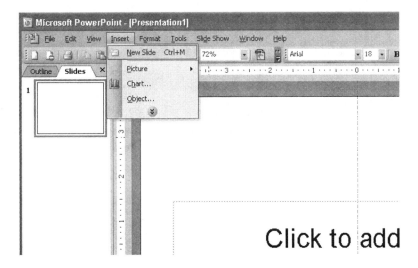

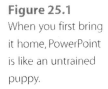

Figure 25.1
When you first bring
it home, PowerPoint
is like an untrained
puppy.

Pardon my sarcasm, but as you can tell, I really do not like this interface design decision at all.

This was done in the name of user-friendliness: provide the most com-
monly-used commands in a visual environment that will be friendly
and approachable. Let's please reverse this misguided interface setting:

1. Go to Tools | Customize and click the Options tab.

2. Find the Always Show Full Menus option and check it.

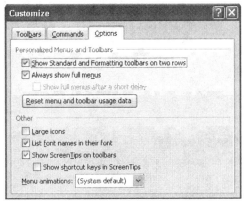

3. While you're here, consider checking Show Standard and Formatting Toolbars On Two Rows. Unless you run at high resolution,
   you will probably prefer using two rows. PowerPoint truncates
   toolbars that don't fit and arbitrarily hides icons behind an inconspicuous arrow.

We suggest you do Steps 1 and 2 and leave them that way forever.

▶ The Always Show Full Menus option is an Office-wide setting. Perform those two steps in any Office application and it will be set across every Office application. Thank goodness for small favors...

While you're at it, head to Tools | Options, where several other choices can make your time with PowerPoint more efficient. Here is a quick tour and a few of our favorite stops:

The View tab

Do you like your presentations to end with a black slide? We would not mind it so much if the slide actually were all black, but it's not—it displays "End of Show" at the top. No thanks—we turn this one off. And if you regularly open several presentation files but don't want the Windows taskbar cluttered with them, uncheck Windows in Taskbar.

The Save tab

We recommend turning off Allow Fast Saves and never turning it back on. This was a failed initiative to allow slower systems to save files faster by not completely rewriting the file with each Save operation. Instead, it does the digital equivalent of "tacking on to the end" any new content. This creates bloated files that are crash-prone. Today, even a 50MB presentation file saves fast, so turn this one off.

If you have a specific location in which you create your presentation files, define it as the Default File Location. If you have a network of folders and sub-folders, define the top level here. I create a Drive P for all of my PowerPoint files and designate that Save and Open commands look there first, not in My Documents.

The General tab

The important setting here is the Link Sounds value, which really should be called Link WAV files, because a WAV file is the only type of audio file for which there is any storage choice (all others are always linked, end of discussion). This threshold gives you an option of embedding the WAV file with the presentation, ensuring that the audio clip always travels with the file. We find that most users like this to be an either/or proposition and so they either set a very small number here (ensuring that all WAV files will remain external) or they set a very large number (designating that all WAV files will be embedded). The setting maxes out at 50MB.

This carries potentially significant implications for those who work with audio. Embedding a large WAV file would balloon the size of the presentation file, while keeping it externally linked makes it inconvenient to transport or distribute. Choose your poison.

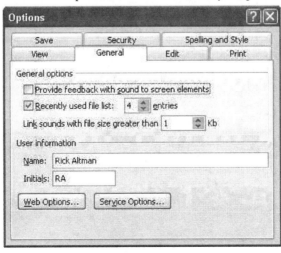

The Security tab

Macro security is worthwhile to study for those who expect to create or receive presentation files that include VBA scripting. Password-protection is also worth understanding, as it allows you to restrict access to a presentation file. We frequently distribute presentation files that can be opened by anyone but modified only by those who know the password.

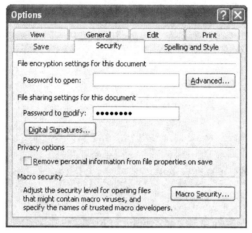

The Edit tab

Most of these settings are self-explanatory and not earthshaking. However, if you work in a mixed environment with colleagues still using version 2000, it would be helpful and not nearly so frustrating to essentially turn off the significant features added at version XP. This also applies to a workstation that you could set up for a co-worker who goes totally overboard with exits, motion paths, and simultaneous animations: sneak onto his computer and disable New Animation Effects...

The Spelling and Style tabs

Yawn. Use as desired.

The Print tab

How many times have you intended to print your notes or create a set of handouts but have inadvertently printed the slides themselves? I do this all the time and it steams me. Therefore, I have changed the default to print the Notes page to my black and white laser printer. I print notes much more often than I print slides, so I appreciate having that as the default.

Flying Tools

Let's start with a basic technique that works across all of PowerPoint 2003's many toolbars and flyout menus. If you look closely at one of the toolbars on your screen, you'll notice a row of vertical dots on its left. That is an indication to you that the toolbar is portable—if you click and drag those dots, the entire toolbar will disengage and float to wherever you take it. You probably won't find a reason to move the toolbars from their positions on top, but here's a handy maneuver that you might find useful:

1. Open the Draw menu from the Drawing toolbar along the bottom.

2. Click Order to open the flyout menu used for all layering and ordering of objects. Notice that it too has the row of dots.

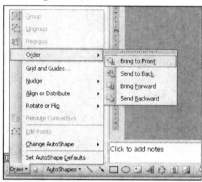

3. Click on the dots and drag the flyout away from its menu. Release the mouse and it becomes its own toolbar, floating on the slide.

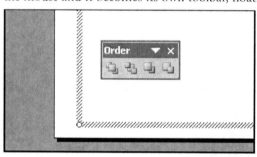

4. If you're like me, you don't like toolbars floating in the middle of your work area, so drag it down and to the right of the Drawing toolbar. It will automatically attach itself adjacent to the toolbar.

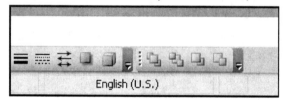

With this menu torn off and docked, ordering objects will be much, much easier—one click instead of click | click | wait for menu to appear | move mouse to desired choice | click.

This menu will remain attached in that location until you move it. Most of the flyouts off of the Drawing toolbar can be handled in this fashion:

- Align and Distribute

- Rotate and Flip

- Lines and arrows

- Other autoshapes

- Font, fill, and line attributes (these can be torn off, but not docked)

Figure 25.12 shows my Drawing toolbar, with one-click access to all of the layering and alignment commands that I use constantly.

Figure 25.12
Precision placement and sequencing of objects is much easier with the tools attached to the interface.

Portable Icons

Flyout menus are not the only elements that can relocate. In fact, just about anything that you click on can be relocated. For that you need to know the two maneuvers that unlock the interface for you:

The Alt key

Press and hold Alt while you click on an icon. When you do that, the icon becomes portable and you can move it to a different location or remove it altogether. Press and hold Ctrl at the same time and you create a copy.

The Customize dialog

Go to Tools | Customize | Commands, at which point the entire interface unlocks for you.

- Click and drag any icon from its location to another one (you don't have to hold Alt).

- Find any command on the list and move it onto a toolbar or an existing menu. This tab of the dialog box is your gateway to every single command that exists in the application.

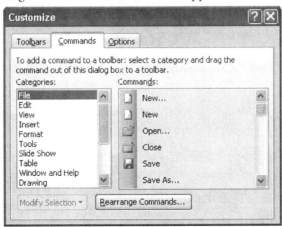

Part Five: Working Smarter

- From the bottom of the Categories list, create a new menu entirely, attach it to the Menu line, and then drag commands onto it. Notice that last command on Rick's Favorites—we'll talk about that soon.

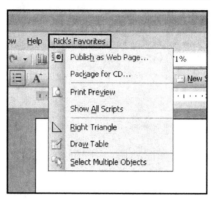

- From the Toolbar tab of that dialog box, create a new toolbar, populate it with commands, and float or dock it anywhere you want.

Select Multiple Objects? Did you know about that command? It brings up a dialog box showing every object on a slide, allowing you to select any of them. This is terrific when you have objects hiding behind other objects, but you've probably never seen that command on the standard interface; the program developers did not place it on any toolbar or menu. It lives only in the Commands list of Tools | Customize (in the Drawing category). You'll find several other commands you probably never knew existed there. A version history dialog...a command to change an OLE link...view HTML source code...nudge leading—these are just a few useful commands that were left off of the interface by the developers. You can fix this.

Your Personal Litmus Test

Let's remember the premise of this chapter: it is for experienced and ambitious PowerPoint users who know what tasks they want to achieve, who know what commands they need in order to achieve them, and want quickest possible access to those commands.

Armed with the techniques discussed above, you have total freedom to place at your virtual fingertips any command you want to.

So what would you choose? What are the commands you use most often and how accessible are they? Away from the pressure of a deadline, ask yourself those questions. I'll go first:

I switch between editing the slide master and regular editing dozens of times during the initial stages of a project. The conventional steps are as follows:

1. Pull down the View menu.

2. Head down to Master.

3. Wait for a moment for the flyout to reveal.

4. Carefully head directly across and down to Slide Master (if I take the diagonal, the flyout will close).

5. Click on Slide Master.

That fails my personal litmus test. In fact, it isn't even close! For a task as important as working on my slide masters, I want to do that with one click of the mouse. Here's how we would accomplish that:

1. Go to Tools | Customize | Commands.

2. Select View from the Category list on the left.

3. Find Slide Master from the Commands list on the right and select it.

4. Drag it onto your Standard Toolbar (the one closest to the menus).

5. If you did it right, you should see an anemic looking little blob residing on your toolbar.

Don't even get me started on anemic-looking icons that bear no resemblance to any part of reality. Fortunately, that whole debate can be rendered moot.

6. With the Customize dialog box still open, right-click on the new blob-um, the icon on the toolbar.

7. Change Default Style to Text Only (Always).

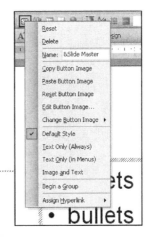

8. At your option, change the name. The optional ampersand indicates which Alt+key combination would trigger the command.

9. Close the Customize dialog and test out your new creation.

A button on my toolbar labeled Slide Master—now that passes my litmus test. Determine for yourself which commands you use most often. Create one-click access to them or place them directly onto a menu. And if you hate icons as much as I do, turn them all into text.

Optimizing Toolbar Space

If you are like me, your toolbars are going to get crowded before long. They already were crowded, and now you are adding more elements and converting them from blob to English.

Your toolbar is prime real estate: commands need to earn their way onto it. So before you go any further, scrutinize every icon that's there. Here's how my scrutiny session would go...

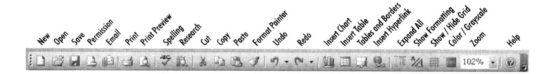

New I press Ctrl+N for this command and do not need it here on my toolbar. I would send it to oblivion by pressing and holding Alt and dragging it out onto the slide.

Open I have Ctrl+O for that. Gone.

Save I have been pressing Ctrl+S to save documents since WordStar 2.26 on my Osborne I in 1981. Gone.

Permissions I have never executed this command in over 15 years of using PowerPoint.

Email I use this command about a half-dozen times each year. I can find it on the File menu when I need it.

Print That's Ctrl+P for me.

Print Preview This is a potentially useful command that I often overlook. I'll tell you what I'm going to do: I'm going to put this command on probation. It can stay on my toolbar for the rest of this month. If I click it even once, it has earned itself another month. But if I haven't clicked it in that month, it's gone.

Spelling I probably should run spell-check more. If I do, I'll find it on the menus. Where is it, somewhere in Tools?

Research I have never clicked this and I have no idea what it is.

Cut / Copy / Paste I use Ctrl+X, Ctrl+C, and Ctrl+V for these.

Format Painter This is a good command and it even has a decent icon. It stays.

Undo I use Ctrl+Z for that.

Redo I never remember this keystroke, so the icon is useful. And because I consider Undo and Redo as sort of a package deal, I'll leave them both here.

Insert Chart I hate charts. Gone.

Insert Table I use this maybe three times a year. I'll find it.

Tables and Borders Say what? Gone.

Insert Hyperlink Once per quarter. I'll find it.

Expand All I guess this is for outlining? I'm sure it's a perfectly fine command, but I don't outline in PowerPoint.

Show Formatting I never knew this command existed until 15 minutes ago. It appears to show typeface and size in Outline view and on the Notes pane that appears below the slide. I want to see formatting on the Notes page, but I don't care about seeing it on the small pane in Normal view.

Show / Hide Grid This is a good command and quite useful. It stays, but can I please have something other than a barbed wire icon?

Color / Grayscale This command stays, and I don't mind its icon.

Zoom PowerPoint has the worst zoom controls on the planet. And as this drop down is pretty much it, I guess it stays.

Help I don't need no stinkin' help. Kidding...I use F1 to get it.

By the time I was done, I had cleared up quite a bit of space on my Standard toolbar, the one right below the Menu line:

With all of that space available, I can fit many of my favorite commands and have them display in English. Big readable buttons labeled "Animation" and "Layout"—now that's a toolbar I could learn to love!

▶ If you move an icon or a menu item a tiny bit in one direction or the other, PowerPoint creates a separator line. This is very helpful for creating logical divisions between commands.

Figure 25.19 shows the result of about 20 minutes of earnest time spent with the customization controls. Here's a brief tour:

- The bracketed menu item is a non-functioning empty menu. I use it for identification purposes: If I see Rick's Interface up there, I know I have my preferred interface activated.

- The second item from the left on the Standard toolbar looks like the Paste command but is actually Paste Special. I recommend its use over Paste for all Clipboard elements coming from other applications.

- There are two sets of Group/Ungroup commands, as I find myself needing them when my cursor is near the top and the bottom of the screen.

- All layering, aligning, and distribution commands are available from the Drawing toolbar.

Figure 25.19
Here is the author's perfect PowerPoint interface.

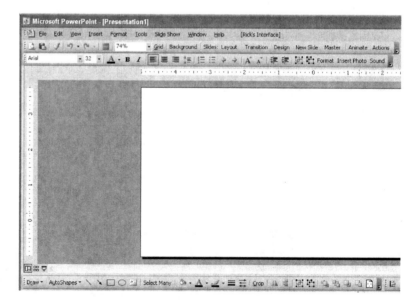

Managing Your Personal Interface

Once you get your interface just right, how do you save it, restore it, protect it, share it, and transfer it? It's not like a presentation file that you can simply save and open. PowerPoint keeps track of all of the customization work you do by storing it in a well-hidden file. It writes these changes to that file when you exit. Let's be more specific: when you exit the program *peacefully.* If you happen to crash, none of your changes will be recorded.

Therefore, when in the middle of a customization session, exit the program every ten minutes or so. This is equivalent to saving. It doesn't matter how you answer should PowerPoint ask you what you want to do with the current file. You don't care about that—just quit the application and then come right back in.

PowerPoint writes to a file that is buried in the Documents and Settings folder. Here's the path to it for Windows XP users:

c:\Documents and Settings
    [your profile]
        Application Data
            Microsoft
                PowerPoint

And for Vista users:

c:\Documents and Settings
    [your profile]
        App Data
            Roaming
                Microsoft
                    PowerPoint

Not Just a Question of Speed

Creating an efficient and easily-navigated interface is about more than being productive; it's about staying healthy. Risk is high these days for repetitive stress injury, what with feeling chained to our desks and pounding away at our computers for hours on end. One of the biggest risk factors is the excessive pressing of mouse finger to mouse button and the tensing of the arm muscles during same.

Reducing the number of clicks and mousing around provides measurable relief for tired muscles.

▶ Windows XP and Vista both hide their application data folders by default. See Chapter 30 for information about accessing this important location.

In that folder, you will find a file with a .pcb extension. If you are still using PowerPoint 2000, the file is named PPT.pcb. Those using Power-Point XP will find a file named ppt10.pcb; PowerPoint 03, ppt11.pcb. For the rest of this section, we will use the PowerPoint 03 filename, ppt11.pcb, but the following discussion applies to earlier versions, also.

Treat that file like important data. Back it up, store a copy in a .zip file, move it to a different computer, send it to a colleague. Here are a few items of varying degrees of usefulness about the .pcb file:

Return to sender

If there is an active .pcb file, PowerPoint looks for it upon launch. If it doesn't find it, it starts with factory settings. So if you ever delete your .pcb file, you'll get factory settings.

Multiple people, multiple personalities

You can keep several files in that folder—whichever file is named ppt11.pcb when the application is launched determines the look of the interface. If you want to change out your interface, you can take some-one else's .pcb file or a renamed file and overwrite the current ppt11.pcb with it.

Is your computer shared among multiple users? Each can have his or her own interface file.

If you have occasion to work PowerPoint in radically different ways, you can create multiple .pcb files and shuttle them in and out. Perhaps you would want one interface for full-scale content creation, one for outlining, and another one for reviewing. After creating each interface, quit the program, find the ppt11.pcb file and copy it to, say, con-tent.pcb, outlining.pcb, or reviewing.pcb. Then to activate any one of them, copy it over ppt11.pcb. We've seen some elaborate batch files written that ask you to pick a work environment and then activates the appropriate .pcb file before launching PowerPoint.

Do you remember your first time?

If you have never made an interface change, PowerPoint does not expect to see a .pcb file and therefore doesn't even look for it. If you were to acquire a .pcb file and put it in the correct location with the proper filename, PowerPoint would not use it on its next launch, because it thinks that there is no need for it.

So before you activate a .pcb file that you have gotten from elsewhere, make a change, any change, to the interface. Drag any icon off of any toolbar, then quit the program. The first time you make an interface change, PowerPoint wakes up, creates the .pcb file, and begins looking for it on subsequent program launches. Now you can replace it with the .pcb file that has the settings you want to activate.

Give Me Back My Interface!

At a recent PowerPoint Live, I played a practical joke on a co-presenter and replaced his .pcb file with one that I crafted just for him. I gave him a jump drive and told him to run the file called prep.bat. This file automatically performed the following actions:

1. Determined the name of his user profile and went to the folder that housed his .pcb file.

2. Backed up his current .pcb file.

3. Replaced it with the one that I created for him.

4. Launched PowerPoint, whereupon he found no toolbars, no task panes, no thumbnails, and only one menu item with one command on it.

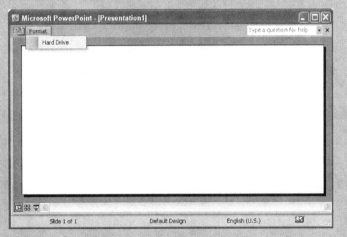

Did I mention that this took place in front of all 220 patrons in attendance that year…?

We like to blow stuff up

We conducted a sadistic experiment to see how much abuse Power-Point could take. We had quite a fun time creating all sorts of "accidents":

■ We deleted all of the .pcb files. PowerPoint just recreated them.

■ We deleted the entire PowerPoint folder. PowerPoint didn't com-plain—it opened with factory settings and recreated the subfolders that it needed.

■ We took the .pcb file and replaced it with nonsense files—like autoexec.bat, SexyBack.mp3, a YouTube video, and a text file that said "Mary had a little lamb" about a thousand times. PowerPoint never flinched—it ignored the file entirely and when it needed to record an interface change, it replaced the file with a real .pcb file.

We were impressed...if a bit disappointed.

Chapter 26

Creating a Smarter Interface in Version 2007

When we first began to dive into version 2007, we were disappointed in the program's apparent lack of support for customization. Most of the cool techniques reported in the previous chapter are not available in V07.

We advanced users were initially disappointed with the bone that it seemed Microsoft was throwing us with the Quick Access Toolbar. However, I have discovered some aspects of the V07 interface that mitigate the situation to some degree. It might not be enough for the truly disgruntled; be that as it may, this short chapter explores several important solutions, most built into the program and one that requires extra software.

The Version 2007 Downgrade

While PowerPoint 2007 reflects improvements in many areas, interface customization is not one of them. Program developers are so enthused about the Ribbon and the way it has been designed, they do not want us tinkering with it. At the Office website, the word is pretty clear about this. Here is what you cannot do:

- Add to or rearrange the commands on the Ribbon.

- Change or remove a command or group on the Ribbon.

- Add tabs to the Ribbon without programming code.

- Use toolbars and menus from earlier versions of PowerPoint.

- Change the font or font size used on the Ribbon.

- Remove seldom-used commands and replace them with other commands.

- Save, swap, and migrate your customized interface to other places and to other people.

Version 2007 sports a much-improved look and accessibility for all of the settings within the PowerPoint Options dialog, including an Advanced tab shown in Figure 26.1—sort of a one-stop shop for all geeky stuff across the application. You access these options from the Office Button, the round icon at the top-left of the PowerPoint screen.

The less fulfilling interface change for advanced users is called the Quick Access Toolbar (QAT), a row of icons across the top of the interface. You can place any command you want there and it will hold many. But you cannot change them from icon to text and the QAT can only live in one of two locations—above the Ribbon or below it.

This seemed very meager when compared to the extraordinary capabilities described in the previous chapter. We'll outline here the tricks that we have learned about the V07 interface that help soften the blow a bit.

If You Know It, Type It!

If you're like me, one of the more frustrating aspects of PowerPoint 2007 is the where-did-they-put-it syndrome that has us searching every ribbon for a function that we used to access in our sleep. For instance, in V03, I would type Alt+D | S to reach the Set Up Show dialog box in about two seconds. I could pull down the Slide Show menu and then click Set Up Show, but the keystrokes are faster and seem easier to me.

Figure 26.1

Version 2007 enjoys a redesigned and much more accessible set of options.

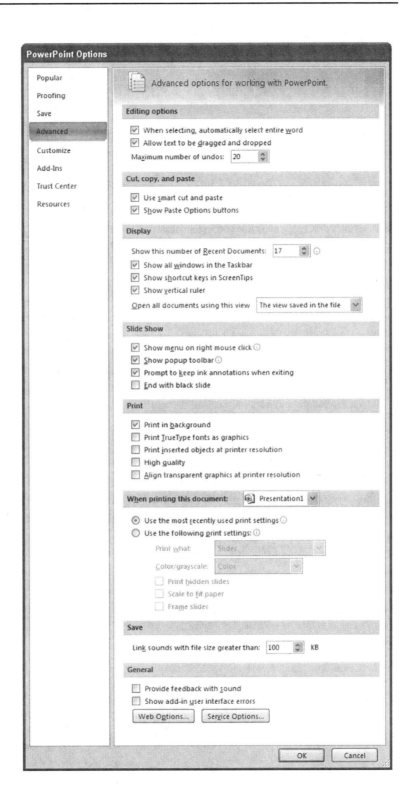

So imagine my pleasant surprise to discover that V07 honors V03 keystroke access. Alt + D by itself doesn't mean anything to V07, but if you just keep going and complete the sequence, the software figures out what you mean and executes the command for you. So...

Alt + F | U   To reach Page Setup
Alt + E | S   To invoke Paste Special
Alt + V | P   To switch to the Notes page
Alt + I | P | F   To insert a photo
Alt + O | R   To open Replace Fonts

All of these keystrokes work in V07. There are no cues on the interface—you just type them blind, as if you were in V03.

When in Doubt, Press Alt

While learning your way around might be a chore for months to come, there is an easy way to embark on that journey, and once you find what you're looking for, an easy way to access it. Just press Alt once and note the keys that promptly appear under the main menu:

From here, press the corresponding letter to activate the desired ribbon. Once you learn the key designations, you won't have to wait for them to appear: press Alt+N to go immediately to the Insert menu. And once there, note all of the keystrokes that appear:

This becomes a handy cheat sheet as well as the door to fast access.

The QAT: Blunt but Effective

Because I'm a keyboard-aholic, these two techniques were tremendously gratifying for me to discover. Mouse-centric users, on the other hand, won't find much cause to celebrate here. For them the QAT is as good as it gets without purchasing extra software.

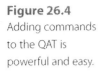

Figure 26.4

Adding commands
to the QAT is
powerful and easy.

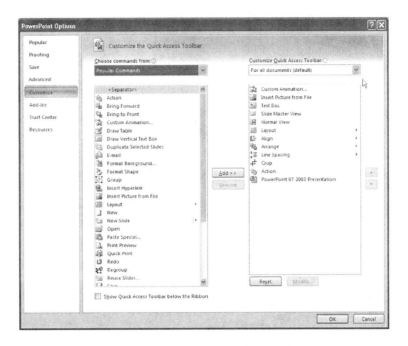

The QAT's virtue is the ease with which you can place onto it any command you can find. And as you can see in Figure 26.4, it's pretty easy to do: browse the commands on the left and add any you want to the list on the right. The Choose Commands From dropdown includes sets of commands based on category as well as a vast master list of every command that exists within the application, including a few dozen that do not live on the Ribbon and would therefore never be found except via a trip to this dialog.

I wish you could save your QAT settings, create different sets, and load and unload them at will. You can't. The best you can do is define a QAT for the current presentation file, distinct from your master QAT.

The other mystery is where QAT information is stored. It is not in an accessible file like the .PCB file described a chapter ago. Instead, it is buried in the Registry in a location seemingly requiring security clearance to learn about. So transferring your QAT settings to your notebook or to a colleague is not possible. You will have to recreate them for each machine that is to have them.

Figure 26.5
The author's QAT

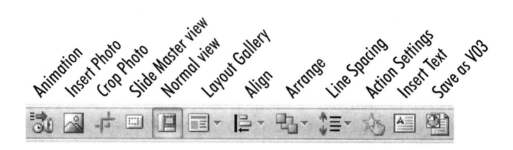

Figure 26.5 shows the 12 commands that I have placed on my QAT. I will no doubt continue to grow this list as I discover more and more commands that I would prefer to access with one click instead of a hunt across the menus and then a dive into a particular ribbon. But the first nine are essential and I chose them carefully. This is because the Alt key works on the QAT, also. Press it and you'll see this:

This brings an unprecedented level of access to my most-used commands—better, in fact, than in version 2003:

In order to	I press
Invoke the Animation task pane	Alt+1
Crop a photo	Alt+3
Switch to Slide Master view	Alt+4
Change a Layout	Alt+6
Adjust Line Spacing	Alt+9

As you can see from the image above, once you get past nine, you need to press two keys along with Alt. As the list grows, it will reach 01 and then begin counting up from 0A through 0Z. We haven't gotten past 0Z to see what happens next—our video card runs out of resolution...

As I get more experience with V07, I find my creative workflow is exceptionally high when working with my bread-and-butter commands, and then it falls off markedly when I have to hunt through the ribbons to find an uncommon command. When I am working on a project that takes advantage of V07's expanded feature set, it is worth the tradeoff. When I'm just doing mundane things, I am tempted, and often succumb, to issue the QAT keystroke of Alt+07, which quickly invokes the Save as Version 2003 dialog so I can resume work there.

Customizing the Ribbon

Download a copy as a trial or for purchase at www.pschmid.net.

This final section of the chapter involves an add-in software program created by Patrick Schmid, a member of Microsoft's Most Valued Professional team of volunteer specialists. His RibbonCustomizer enables you to arrange, rearrange, change, remove, and add ribbons and groups of commands. It's pretty slick software, only costs $30, and can be downloaded on a trial basis.

In working with the software, there are a few things I have observed and concluded:

- The software does not work with individual commands but command groups. In Figure 26.7, you can see the personalized ribbon that I have created, and on it are the Animations group, the Background group, Slide Show Set Up group, etc. PowerPoint does not provide access to individual commands. You can't place just Set Up Slide Show command on a ribbon; you must add the entire Set Up group. It is rare that I want direct access to every function of a command group, so there remains a bit of flotsam on my customized rib-

Figure 26.7
With Ribbon-Customizer, you can create your own ribbons, with whatever groups of commands you want.

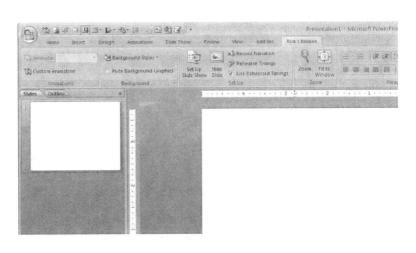

bon. I hope this changes, but I suspect that the change needs to come from Microsoft.

- With RibbonCustomizer, you can completely rearrange and redesign any of the existing ribbons. If you do that, make sure that you familiarize yourself with the Reset Ribbon command should you find yourself in close collaboration with others. Version 2007 is confusing enough to your co-workers without adding in the additional element of you completely changing around the interface.

- Unlike the QAT, you can create more than one customization scheme, save them, transfer them to other computers, send them to colleagues, and swap them out on the fly.

- Because the Ribbon is context-sensitive, PowerPoint will switch to other ribbons as you work...whether you like that or not. I was disappointed to observe—after creating the perfect custom ribbon with all of the commands I could want—that inserting a text box caused PowerPoint to switch to the Home ribbon. Again, this behavior is imposed by PowerPoint, not by RibbonCustomizer.

◆

All in all, I find reason for optimism that the Office 2007 interface will continue to evolve. With creative developers like Patrick Schmid, the user community will get a chance to participate.

In other words, perhaps it takes a village to raise a software program these days.

Chapter 27

Creating Intelligent Presentations

I have written a significant chunk of this book while seated in the same chair. I have begun with Chapter 1 and have written most of the book in order. I am a creature of habit and I am most comfortable when there is order to the things I do. I don't view this as unusual behavior—most people display this same tendency in one or more areas of their lives.

We're a race of linear thinkers and most of our presentations reflect that trait. We start at the first slide, end with the last slide, and expect to advance through them in order. This is not broken and I'm not here to try to fix it. However, leaving that mindset, even temporarily, stands as one of the most important improvements you can make as a presentation designer, content creator, or presenter.

This chapter is all about how you can breathe life, flexibility, and creativity into your presentations by thinking in a non-linear way. This is an impossibly vast topic, about which entire books have been written. Like the chapters before, we'll get to fifth gear in a hurry and will be speaking to you as if you are an advanced user who knows his or her way around the program. Seat belts optional but recommended…

Click Here, Go There

The irony is not lost on me that we will work through these non-linear topics in a very linear way. The path to excellence might be circular, but the path to learning it goes in a straight line. Here are the topics we'll be discussing:

- Moving at will to a specific slide

- Jumping to a different presentation

- Opening a non-PowerPoint document

- Creating a menu-driven interface within PowerPoint

The classic example to illustrate this idea is the presentation that runs long. I'm sure this has *never* happened to you, but you've no doubt been in the audience when a presenter, we'll call her Kathleen, allows a midway Q&A session to run long and now finds herself with five minutes left and three complete ideas yet to explore. So what does she do? She flies through her slides so she can get to her final idea, which promises to crystallize everything she has tried to say over the last 45 minutes.

Will you remember Kathleen's dramatic and powerful close when you drive home that afternoon? Not likely—instead, you'll remember all the content she dismissed as so much slide junk as she whizzed through it. You might even wonder about a slide that looked pretty good as it flashed before your eyes, because that's the way we humans are: we're more interested in what we can't have than what we can.

Your first impression is likely to be of a person who did not completely have her act together. She became imprisoned by her own linear thinking and she paid for it.

At the core of the solution is your understanding of the basics of hyperlinking. As with a web page that offers you a way to jump somewhere else, a presentation can be programmed with this same intelligence. It's done through the Action Settings dialog, a powerful set of controls that has earned a spot on my Standard toolbar.

Any element that can sit on a slide can be programmed as a hyperlink, and Figure 27.1 shows the list of choices for standard hyperlinking. When running a presentation (i.e., when in Show mode), clicking an object programmed with a hyperlink will cause you to promptly move to the location you have set.

If Kathleen had programmed a hyperlink to her concluding slides, her audience might have never noticed that she was running long.

Figure 27.1
The hyperlink is the cornerstone of non-linear thinking.

Hidden vs. Visible Hyperlinks

There are two basic methods of implementation and the one you choose is a matter of situation, preference, and even philosophy.

Roadmaps

We know many accomplished presenters who place their hyperlinks directly on the slide, in plain view of the audience, where they will never forget about them. For times when you want your audience members to see that you are making a turn onto a different street, a visible hyperlink is perfect. When I presented on this topic last year, one of my main slides looked like Figure 27.2 on the following page. Using those example buttons accomplished three important objectives:

- It helped keep me in the flow by reminding me what to do next as I worked through a complicated set of tutorials. I was seated at the computer, in full-scale building mode, and I appreciated not having to retreat to my notes. I knew exactly what to click next to take me to the next point I wanted to make.

- My audience could create a visual of my progression of topics, helping them understand the concepts better.

- They could see examples of the very techniques I was teaching.

Figure 27.2
Visible hyperlinks are invaluable for working through complicated tasks.

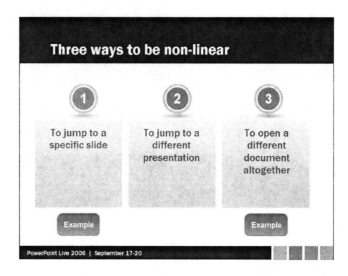

▼ To see these hyperlinks in action, download Figure 27-02.ppt from the whypptsucks.com web site.

Many presenters have no reticence about showing their inner workings to their audiences, and I count myself among those who are comfortable with this way of thinking. This just says to your audience that you have given considerable thought to how you want to approach a topic. It says that you are organized.

Secret passages

Invisible hyperlinks are equally handy for those times when it is not essential that your audience members follow how you get to a certain place. This is how Kathleen would have used the technology to jump to her conclusion without anyone noticing how far behind she got.

A hidden hyperlink can take one of two forms: 1) an object that is almost literally invisible, devoid of fill or outline; or 2) an object that is part of the slide design. We favor the second approach, as it is all too easy to forget the location or even the existence of invisible objects. In Figure 27.2, the small square at the extreme bottom-right of the slide has been programmed with a hyperlink that jumps to my last topic. If I run out of time, I can just click that rectangle and begin my conclusion. Nobody has to know about the dozen slides that I skipped over.

Flexible Intelligence

In Kathleen's case, she would have been grateful enough for a one-way ticket to her concluding slides. You, however, can build further intelligence into your slides by creating a way to return to whichever slide you were on before making the jump. Your web browser has a Back button and PowerPoint offers the Last Slide Viewed hyperlink choice.

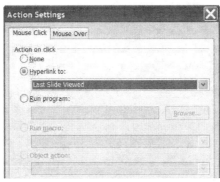

Program this hyperlink into a permanent object and you know you can always return to whichever slide you were on before the jump.

This argues for a more global view of your hyperlinking scheme, so ask yourself the following questions:

■ What are the specific slides that I might need to visit at any given time during the presentation?

Hyperlinks Never Get Lost

Hyperlinks jump to specific slides in a presentation and it is important to note how PowerPoint identifies the slide. When you create a hyperlink, you identify the destination by its content, not by its position in the slide deck.

You are not creating a hyperlink to whatever slide happens to be the fourth in the deck; you identify a specific slide. If you were to move the Navigating Your Slides slide to a different place in the presentation, the hyperlink would find it just fine.

And while you identify a slide by its content, PowerPoint understands that you might change the slide's content. You can rewrite the title, change out all of the text, convert it to a chart layout, or remove all content entirely—PowerPoint will still keep the hyperlink in place.

▪ Do I want to show my links or not bother my audience with them?

▪ If the latter, are there slide elements that I could use for them?

It is unlikely that you would know the precise slide that you would be on when you wanted to employ a hyperlink, so they are best created on the slide master.

Figure 27.5 shows a slide for a presentation on creating graphics for PowerPoint. There are four topics to be discussed and as serendipity has it, the design incorporates four small square in the corner of the slide. If you were creating this slide deck, you could ensure your ability to reach any of the four main topics with these steps:

1. Go to the slide master.

2. Select the first small square and create a hyperlink to the slide that introduces the first main topic.

3. Select the second square and make a hyperlink to the second topic.

4. Repeat for the third and fourth topics.

5. Select the long rectangle along the bottom and create a Last Slide Viewed hyperlink.

6. Select the Title placeholder (not the text itself) and create a hyperlink to the presentation's conclusion.

Now this PowerPoint file will serve you, its presenter, much more ably. No matter where you are in the presentation you know that you are one click away from any of your four main topics and from your

Figure 27.5
This slide could function as home base for your presentation, and those four little rectangles at the bottom could take you to each topic.

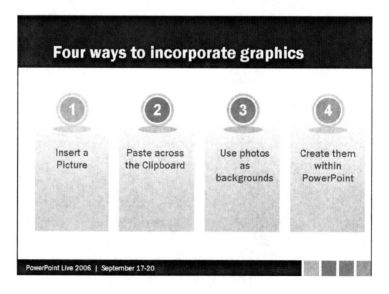

conclusion. And if you needed to make a quick, temporary, jump to one of those slides, after going there you could return with one click.

Not all PowerPoint templates are so ideally-designed for creating hyperlinks, but we've not yet met a slide design that couldn't accommodate hyperlinking needs. Even if you were just to define quadrants of the slide—top-left takes you to the beginning, bottom-right to your conclusion—you'd be better off than being confined to a linear progression of slides.

▶ Make sure not to obscure hyperlinks on your slide master with content on the slides themselves. If that happens, you won't be able to click on the hyperlink. Version 2007 allows you to create a custom placeholder as a hyperlink and ensure that it is always on top. With earlier versions, you need to be careful about your layering.

Nay-saying

There are three typical criticisms against the use of hyperlinks, none of which we accept:

You might accidentally click a hyperlink   Well, yes, I suppose, but so what? If you accidentally clicked anywhere on a slide, you would advance without wanting to. With your Last Slide Viewed button, you can always return with just one click.

You might forget that they're there   And you might not. What does it hurt to have them there?

You can just use the built-in navigation   It's true that you can advance to any slide by simply typing its number and pressing Enter, pressing End to reach the last slide and Home to go to the first. But this is not nearly as good as building in your own navigation. Using the built-in navigation assumes three things that you can't really assume:

- You remember the exact number of the slide you want. I never do.

- The last slide of your deck is the concluding slide that you would want to jump to. Rarely is that the case with my presentations—I usually design a conclusion slide before my thank-you-and-goodbye slide.

- Ditto for returning to the beginning of the presentation. Usually, menu-type slides that you would want to return to are not the first slide of a presentation.

If you have never tried creating your own navigation to make a presentation more flexible, you owe it to yourself to experiment with it.

Linking to Custom Shows

One of the most powerful combinations available to the non-linear thinker is the marriage between hyperlinks and custom shows (a group of slides defined as a subset within a slide deck—see Chapter 12). With these two features working together, you can create the kind of menu for a flexible presentation as shown in our photo-cropping tutorial discussed in Chapter 19.

1 Here is the menu slide for that self-running tutorial with the three titles acting as a hyperlink. The idea is that you, the viewer, choose which form of tutorial you want by simply clicking the big number associated with each one.

2 To assign a hyperlink to a custom show, you simply designate it from the Action Settings dialog. The key requirement is to check Show and return, which ensures that when the custom show is finished, you are returned to the primary show that is running.

3 The primary show has been defined as only one slide—the menu slide. And when you are "finished" with the show, the Loop Continuously Until Esc option ensures that you always return to it. If you were to simply advance past the first slide, you would finish the show and start over, the result being that advancing the slide show seems to do nothing. The only way to get anywhere in this show is to choose one of the three options on the menu slide and run the respective custom show.

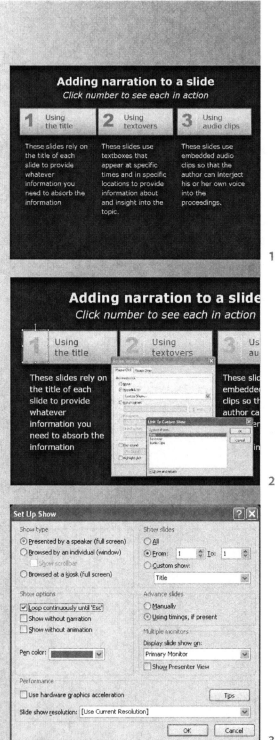

1

2

3

Navigating Outside a Presentation

With the basic hyperlinking engine, you can seamlessly integrate content from outside of the PowerPoint file. You can create the following types of links:

■ **To other presentation files** Link to another presentation and it begins playing without delay or prompting. When that show ends, you are returned to the show you were in and the slide you were on when you launched the second show.

■ **To a web page** Click on a URL link and that page opens in the default browser, as defined by your system. The presentation remains running underneath and you can Alt+Tab to it anytime.

■ **To any document** Any file that you can double-click on in a My Computer window can be linked to from within PowerPoint.

■ **To an application** With one backdoor maneuver, you can call up any Windows application without actually opening a docuement.

Are you pro-choice or pro-freedom?

There are two factors that take the discussion deeper, and the first one is how you activate a hyperlink. Few things in the presentation business are more satisfying than watching an accomplished presenter who is adept with a wireless remote and has designed a presentation to take advantage of it. He can be all the way across the room and still command the screen. She can work the crowd, knowing just when to send her audience's attention back to a slide.

At the same time, there is quite a rush in creating a rich presentation that is full of hyperlinks and flexible navigation. Click here and go there. Click there and go here.

Hyperlinking is at its most flexible when you are able to move your mouse to objects and click them. You have as many choices as you have programmed onto a slide and you make the choice during the course of your presentation. I'm going to coin a term for this action: mouse-centric navigation.

On the other hand, hyperlinking is at its most seamless when you can simply click Advance on your remote and be taken places. You make all your choices ahead of time and you advance in a linear fashion through the presentation, but with the techniques discussed in this chapter, the places you can go in that straight line can be exceptionally inventive. Here's another made-up term: remote-centric navigation.

Part Five: Working Smarter

Work the room or work the computer? Which approach is better? Are you pro-choice (mouse-centric) or pro-freedom (remote-centric)?

That question has no right answer and we're not interested in establishing one. Our interest is in helping you determine when to adopt each strategy and ensuring that you get maximum value out of whichever one you choose.

In the next section, we'll create mouse-centric navigation that will make your head spin. First, let's discuss remote-centric navigation because to maximize its use, it requires familiarity with a technique that most Windows users do not explore:

Inserting Objects

An inserted object (or OLE object, for the Object Linking and Embedding engine) is different from an imported graphic or a hyperlink. An object represents the contents of a different file and it can be animated in a unique way.

If you have never worked with OLE objects, you're going to need an example, so let's say that in a presentation that you're giving about home mortgage refinancing, you want to show a set of slides, called payments.ppt, that graphs interest payments. You could simply import the slides into your current presentation, but the information in payments.ppt is constantly changing and you will use this data in several different presentations. When the data changes, you don't want to have to edit every presentation that uses that data; you want to update just the payments.ppt file. Here is how you would establish this relationship in both Versions 2003 and 2007:

1. Find the precise point in your current presentation where you want to show payments.ppt. In our case here, we want it to appear after the third bullet on this slide.

When is the right time to refinance?

- How much principal do you carry on your first mortgage?
- How much equity can you pull out in an emergency?
- Have you run the numbers with the new fees?
- Do you have the time to manage the move?

2. Those bullets are animated with a fade, the first three happening automatically, and the fourth one set to enter on a click.

3. Go to Insert | Object, click Create from File, and click Browse to find the file.

4. Locate the file and then check both Link and Display as Icon.

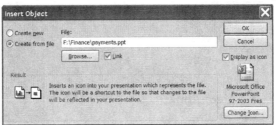

The Result section of this dialog is quite helpful. In this case, it verifies that you are creating the equivalent of a shortcut on your Desktop: an icon that represents the file. If you did not check the Link box, then PowerPoint would take the contents of the file and stuff them into the current file. This is important if you were sending the file off to someone else or posting it for distribution (all data is in one file), but not at all helpful if you want one dynamic file to be pushed out to several presentations.

If you did not check Display as Icon, PowerPoint would create a thumbnail of the first slide in the file and show that on the slide. There are plenty of times when that would be useful, and you can decide that for yourself. In this scenario, we are not interested in providing a visual cue for the hyperlink.

5. Click OK and note that a small icon appears in the middle of your slide.

6. Move the icon off the slide. In the image below, the gray area to the right of the slide is not the slide background; it is actually outside the slide boundary.

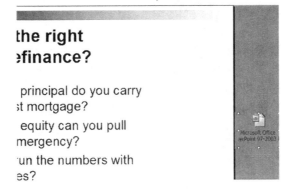

7. Open the Animation task pane, and with the icon still selected, click Add Effect. Notice the fifth choice: Object Actions.

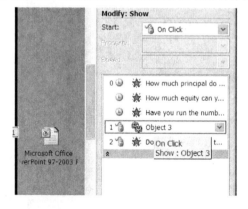

The purpose of this animation is not to determine how the object makes its appearance on the slide—it's not even on the slide, so you don't care about that. This animation determines what the object does when its turn comes around.

8. Click Object Actions and then Show.

9. Verify that the animation will start On Click.

10. Move it inbetween the bullets so that it is fourth in line.

Here is a play-by-play of this slide in action: 1) The title and first three bullets appear; 2) You advance and the payments.ppt slide show promptly appears; 3) You advance through it, and when it ends, you find yourself right back where you were.

Audience members have no idea that you ran a secondary presentation file. They just know that a relevant set of data appeared on screen to help them understand the question of interest for a refinance.

▶ The critical requirement to this method is that the payments.ppt file continues to reside where PowerPoint originally found it. Each time you open for editing the file that contains the link, you'll be asked whether you want to update the presentation with current data. If you made changes to it recently, click Update.

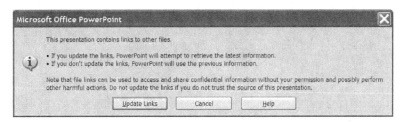

The safest course of action is to place all linked files in the same folder as the .ppt file that contains the links.

Thanks to the ability to place the linked object in the animation sequence, this is by far the most elegant technique for running a secondary presentation within a primary presentation. If you know when and where you want it to run, you can reduce the task down to a single click of a wireless remote or mouse. No other technique approaches this level of simplicity:

▪ If you created a standard hyperlink to the presentation, you would have to use your mouse to click on the hyperlinked object, requiring you or someone to be at the computer.

Using PowerPoint to Teach PowerPoint

At the conference, we find ourselves in an interesting conundrum: how best to use PowerPoint to show how to teach PowerPoint, all the while aware that everyone is watching how we use PowerPoint and how we behave as presenters. *Paralysis of analysis* comes to mind as the operative phrase for the risk we undertake of calling so much attention to the process of presenting.

The particular challenge is how we transition from showing a presentation, which we would normally do to frame the topic and introduce the technique to be discussed, to editing a presentation, which we would need to do in order to teach the technique.

Inserted objects can help smooth and integrate this transition, because you can call for a secondary presentation to be opened for editing, instead of opened as a show. In Step 8 on Page 312, choose
continued...

- If you chose to embed the presentation instead of keeping it linked, you would have to re-insert the file as an object anytime changes were made to it.

- By dragging the icon off the slide, you make the transition completely seamless to your audience members. If instead you wanted to create a visual cue for the jump to a secondary presentation, you could choose to show a thumbnail of the slide. And if you did that, you might want to add a conventional animation to it, so that it would fade onto the slide at the right time.

Using PowerPoint to Teach PowerPoint

(from previous page)

Edit instead of Show—that will cause the PowerPoint file to be opened normally.

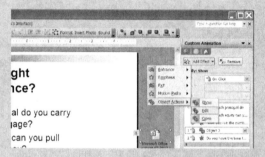

You can no longer navigate with your wireless remote—the only way to return to your primary presentation is by Alt+Tabbing back to it; by closing down the secondary presentation file; or by clicking the Resume Slide Show button that appears on the toolbar. But that's okay, because the whole idea here is that you are about to actively use PowerPoint to teach an aspect of it, so you inevitably have your hand on the mouse, ready to drive.

We've found a caveat to this that is worth noting: PowerPoint normally tunes the external display correctly when you are displaying through a projector, so your audience usually sees everything correctly. But sometimes your own internal display can go bonkers when you switch back and forth between showing a presentation and editing one. To prevent this problem, make sure that your internal display is running at the same resolution as your external one.

You can't go wrong if you set everything up for good old XGA, 1024 x 768. All components will behave well at that resolution, and even though today's equipment can run at higher resolution, your audience members and their aging eyesight might not appreciate how small everything gets at higher resolutions.

▶ If you use a wireless remote that includes cursor motion and click capability, you might be able to have it both ways: work the room and move your cursor to a hyperlink and click it. Our observation, however, is that few presenters are deft enough to perform this action elegantly while commanding a room full of people. At a minimum, you will want lots of practice if you want to have your cake and eat it, too.

Opening non-PowerPoint content

Using inserted objects is useful for just about any secondary data or application you want to show, whether it is a PowerPoint presentation or some other document. I regularly call upon PowerPoint to open Photoshop files, databases, fully-designed illustrations, even applications that take control of digital cameras when tethered by a data cable. It bears repeating and emphasizing:

> **Anything that can be launched from My Computer can be launched from within PowerPoint.**

You would use the same procedure detailed in the sidebar on Page 313:

1. Use Insert Object and Create From File.

2. Browse to the file and create a link.

3. Add an animation to it, choosing Edit as the action.

There are only two prerequisites:

- The application must be installed on the computer running the primary presentation.

- The document, if there is one, must exist.

The document…*if there is one*…hmmm…

Indeed, you don't need to open a document; you can ask PowerPoint to simply open the application. When you issue the Insert Object command, choose the other radio button, Create New, and find the program you want to run in the Object Type list. If it is there, select it and finish the process of inserting an object and including it in the animation scheme. You're done.

But what if the program is not on the Object Type list? Many installed applications do not announce their availability to the OLE engine because they do not have conventional data files associated with them. One example is iTunes. You could probably start iTunes from within PowerPoint by finding a downloaded song on your hard drive and inserting it as an object. Finding iTunes songs on your hard drive is no easy task, however, and as soon as you triggered it in the animation scheme, the song would start playing.

If the application is not readily available to you through the Insert Object dialog, you can go back to the Action Settings command and create a hyperlink to it:

1. Create an object to act as the iTunes icon (or import a graphic of its actual icon).

2. With the object selected, go to Action Settings and click Run Program.

3. Navigate your primary hard drive to where iTunes is installed, probably under Program Files, and find the iTunes.exe file.

4. OK your way back out.

Now when you click that object, iTunes will launch.

With this technique, you cannot automatically run the program the way you can with Insert Object—the object behaves like a standard hyperlink, requiring you to click the object that contains the hyperlink.

> While attempting to launch executable files as hyperlinks, you will be stopped if your Macro Security setting is anywhere except on the lowest setting. You will be required to acknowledge the risk by answering Yes before being allowed to proceed. On the lowest setting, PowerPoint does not intervene at all.

PowerPoint as operating system

If you regularly use PowerPoint to demonstrate or to teach, you'll find that it can function quite ably as a main platform, almost like an

Super-Geeky Tip No. 34B: Open Any File Like a Program

If you prefer the above technique of creating a hyperlink to run a program, you can use it to open files, too. Choose Run Program from Action Settings, but before you begin looking for the file you want to open, change the file type filter from Programs (*.exe) to All Files (*.*).

Now go find your document and OK your way out. When you click the hyperlink, PowerPoint automatically launches the application that created that document and opens the file.

operating system. You could build slide masters with inserted objects and hyperlinks and create templates tuned for teaching specific skills. Coupled with navigation buttons and prompts for choosing one path or another, you can create a completely interactive, self-paced set of tutorials or demonstrations on just about any topic.

I'm not at all certain how many different types of elements can be inserted into PowerPoint and I learn about new ones almost on a daily basis. Just the other day, I discovered that the digital slide shows I create in ProShow Producer can be run as objects within PowerPoint by finding and inserting a behind-the-scenes file. Once you understand the plumbing, you will make similar discoveries on the road toward using PowerPoint as the means by which you can open anything.

Creating Killer PowerPoint Menus

Here's the scene: you are speaking to a room of—whom would you like to be speaking to?—let's say, a group of A List Hollywood celebrities, and you are offering them advice on—what would you like to be an expert on?—let's say, you're advising them on how to better interact with the public.

Brad Pitt asks you the following question:

Brad: There's public and there's private-public. If I'm at a ballgame, I expect that I'm going to be asked to sign a few autographs. But when I'm in a small restaurant, in a corner booth, with Angelina—that's the time that I really need for my privacy to be respected.

You: That's a really good issue you raise. It's not on our agenda, but it's worth taking a few minutes to explore.

You walk to your computer and click once. Up pops a row of topics on the top of the slide, one of which is entitled Privacy. You click it to retrieve a rich presentation of photos, quotes, and advice to celebrities who feel stalked in public.

Brad gives you a seated ovation (he stands for nobody), and other audience members are so impressed with your ability to provide this level of detail on the fly that they all text their agents and tweet their followers to recommend you being hired as special advisor.

All this because you clicked once on a slide.

This fantasy was brought to you by one of the most powerful techniques that we know for infusing a presentation with flexibility and intelligence: a customizable menu that you can make appear at any time. If you can anticipate the kinds of questions that might arise during a presentation, few things are more impressive than being ready to address them.

▼ To see a video on this topic, visit www.pptlive. com/video/intellig entpres.htm.

You already know part of this solution: hyperlinks to other presentations or to custom shows within your presentation. When done properly, the objects containing the hyperlinks are never more than one click away, and upon that click, they appear on screen, not unlike the Windows Start menu, ready to take you somewhere.

Triggering the menu

The key ingredient to this capability is the trigger: a technique whereby clicking on one object triggers the animation of another object. Figure 27.10 shows the basic mechanics of this technique. The rectangle has been given a fade, set to appear On Click. The question is what click? The answer comes from the Timing dialog of the rectangle's animation, where we have instructed the animation to take place when we click the oval.

Click the oval and see the rectangle.

Those are the basics of a trigger. As with a standard hyperlink, the idea is to find a design element on the slide and make it be the trigger for the menu. Once the menu appears, standard hyperlinks take over. Here is how we would build one for our Hollywood audience.

First off, the whole idea of this menu is that it be just a click away, anytime, anywhere. That means that it must be built on the slide master,

Figure 27.10

The idea of clicking one object to make another appear is central to a good menu. This technique works the same way in both Versions 2003 and 2007.

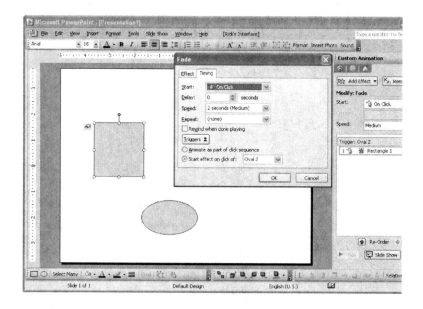

Figure 27.11

The stage is set for this menu: room for it top-right, and rectangles to act as triggers lower-right.

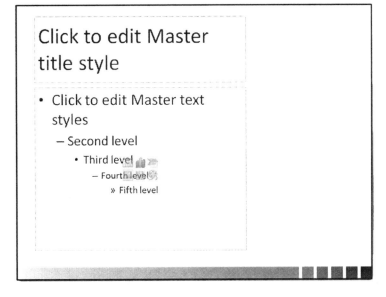

and Figure 27.11 shows the one that we built for it. This exercise takes place in version 2007, but all of it can be done in version 2003, as well.

The rectangular quadrants along the bottom provide a good opportunity to create triggers, and we have shortened the size of the title and content placeholder to accommodate the menu's appearance at the slide's top-right corner.

I do not like the look of hyperlinks applied to text (they get underlined and they change color, just like the old-style web-page hyperlinks in the 1990s). Therefore, I take on a bit of extra work when I create hyperlinks for text strings: I either apply the link to the entire text string, or when I must hyperlink text that is part of a larger string of text, I create nearly invisible rectangles over the text and apply the hyperlinks to them.

Creating the text is easy—in this case, just five short items. Notice that I am zoomed way in, as is my standard practice for performing precision placement on a slide.

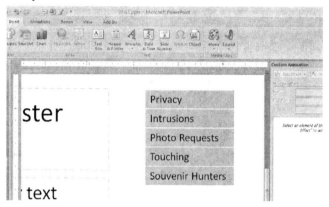

Once the text is in the correct position, I use the Action Settings dialog to create the hyperlink, in this case to a separate file called privacy.ppt. Each of these five text strings will be given a hyperlink to a file. In the alternative, I could create custom shows made up of hidden slides and hyperlink to them.

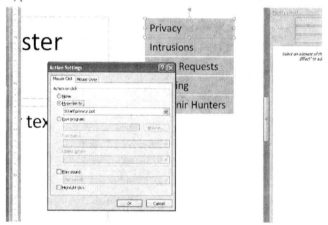

Once I have drawn and positioned the text strings and created the hyperlinks, it's time to animate them. So I drag a marquee around all of the text and group it (this is not essential, just recommended for keeping the animation sequence easier to deal with). I apply a fade to the group and set it to appear On Click, Fast. If you are using version

2007, as I am here, you can use the Selection and Visibility pane to name your group something better than Group 19.

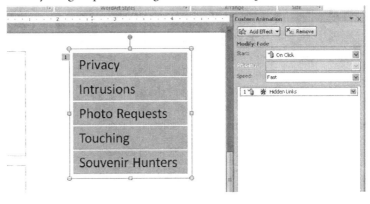

With the animation in the task pane selected, it's time to create the trigger, using the Timing dialog. But first I must know the name of the object that's going to act as the trigger. PowerPoint 2003 does not make this easy on me, as the only time that an object's name appears is when you animate it. So I must scroll down to the bottom of the slide, select the right-most rectangle, and then apply a temporary animation to it, just so I can get its name. It's called Rectangle 23. With version 2007, I have named the rectangle Menu Trigger.

I select the group, right-click, choose Timing, click Triggers, and then choose the rectangle as the object that will start the animation.

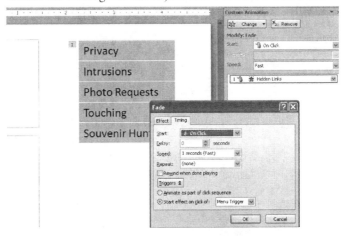

To make the effect a bit more refined, I also create an exit fade for the menu, triggered to the same rectangle. Now my little rectangle acts like a toggle to my hidden menu.

Letting go of our Brad Pitt fantasy, however reluctantly, you can use this technique successfully if you have any inkling at all about related topics that might be raised in a presentation. These would be questions not quite germane enough to be part of your main talk, but worthy of discussion should your audience ask.

Design your main slide master so it can accommodate a block of text and then think of five or six topics that you might be asked about during the presentation. Prepare short slide decks for each one (or hidden slides on the main deck) and hyperlink to them. Your audience will be impressed beyond belief—chiefly with your ability to anticipate their questions, but also with a technique within PowerPoint that they probably have never seen before.

▶ Over the course of a four-day PowerPoint conference, I can think of about 10 topics that are sure to come up at one point or another. You can download a .zip file containing my collection of linked presentation files as pptlive.zip.

Trainer Heaven

The techniques uncovered in this chapter can be put to great effect in countless situations. Of all the strategies discussed throughout this book, the ones in this chapter carry the greatest potential of taking you to an altogether different level of proficiency as a presenter and as a content creator.

And if I had to identify one group in particular that would benefit the most, it would be those who use PowerPoint as a training tool. The demands put upon students learning from a PowerPoint presentation are different than with an audience listening to a sales pitch or a keynote address. In short, the demands are much higher. They need to pay closer attention to details, they usually take many more notes, they are often following along with their own notebooks, and if they are learning a software program, they are likely watching smaller elements on screen, like icons, tools, and menus.

As the trainer, this increases your burden, also. You have to minimize extraneous screen activity, avoid being herky-jerky with the mouse, and eliminate unnecessary dialog boxes and windows that are not relevant to the task.

You can achieve all of that with effective use of hyperlinks, linked objects that automatically open data files, visual cues, and interactive menus. These are the ingredients to a cleaner and more enjoyable experience, both for you and for your students.

Chapter 28

Fabulous Photos

We have made no secret across the first 322 pages of this book of our affinity for photos. Big photos, loud photos, evocative photos—the bigger, louder, and more evocative the better. Ask anyone who has had to sit through an endless procession of bad bullets—they would kill for a slide with a photo on it. Even a bad photo.

Indeed, most of us love a good photo...even if we don't understand it. Our experience suggests that most people take digital photos for granted and don't really have a good handle on how to best make use of them. So consider this chapter a primer on all that you need to know and all that you need to forget with respect to using photos in your presentation files.

Resolution Confusion

Are you ready to hear the most widely-circulated misunderstanding concerning the use of photos with PowerPoint? Here it is:

When imported to PowerPoint, a 300-dpi photo will look better than a 72-dpi photo.

This is an incorrect statement. In fact, two photos of the same dimension (let's say 1024x768), one exported at 300 dpi, one exported at a lower resolution, will look exactly the same and will have the *exact same file size.*

One reason that you're probably shaking your head in the general direction of my book right now is because most software programs have misled you all these years. They have allowed you to speak the language of the print industry while working with display technology.

Get the dot out of here!

What exactly does it mean to have a photo appear on your screen that is 300 dots per inch? You might be able to explain to me the part about the dots, but an inch? What's an inch? On the monitor that's resting on my lap right now (yes, while my wife sleeps and my dog sneezes...still), an inch is over 7% of the total width. When this same image is projected before my audience, an inch would be less than .01% of the width. Same image, same computer, same photo, very different inch.

▶ Before you resize photos, make copies so you preserve the original fidelity. See Page 333 for details.

Measuring in inches has absolutely no meaning when discussing an image on screen, and therefore the term for resolution known as dots per inch is equally irrelevant. The dot refers to an actual placement of ink or toner on a printed page and that page has a measurable size. You really can measure how many dots of ink fit within one inch when you are printing.

We can do no such thing when we are discussing a photo that appears on screen, because there is no such thing as a dot and there is no such thing as an inch. There are only pixels—the basic unit of measure on a computer screen, the single grid point in an image, the abbreviation for "picture element."

The only measurement that is relevant with respect to the quality of a photo being prepared for PowerPoint is its size in pixels—1024 pixels

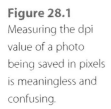

Figure 28.1
Measuring the dpi value of a photo being saved in pixels is meaningless and confusing.

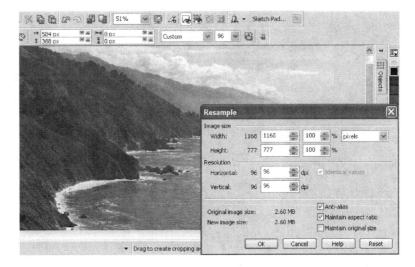

wide...800 pixels wide...600 pixels tall, etc. This is why software that implies otherwise, as we see in Figure 28.1 does us all a disservice.

This application here is just one of many programs that commits this error. If you were to adjust the dpi value in this dialog box, the software would compensate by changing the image size. This might lead you to believe in the relationship between dpi and screen resolution, but it is really tantamount to two wrongs making a right. So just remember this:

> **When sizing a photo for PowerPoint, the only thing that matters is its size in pixels.**

If the image were destined for a magazine and were being measured in inches, that would be different. But it's not, so please stop thinking about dots and inches. Instead...

Think pixels

Let's start by making this really simple, so if you get fed up with this chapter right now, you'll already have the important part:

> **Try to use photos that have at least 1024 pixels of width or 768 pixels of height.**

Over 90% of all presentations delivered today are projected at XGA resolution—1024 pixels across by 768 pixels deep. If your landscape photo is sized at 1024 pixels wide or your portrait photo at 768 pixels high, you guarantee its fidelity when projected full screen. You'll be exercising overkill for photos less than full screen, but the increase in the file's size is utterly insignificant (read on for our feelings about overkill). If you deliberately decrease the size of your photo because you don't intend to use it full-screen, Murphy's Law will immediately activate, your design will change, and you'll need it full screen. Just keep it at that size, even if you're using it smaller.

This discussion assumes that you have control over the size of the photo, but many times you don't. Like when you get sent a 150-pixel wide thumbnail and you're expected to do something with it. As soon as you take the dpi nonsense out of the equation, you can think rationally about this situation and reach an intuitive solution:

You must display it in PowerPoint at a small size!

And how do you know what size to make it? How can you size it to 150 pixels? You can't, because PowerPoint is brain-dead this way, also! Look at Figure 28.2 and you'll see that PowerPoint insists on measuring this photo in inches.

For more detail on the resolution misconception, visit the PPTFaq site and read www.pptfaq.com/FAQ00075.htm.

Fortunately, you are operating in a very forgiving medium. It really doesn't take a lot to make a photo look good on a computer display or out of a projector. You don't have to worry about color-matching, trapping, registration errors, CMYK conversions, or any of the issues that send those in the print business to early retirement. If it looks good on your screen, there's a good chance it will look good when projected or shown. If you can test it out on the ultimate output device, so much the better.

Just use common sense here: a low-resolution photo (i.e. one that has a small size, like 150 pixels wide), will not look good if sized to full screen. Plan on using it as a small image in your slides.

Figure 28.2
PowerPoint suffers from inchitis, just like other programs do.

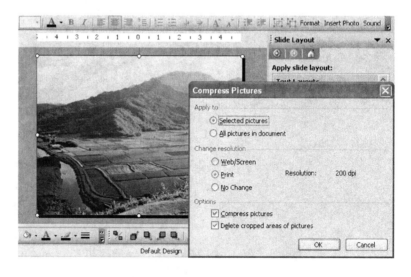

Figure 28.3
This photo was taken by an 8.1 megapixel camera, a typical resolution by 2007 standards.

Welcome to the BetterPresenting PowerPoint Photo Lab

In order to make these points real and practical, we need to use real photos, talk about real numbers, and see real results inside slides.

Figure 28.3 is a photo of my two daughters outside on a sunny fall day in San Francisco. It was taken with my Canon EOS XT, a digital camera that takes photos at 8.1 megapixels.

Dimension	3456 pixels wide
	2304 pixels high
Filesize	3.3MB

By 2009 digital SLR standards, this camera is considered low-resolution—the current Canon EOS model shoots at 13 megapixels, producing images that are 4272 pixels wide. (And my older daughter no longer wears braces; such is progress.) Given that most of us project our slides at 1024 pixels wide, you can see how much extra resolution we have to work with.

It also gives you an idea of how large your PowerPoint files might grow, but stay tuned—we'll discuss that in detail, also.

Figure 28.4
When imported to PowerPoint, this photo is many times larger than the slide itself.

When imported into PowerPoint, it is such a large photo that my older daughter's head barely fits on the slide. In Figure 28.4, we have super-imposed the size of the actual slide so you can get a sense of how large the photo is. The slide thumbnail on the left of the figure will give you the same indication.

With just this photo, the PowerPoint file is 3.5MB, but before you go on auto-pilot and conclude that it needs to be shrunk down, consider

■ You could zoom and pan this photo and maintain high fidelity.

■ You could confidently use this photo as an extreme close-up:

Above all, you want to be free to make these kinds of decisions later in the project, which is why we advise keeping your photos at full resolution. Let's continue the experiment and you'll see for yourself...

At 1024 pixels wide...

We have taken the photo into an image editing program (Photoshop, PhotoPaint, Paint Shop Pro, ACDSee, et al) and reduced it in size to 1024 x 682 (we told it to size the width to 1024 and allow the height to adjust in proportion).

 Download photo_lab.ppt for a complete analysis and recap of the experiments discussed in this chapter.

The result is a photo that looks great when displayed at full-width and yet is a fraction of the size of the original: 254KB, down from 3.3MB.

For most people and most situations, this photo will fill your needs, from full-slide down to thumbnail. But if you get ambitious and strive for the extreme close-up shown earlier, you will be disappointed with the results if you have already downsized your photos. Even on the black and white pages of this book, I'll bet you can see the difference between the 1024-wide image below and the full-resolution one on the opposite page.

Look at her hair, the texture of her skin, and the eyelashes. Whatever differences you see here, shown three inches wide and in grayscale, multiply many-fold for color output on a high-resolution display.

Once you size the photo down to 1024 pixels of width, you close the door on close-ups like this one. There are no longer enough pixels in the photo to provide the detail needed.

At 800 pixels wide...

When downsized to 800 pixels wide and then shown at full-slide, we see almost no drop in image quality compared to a higher-resolution image. This suggests to us that the relationship between resolution and file size is not linear. We saved a bundle of file space in the first decrease in size, but not nearly so much this time: only 70K, from 254KB to 185K. Even sized up full-slide, this one looks almost identical to the 1024-pixel-wide photo.

At 640 pixels wide...

When displayed at full-slide width, you can clearly see that this photo does not have as much detail. Given that you're only saving about 40K (file size of 144K), sizing down to 640 pixels or lower seems pointless.

Figure 28.8 shows the four resolutions that we worked with in this little experiment, and displayed at this small size, I'll defy you to see a difference. On my 24-inch display, I have to practically touch my nose to the screen to discern the subtle differences in Erica's lashes.

But in Figure 28.9, it's a different story altogether, as once again, the demands of such a tight zoom are too much for the versions of this photo that have been reduced in size. The other scenario in which lack of resolution shows up is with a sweeping pan across a photo, available for you to see if you download photo_lab.ppt. An effective pan requires that the photo start out significantly larger than the slide itself, and that spells trouble for photos that are only the size of the slide or smaller.

Keep those pixels!

This is one of two reasons why I recommend that you *not* downsize your photos before importing them to PowerPoint.

When I have a rich presentation to prepare that will be run on my own computer, I really don't care how large my PowerPoint file becomes. I just want every possible creative option available to me. Pans and zooms are standard operating procedure when I'm hoping to evoke emotion with a photo montage and for those two maneuvers, I need every last pixel.

Figure 28.8
One of these photos is 3.5MB in size and the other is 104K, but at this size, you wouldn't be able to determine which is which.

Figure 28.9
Close-ups like these, however, expose the photos that have given away too many of their pixels.

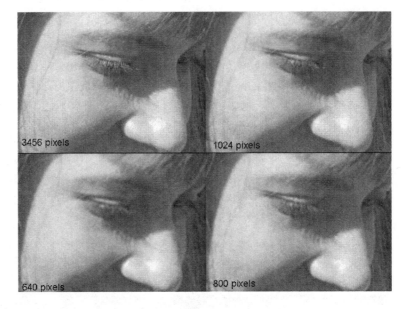

On some computers, there might be a drop in performance with photos this large, but on any of the desktops or notebooks that I have purchased since 2003, I have noticed none whatsoever.

Furthermore, I would be nervous on your behalf if you were aggressively reducing the resolution of your JPGs before using them in slide decks. Have you carefully tucked away the original file, in case you want to make a print? It's just too easy to forget to do that and I argue that it is unnecessary to have to burden yourself with that responsibility.

If you have a slide deck you have to send to someone else or make available as a download, you would want to take measures to keep the file size down. Nonetheless, I still do not recommend you downsize your photos before import; there are better ways to address this situation.

Managing the Move

Should you choose to get aggressive with the size of your rich presentation files, there are three courses of action available to you:

- Resize your photos with image-editing software before importing them to PowerPoint.

- Let PowerPoint do it for you, with the Compress Pictures command.

- Use third-party software that compresses the entire PowerPoint file.

If you have a preferred image-editing application, you not only know how to size a photo, you've probably done it countless times already. For those with less experience, I recommend picking up a copy of ACDSee Photo Manager, the versatile image viewing, organizing, and editing tool from www.acdsystems.com. With a buy-in starting at $50, you get a handy array of tools and a friendly interface, as shown in Figure 28.10. I own Photoshop, PaintShop Pro, and PhotoPaint, and yet I often reach for ACDSee for quick crops, format conversion, and changes in size, thanks to the program's quickness and accuracy.

PowerPoint has its own built-in compression function, available for any selected photo in a file (via the Picture toolbar or the Format Picture dialog) or for every photo in the file (using the Tools drop-down in the Save As dialog).

Figure 28.10
ACDSee proves to be a handy investment for anyone who works ambitiously with photos.

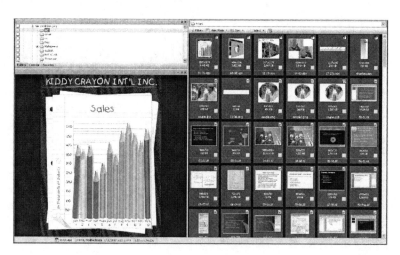

This procedure works according to algorithms that nobody has satisfactorily explained to me. Sometimes it reduces the size of a file by many factors and other times it does nothing. And as mentioned earlier, PowerPoint muddles the whole dot-per-inch/pixel situation, associating web quality with 96 dpi.

▶ In versions 2003 and earlier, you cannot compress photos that have been placed into a shape. With version 2007, you can.

Still, it doesn't hurt anything and is worth trying when you need to keep file sizes down and when you don't anticipate using photos that are larger than the slide itself.

As for after-market tools for file compression, we like NXPowerLite from the London-based Neuxpower company. For $45, you get an easy-to-use utility that takes care of business with no backtalk. And wow, does it work—our photo_lab file went from 3.9MB to 850K with no discernible picture loss. www.neuxpower.com.

Microsoft MVP Steve Rindsberg and his PPTools suite of programs offer an optimizer, among many other useful PowerPoint utilities, and you can find out about them at www.pptools.com.

We also like MVP Bill Dillworth's SizeMe utility, which reports in detail on what might be responsible for your file bloat. http://billdilworth.mvps.org.

The most important part of this whole process is insuring against downsizing your photos without having originals tucked safely away. If you are in Photoshop about to downsize an image, take a moment and save the file in native .psd format. Ditto for PhotoPaint and a .cpt file.

Once again, because we know how easy it is to forget to save photos in native formats, we like the post-production compression tools such as NXPowerLite. Reducing images once they are already in PowerPoint removes all risk to the original photos.

Version 2007's Treasure Trove

There is an awful lot to like about the current version's handling of imported photos—enough to make you think twice spending anything, let alone $1,700, on image-editing software. We alluded to version 2007's better graphical engine in Chapter 13 but it deserves more ink—its prowess is impressive.

The Format ribbon positively comes alive when you double-click an imported photo. Most of the offerings are one-click operations, making the following variations of a photo all trivial:

In clockwise order after the original photo (left) are brighten, darken, increase contrast, place inside shape and apply shadow (technically two separate operations), double-frame style, and monochrome recolor.

Yes, one-click operations are impressive—even more important is the type of control you can wield over a photo if you actually spend a few minutes with it. The gateway to quality time with a photo is the inconspicuous and easily-missed arrow pointing down from the Picture Styles group on the Format ribbon, shown below:

That is your gateway to the Format Picture dialog, an evolved and interactive dialog that combines many of the most powerful functions available for photo editing: shadowing, three-dimensional formatting, rotation, and recoloring. This dialog does not require that you close it in order to see the effect you have requested; it occurs in real time, inviting experimentation. The effect below would require a significant effort in an image-editing program like Photoshop. In fact, if I'm being honest, I would have to say that I wouldn't know how to accomplish it.

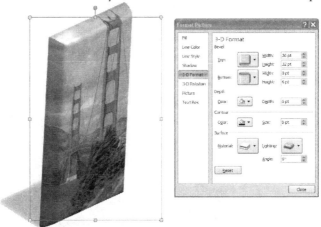

You can see from the selection handles how much this photo has been altered—it has been rotated counter-clockwise, been given depth and realistic lighting, and a shadow at the imaginary point where it would be resting on a surface.

◆

The important proviso to all of this is the reminder that none of these impressive features will make you a better presenter or a better designer of presentation content. If you use it gratuitously, it is just as bad as if you were to apply a spiral or a boomerang animation to your text. And as with the emphasis syndrome, if you apply a bevel and a shadow to every single photo in PowerPoint, the impact will be lost entirely. But if used appropriately—to color-correct a photo that was poorly-exposed or damaged, or to create emphasis to a singular element that warrants it, these capabilities can be invaluable and breathtaking.

Digital Photo Survival Skills

If digital photography does not prove to be the killer app of this decade, it means that something really huge is coming tomorrow. Using a digital camera, even an inexpensive one, is a liberating experience for so many reasons beyond the fact that it is much, much cheaper than using film. Here are a few of the dozens of reasons why digital photography has become one of the most popular pastimes for anyone who likes taking photos:

A digital camera makes you a better photographer Even if we're just talking dumb luck here, we take so many more photos of a given scene than we ever would have before, one of them is bound to be good. Furthermore, you get instant feedback through your LCD and that helps you develop an eye for what works and what doesn't. Waiting three days and relying on memory never worked for me across three decades of using film cameras; I learned more about composing shots in one year of using digital.

A digital camera makes your subjects better models I've observed that people are willing to pose for about three shots; after that, they begin to ignore you. Start snapping, my friend, because that's when you'll get some really good shots.

If you are paying for film, you are likely going to take only one or two shots of friends or family, and they're probably going to pose for you, like these photos here:

But if you know that you've got 120 shots left on your 1GB card and you can delete bad shots moments after taking them, you're going to shoot more. And when you do, your subjects are going to get tired of smiling for you. That's when you start to get photos like these:

Traditionalists are welcome to disagree, but to my eye candid photos tell more about somebody. On the left is a father and his adopted daughter, for whom he went to hell and back when she was just months old. They are very close and the quiet moment they share in the second photo conveys that. On the right are my daughter and my sister and they are best friends and confidants. That comes through much more in the non-posed shot.

You can fix your foul-ups There are entire books on this subject, and the world of photo-refining can be an intimidating place. Coming soon will be some tips that anyone can follow for making better photos.

Whether they are your own photos or ones supplied by others, understanding the basics of photo taking, exposure, focusing, and cropping will make your presentation content that much stronger. Here are a few topics to consider...

Depth of field

Even today's point-and-shoot cameras are capable of manipulating light to affect how a camera focuses. On a bright day, you can really learn a lot about this dynamic, because you have a lot of room to adjust. These two photos were taken just 10 seconds apart:

The one on the left was taken with a slow shutter speed, and to compensate, the camera closed ("stopped down") the lens by a considerable amount. This results in a greater focal length ("depth of field"). The photo on the right underwent the reverse: very fast shutter speed which

caused the lens to open much wider. That results in a much shorter
focal length. You can see all the way across the street in the left photo
but you can barely see five inches past the flowers on the right photo.

If you need a photo to be descriptive, the greater depth of field would
serve you well. If you want to be dramatic, the shorter depth of field is
what you want.

If you didn't do this out in the field, the digital darkroom can help you
in one direction. While making a blurry photo sharp is next to impossible, going from sharp to blurry is quite possible. It requires proficiency with your image editor's selection tools. With them, you can iso-
late the background and make it blurry. That helps bring focus and
drama to the foreground.

Figure 28.17 shows a photo undergoing such a transformation. The
coach has been "masked" (appearing in these pages with a white glow
around his periphery). Masking allows us to work on just him or just
the background. In this case, the coach was unaltered and the background behind him underwent a "Gaussian Blur," so named for the
mathematician who developed the algorithm two centuries ago.

Zoom

There is nothing like a good telephoto lens to allow you to sneak up on
people and get good candid shots. A good zoom feature on your camera also lets you alter reality. Witness these two photos, both taken
from the exact same position.

With a normal 35mm lens (left), you get a good sense of the distance between the foreground tree and the background tree. A telephoto lens tends to shrink the observable distance between foreground and background and the 300mm lens used on the right gives the impression that you can practically touch the tree in the back.

As with a short focal length, zoom can add energy and emotion to a photo, but it does so at the expense of realism. If you need your photo to be accurate, use a normal lens.

The most important thing to know about zoom is to avoid "digital zoom" at all costs. If your camera offers it, scroll the menus until you find out how to disable it. If a camera you are considering for purchase makes a big deal about it—if that's the best feature they have to advertise—run away fast! To reiterate

Avoid using your camera's digital zoom!

Optical zoom uses the lens itself to bring the subject closer—the physical elements of the lens move in order to change the field of vision. Digital zoom does nothing more than enlarge a portion of the image using an interpolation that has nothing to do with making the image better. Only bigger.

This treatment is similar to what you could do using the crop tool of your image editor, with one important difference: your software is much better at it than the camera is.

Figure 28.19 is a photo taken at the maximum level of optical zoom. It is a sharp, focused image taken with a 5MP point-and-shoot camera.

In order to zoom in even more on the oranges—in PowerPoint, in another application, or in a print—you have two choices: 1) use your camera's digital zoom; or 2) crop this photo and then enlarge the remaining area. While it's easier to push a button on your camera than work the photo with software, the results aren't even close.

The photo on the left is a product of 30 seconds spent in PowerPoint cropping and then enlarging the photo. The one on the right is my camera's pathetic attempt to do the same thing. Turn off digital zoom and pretend you never heard of it.

Flash and exposure

This one's easy, right? You use it when you are indoors and you turn it off when you are outdoors.

What if I told you that you might have better results if you were to do the exact opposite? Using a flash indoors tends to overpower the existing light, creating bright and often harsh images. If you can shoot without flash, the natural light of a room tends to be warmer. Here is a simple example:

On the left, the candle is overwhelmed by the flash and the granite counter looks cold and harsh. But on the right, the scene is captured more realistically—the candle was the only illumination at the time. The shot on the left is plenty bright and descriptive, and it's easy to take. The one on the right requires a steady hand (much slower shutter speed), but if you seek realism of a scene, the effort is worth it.

Meanwhile, a nice bright summer day, with the sun directly overhead, could spell death for your ability to capture facial features. Witness these photos of a nice Yosemite hike at Vernal Fall:

All of that rushing white water in the background captured the lens's attention (left), and everything else was underexposed. But the addition of flash (right) provides enough light to cut through all of that glare.

Outdoor flash is much more subtle—you rarely have to worry about it looking artificial, as you do indoors. It just provides a bit of illumination to fight backlighting and dark shadows from midday sun. The auto-husband removal is an optional feature, usually costing extra.

The risk of shooting indoors without a flash is that your images will be blurry. As the camera struggles to get enough light, it slows down the shutter considerably, amplifying any bit of shake you might introduce. You can help by telling the camera that it doesn't have to try so hard to get sufficient light. Find your camera's exposure setting and reduce it, effectively telling it that it is okay if the image is a bit dark. With that requirement eased, your camera will use a faster shutter speed, allowing you to take sharper photos.

And what about those dark photos? While it is very difficult to save a photo that has been overexposed, you would be amazed at how much information can be squeezed out of an underexposed shot:

I promise that I did no doctoring to these photos other than what we're about to describe. The photo on the left is exactly how my 10-year-old daughter took it, from inside a mission where flash photography is prohibited. The version of it on the right is the result of increasing the image's midtones. It took about 15 seconds in ACDSee.

The moral of the story: Don't be afraid to underexpose your shots, and don't give up on dark photos.

A load of crop
The single most important difference you can make with your photos is to remove parts of them. You play an important editorial role when you make decisions that help focus attention and bring more energy to

Figure 28.24
This photo suffers from unimaginative composition and too many visual distractions.

Figure 28.25
Twenty seconds with a crop tool and now this photo is ready for a frame.

a scene. We have so many examples of this, we have prepared a download for you, but we'll share one of them here in these pages.

Figure 28.24 is a typical example of a tourist or vacation photo, with the subjects placed right in the center of the shot and a bunch of noise

Figure 28.26
This photo is fine, and the headline is fine, but it will never be better than fine.

Figure 28.27
With one crop and three minutes with a transparent rectangle, this slide gets an infusion of energy.

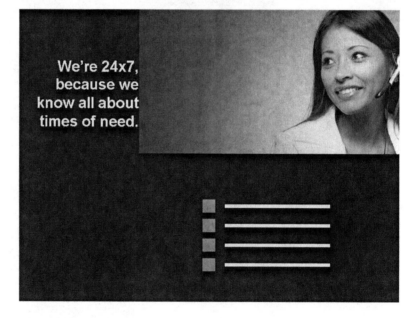

in the background. Like we really need an ugly picnic table and iron barbecue back there?

Most amateur photographers place their subjects in the center and probably will until the day they die. Fortunately, the digital age allows you to make your creative decisions after the fact, and Figure 28.25 on the previous page shows the result of a simple crop. With the unattractive part of the background out of the picture, the truly beautiful part

▼ Download cropping.ppt for an interactive tour of many photos made better with the right crop.

that is the Santa Barbara coastline becomes more prominent. And just by putting the two people a bit off to one side, the photo becomes vital and more interesting. This is not difficult at all to do in PowerPoint, especially if you create better access to the Crop tool. The hardest part is remembering to think about it, instead of just accepting a photo's default placement. It's a matter of thinking asymmetrically: *If I moved this person out of the center of the photo, would it look better? If I moved part of her off the slide, what would that do?*

Figure 28.28
Cute girl...nice message...

Figure 28.29
Cute girl...nice message...powerful visual!

The before and after examples on the previous pages are quite telling. Otherwise plain layouts give off completely different feelings with the help of simple crops. I also like that the subjects in the photo end up being bigger.

I probably use the Crop tool in PowerPoint more than any other, except for animation and layering. I was gratified to discover that if I used the Customize dialog to ask for an English-speaking button instead of an icon, and I labeled it &Crop, I could activate it with Alt+C. I have cut way down on my mousing around by being able to move the cursor to the photo, press Alt+C to activate the tool, and then begin cropping right away.

As you can tell, I love my digital cameras...all six of them. I still have my first one, a 1MP shoebox that Kodak introduced in 1995 for $800. As far as I know, it was the first digital camera made available in this country. When we used it at the 1996 CorelWorld User Conference to take photos and then, 10 minutes later, projected them in the main ballroom, it was nothing short of a miracle.

I am never satiated. At this very moment, my auction software is poised to make an eBay bid on a new camera and I have my eye on about five lenses.

Digital photography is one of the happiest addictions I have ever had...

Chapter 29

Music and Video: Looking Beyond PowerPoint

We're sure you've heard the expression before, or a derivation: "When all you have is a hammer, everything looks like a nail." It describes our human desire to make things work, even if they are not destined to.

We have seen some amazingly deft and inventive workarounds to overcome PowerPoint's shortcomings and we applaud the ingenuity of those who refuse to give up.

Nonetheless, there are times when the wisest course of action is to acknowledge that PowerPoint is merely a tool designed to help you perform tasks. And for some tasks, it is the wrong tool. This chapter addresses a niche that has really exploded over the past three years—multimedia and video. And with it explodes the illusion that PowerPoint can handle our multimedia needs.

Beyond Slides

We have noticed two clear trends over the last few years of hosting the PowerPoint Live User Conference. The first is a growing desire to deliver content on DVD, and the second is an affinity for creating movies, be they promotional videos for business purposes or family videos commemorating significant lifecycle events. Family keepsake videos are big; I have literally formed a secondary business around it.

These two areas of interest share many challenges and rewards, not to mention an entire cottage industry and software niche. They also share the inescapable conclusion that PowerPoint is not the right tool to use.

Would that the Package for CD function contain the magic necessary to convert your PowerPoint presentations into a digital video stream that could be ripped directly to DVD. The cold truth is that there is no easy way—only circuitous, multi-step routes—to convert a PowerPoint presentation into a DVD video. In this particular regard, Apple Keynote enjoys a clear advantage with its ability to export to video.

The more glaring issue is the set of deficiencies that work against you when trying to create an evocative slide show to move or persuade an audience:

■ Unreliable synchronization of music with imagery

■ No support for fading an audio clip

■ Inconvenient handling of photos

■ Limited support for playing video

■ Poor timeline

■ Inability to combine or script zooming and panning

None of these shortcomings is addressed in PowerPoint 2007, and many of us who have cut our teeth using PowerPoint to create digital video are now looking at other applications that are better suited to these tasks. You can spend as little as $50 or as much as $1,700 in the software niche that doesn't really have an agreed-upon name yet. Some vendors refer to their programs as digital video creation tools; others as home movie makers. Some call this niche photo slide show creation; others prefer the more impressive digital production and post-production.

The least sexy phrase is the one that has caught on: non-linear editing. NLE software allows you to slice and dice video and move from the beginning to the end of a movie with one command. VHS is linear; movie-making software is non-linear.

By any name, these programs all offer the following critical set of features:

External referencing of photos Instead of trying to import and digest megabytes worth of imagery, these programs store references to the external files. Any changes made to the source files are instantly reflected in the project, and you needn't worry about downsampling the photos first to keep file sizes down. That is one of your export choices, so you can wait until the very end to determine the resolution and quality of your movie.

Complete audio-video synchronization No matter where you are in a movie's timeline, you can confidently match an audio clip to the imagery behind it. If you want to cut to your Niagara Falls panorama right at the crescendo of Beethoven's Fifth, or when Whitney Houston hits a high note, that's no problem, and you can test it by playing just that slide. (In PowerPoint, you would have to start the slide show on whichever slide the music begins in order to even hear it.)

Built-in facilities for editing audio PowerPoint requires that you edit your audio clip before importing it. Most, if not all, digital video software allows you to fade and trim imported audio, making it much easier to refine your timings.

Support for video These programs make very little distinction between still photos and motion video. If it's a standard format, like TIF, BMP, JPG, AVI, MPG, WMV, they will accept the file and play or display it.

Direct export to video and built-in DVD creation Again, PowerPoint knows no such capability. Migrating a PowerPoint slide show to video involves one of two routes: 1) Using after-market software that converts it to Flash, and if that's not your desired format, going from there to MPG, AVI, WMV, or MOV along a very bumpy route; or 2) Using a program like Camtasia Studio to make a real-time recording of your slide show and save it to a video file. Only then can you burn a DVD. You can be 75% into this process and still be wondering, with good reason, if you shouldn't chuck the whole thing and start over with a different authoring tool.

Creating or Burning?

If you are primarily interested in collecting video, photos, or other data and preserving them on a DVD's 4GB of elbow room, then you have a multitude of software choices, ranging from $30 for a shareware program you can pick up on download.com to $300 for a full-featured menu-creation and quantity-burning application. These programs offer little in the way of creativity – you are expected to already have your content created and ready to be burned.

Most creative professionals will have little need for burn-only programs, because the software designed for content creation usually includes sufficient DVD-burning capability. At the top of the mountain is Adobe's Production Premium Suite, geared for those who work regularly with video (as opposed to mostly with still photography). This behemoth package could keep chiropractors in business for years, offering Premiere Pro, Photoshop, Illustrator, After Effects (a dedicated object animation tool), Encore (for creating menu-driven DVDs), and Audition (a full-featured audio-editing package). This bundle retails for $1,699.

When you pull yourself off the floor, we'll talk about the alternatives that cost a fraction of that price. Many of you already have some flavor of Photoshop or a similar image-editing program, and CorelDraw users don't need to purchase an image editor because they get PhotoPaint in the box. If you need a program like Illustrator for vector-drawing work, you probably already have one of those, too. You can pick up a very good audio-clip editor for free--Audacity (audacity.sourceforge.net) or WavePad (nch.com.au), and the slimmed-down Elements version of Premiere is a much more digestible $119.

Premiere is vintage Adobe: it is chock full of features hiding behind an impossibly vast array of toolbars, icons, and other *interfaciala*. If you already speak Adobe, you'll be comfortable with either flavor of Premiere; if not, then even the $119 for Elements might be more than you'll want to invest. Adobe's user interface philosophy does not vibrate particularly well with me, yet I have become quite comfortable working with Premiere Elements.

Ulead (now part of Corel) and Pinnacle Systems both offer video creation tools, and your comfort zone might be stroked better by either of these two. These choices are often a matter of personal preference, so it is helpful to be able to download a trial; unfortunately, Pinnacle Systems offers no trial software at its website, making it difficult to recommend.

Making Memories, Evoking Emotions

Then there is ProShow from Photodex, the most intuitive and "creative-friendly" application we know of for digital photographers. You can start with a free trial download of the $69 ProShow Gold and within less than 10 minutes (seven to be exact, but who's counting...other than us), you can be creating slide shows from your photos.

The $249 Producer version supports RAW photo formats, hyperlinked captions, DVD menu creation, and perhaps most important, support for multiple layers on a slide, making picture-in-picture and similar effects routine.

ProShow will import all forms of video but it does not capture video. If your work is primarily video capture and editing, you'd be better off with Elements, or offerings from Ulead or Pinnacle. But if most of your work is with photos, ProShow offers unparalleled flexibility. And with Microsoft Movie Maker, available for free to all Windows users, you have a no-cost tool for the occasional NLE work.

ProShow's interface invites experimentation on the path to learning. If you're not sure what you can do with a photo that you have dragged to your timeline, just double-click it and a window full of controls and effects appears. Double-click an audio clip and you will be taken directly to all soundtrack options. Adding a transition between slides is as simple as clicking between the two slides. No other program provides this level of control in such an intuitive way.

Finally, ProShow's output choices are positively dizzying. You can export your slide shows as MPEG-1 or -2 video, compressed and uncompressed AVI, high-resolution executable files for Windows PCs, a web stream, five flavors of video CD, a low-res emailable version, and a DVD, either direct burn or ISO creation. The newest version also offers an export directly to Flash and QuickTime format, addressing long-standing deficiencies in Mac support.

Nothing stirs the senses like still imagery set to music, and ProShow enjoys that almost-magical quality of making sense the moment you begin working with it. This was so pronounced for me that I almost literally established a new business as a result of our ability to connect with the software, and if you visit the Portfolio page at www.PhotosToMemories.net, you will see examples of photo slide shows that were created and published in just days.

Coupled with the $119 Premiere Elements and various free applications, all of your bases are covered. This partnership of software can take you leagues beyond PowerPoint's Photo Album feature.

Walking Through a Video Project

My most recent project was a non-paying gig: my younger daughter's bat mitzvah, akin to a wedding in terms of fanfare, occasion, and (gulp) expense. While the event was in February 2009, Jamie had proclaimed way back in August 2008 that she wanted "New York New

York" to be the theme of her reception. Not so coincidentally, we had planned a week's vacation there last summer. Therefore, my marching orders were clear: to create a slide show of photos, set to music, that would celebrate her life, honor her effort over the past six months, and support the reception theme.

This was without question a job for ProShow Producer.

Step one—identify segments

In conversation with my wife Becky, we discussed all of the parts of Jamie's life that warranted highlighting, as well as the people in her life that would be at the reception that day. We defined four aspects of her life—friends, family, vacations, and softball—and from there, created seven distinct parts to the video:

Parts
Introduction
Just Jamie
Her friends
Vacations
Softball
Family
Finale

If you were to conclude from this itinerary that the video would be too long, you would probably be right. When a once-in-a-lifetime event for a narcissistic 13-year-old daughter collides with a father who creates videos professionally, boundaries of sensibility get stretched. The ideal length for a video like this one, to be played in a roomful of friends and family, is about 12-13 minutes. This one promised to be closer to 18-19. The degree to which our friends forgave us would be directly proportional to the number of photos they see of themselves.

Step two—pick music

On our home network, Jamie's iTunes library shows up inside mine, so I could easily keep tabs on the music that she was listening to at the time. This needs to be balanced with the other generations that would be present, the suitability of her musical taste, the significance of the event, and of course, the theme. Taking all of this into account, we came up with the following:

Parts	Music
Introduction	New York, New York Frank Sinatra
Just Jamie	Everything Michael Buble
Her friends	Beautiful Soul Jesse McCartney
Vacations	Holiday Green Day
Softball	Supermassive Black Hole Twilight soundtrack
Family	New York, New York Liza Minelli
Finale	Al Shlosha Rick Recht

This felt like a good mix of contemporary, traditional, and teenage hip (the finale being a song by a well-known Jewish rock-and-roller). The common element is that all of the songs have a strong melody and most of them have an upbeat tempo—two important ingredients to creating a good slide show. As for how we got this music from iTunes into ProShow, see the sidebar upcoming.

Step three—determine video segments

Gathering photos is easy; shooting and collecting video not nearly so. Nonetheless, I was wedded to the idea of getting various groups of people in Jamie's life to perform their own little versions of New York (*"Start spreading the news...your bat mitzvah's today...it's great to be a part of it..."*) This took almost as much effort as the video itself, to say nothing about ensuring that Jamie's friends didn't say anything to her about it. I had four video snippets in mind and this needed its own checklist:

Parts	Music	Video?
Introduction	New York, New York Frank Sinatra	Yes
Just Jamie	Everything Michael Buble	No
Her friends	Beautiful Soul Jesse McCartney	Yes
Vacations	Holiday Green Day	Yes
Softball	Supermassive Black Hole Twilight soundtrack	Yes
Family	New York, New York Liza Minelli	Yes
Finale	Al Shlosha Rick Recht	No

The softball video is of the final out from last year's championship season, and I already was in possession of that.

Step four—begin gathering photos

It is here where you will find the potential bane of your existence: how many of the photos that you want to use are digital? The more you have that are from the digital photo era or already scanned, the more sane you will remain. The worst-case scenario, which I have lived through twice now, is the photo that lives only in a photo album. These are usually large, heavy books, with photos protected by adhesive plastic. In order to scan them, you have to remove them altogether from the album, or roll back the plastic and carefully place the album on the scan plate.

It's Your Music!

Overcoming the oppressive restrictions of iTunes

I had swallowed my frustration for months. I was only paying 99 cents per song, so on what grounds did I have to complain too much? Still, the notion that a song I buy from iTunes can only be played within iTunes or on an iPod seemed like a policy created by IBM, not Apple.

My frustration bubbled over due to the experiences of a family member, not those of my own. My sister Jody, who has had nothing but trouble with her iPod, shared with me the public venting of a New York Times journalist (www.betterppt.com/editorial/archive/06apr01.htm).

I buy many songs from iTunes, and I find it to be the height of arrogance that a song I rightfully own cannot travel with me outside of something beginning with a lower-case i. When it began to impede on my digital video business, I knew I needed to find a solution.

So I went back to my childhood. I used to spend untold hours recording music to cassette. First it was AM top-40 music, then the higher-fidelity FM stations, and ultimately my records. I would lose a bit of fidelity from the vinyl, but it was worth it to be able to play music from my records anywhere I wanted. Funny how far we've come and yet what a giant step backwards we've taken.

And then I encountered an alarmingly simple shareware program called Any Sound Recorder. It is one of several programs that does

My back never hurt so much as when I scanned a few of those pages and then realized the specter of having to scan about 200 more.

In order to save my back, my sanity, and my schedule, I headed outside with the photo album and my camera and literally took photos of photos. I found a place away from direct sunlight, turned my flash off, and began snapping like crazy. I digitized the photos in a tiny fraction of the time it would have taken me had I used the scanner. I needed a concentrated amount of time with my photo organizer (I use ACDSee Photo Manager) to rotate, crop, and occasionally correct for exposure, but that was a much more comfortable session than leaning over a scanner.

I would not trust this technique for making prints, but for the relatively forgiving medium of XGA projection, it was a fabulous solution.

exactly what its name implies: it digitally records any sound that emanates from your sound card. It has become my answer to Apple.

When I buy a song from iTunes, the first thing I do now is record it to CD-quality WAV format, replace the purchased file with the WAV file, and say goodbye to all restrictions. As far as iTunes is concerned, the WAV file is a piece of music that is entirely outside of its jurisdiction. While the song will play in iTunes, burn to a CD, and transfer to an iPod, iTunes does not nag me about authorization or give me any grief should I ever want to convert it to another format.

The WAV file is much larger than the purchased file, but that is my prerogative: I could have chosen to save it as MP3 or in one of several more compressed (and lower fidelity) flavors. If I wanted to cart tens of thousands of songs on a portable player, I would choose to do that, but I have thousands, not tens of thousands, I have a large hard drive in my PC, and I love the notion of having a high-quality original audio file, from which I could create compressed versions at will.

At $24.95, this program is a trivial expense. The more significant outlay is your time: Any Sound Recorder (ASR) and programs like it do not "convert" your songs; they record them. Therefore, after you have paid your $.99 to buy a five-minute song, you will need to spend five minutes playing it while ASR is listening. If you have a library of thousands, you would probably choose to do this on an as-needed basis.

continued...

I identified each section of the video with a letter and began naming files accordingly. Photos in the introduction were named

a01.jpg
a02.jpg
a03.jpg

And in the second section of the video

b01.jpg
b02.jpg
b03.jpg

Step five—more insanity

Production of the video was proceeding quite smoothly...until I concluded that we needed to end the production with photos from the ceremony itself. I have done this before, so I know the drill:

1. Create the entire video and hold, say, four slots at the end for photos from the service.

2. Find dummy photos, name them according to the naming scheme, and pretend they are the real things: pan and zoom, transition into and out of, time the music to end, and create whatever final caption I want to use.

...continued from previous page

ASR is as good as your sound card, but if your sound card were a piece of junk, you would already know it because your purchased music would sound terrible, as well. And while there might be some measurable drop in fidelity running the music through your PC's circuitry, when compared to what I used to do with my cassette deck, the compromise is so small as to be unnoticeable.

This is all completely legal. You own the music and provided you do not intend to resell it or distribute it illegally, you are perfectly entitled to manipulate it to suit your needs. (My republishing of the NYT article at my web site is probably more of a violation than anything discussed here.)

You can also record Internet radio with ASR. I listen to an iTunes stream and as a song is about to begin, I tap a key to launch a script that activates ASR's record command. If I don't like the song, I stop the recording. If I do like it, I wait for it to end, trim off any

3. At the conclusion of the service, when allowed to take photos, I either use my own camera or work with the hired photographer to acquire about a dozen photos as candidates. In the case of the latter, I bring a portable drive with an SD reader to download photos from the photographer.

4. I choose the four I want and rename them according to the scheme, allowing them to overwrite the placeholder files.

5. I then burn the final cut of the video and prepare it to show that evening at the reception.

All fine and well...except Jamie's reception was not in the evening. It was to take place immediately following the service. Without exaggeration, we were intending to show the video 90 minutes after the conclusion of the service.

This had several implications for me:

- I would need a completely clear idea of the photos I needed (vertical of Jamie holding Torah, horizontal of her and the Rabbi, wide shot of family in front of ark, tight shot of Jamie with her sister).

- Final work on the video would be done during the 15-minute drive from the synagogue to the reception venue.

fat at the beginning or end, save it as a WAV or MP3 file, and drag it into iTunes. These recordings are typically not of the same quality as purchased music (depending on the quality of the stream), but they'll do.

Any Sound Recorder fills the bill very nicely for me and solves a problem that Apple deserves shame for creating. Apple's recent decision to remove DRM from its library is encouraging, but you will likely need a solution such as Any Sound Recorder for years to come to convert music you have already purchased.

◆

This technique is of equal value to conventional PowerPoint use, as iTunes-format files are equally unreadable there. With luck, this will all be moot soon if Apple follows through on its stated intent to remove digital rights management from its songs.

Part Five: Working Smarter

- My buddy Dan would be driving me and I would do the final work while riding shotgun.

- With no time to burn a DVD or even rip an AVI file, the public showing would take place from within ProShow. Most programs have a low-resolution playback option for proofing purposes; Pro-Show offers a setting to control the resolution of the test playback, and by bumping the figure all the way up, it was essentially like watching a DVD.

- Above all, I'd better not screw up, lest I receive psychological and emotional torture from my wife, who was against the whole idea.

Mission accomplished

I'm still married, so by at least one measure, the production was successful. For the February showing, work began in December with the shooting of the video and proceeded in fits and starts until January. Once the photos, video, and music were chosen, the bulk of the work came together in about eight days, with the many tweaks and refinements consuming another five days. The entire project probably consumed about 75 hours.

Were this a paying gig, I would have earned about $750—a whopping $10/hour. And now you know why it is impossible to make a business case for digital slide shows being one's fulltime job.

▶ Download and view a portion of this video at www.PhotosToMemories.net/jamie.

Digital Rights and Wrongs

I own all of the music that I use; I pirate nothing. If I need a song for a client project, I buy it from iTunes and include the $.99 in the final invoice.

This, of course, won't protect me in a court of law if a music company decides that it doesn't like what I do.

I am entitled to enjoy properly-purchased music in whatever form and fashion that I choose, for my own private and non-commercial purposes.

- When I played Jamie's video at her reception, that was a private event, not open to the public. Therefore, I could do with it whatever I please.

- When I produce videos for clients, they pay me for my effort, but as long as my client does not try to sell DVD copies, they are all within their rights to enjoy the production in any private setting.

- But when I place samples of my work at PhotosToMemories.net for prospective clients to see, I violate copyright law.

- And by making a snippet of this video available for you, the public, to download and view, I violate copyright law.

I'm not trying to be glib or cavalier about this; I am simply taking a calculated risk. I am gambling that if a record company discovered my samples page, it would make the determination that there is no value in going after me. I obviously mean no malice and it could be argued that I place its music in a positive light by marrying it with imagery in a pleasing and evocative way. Again, this would not be a defense, but record companies are far more concerned with those who traffic in pirated music.

The alternative is to create videos with copyright-free music, but that is not nearly as fulfilling and none of my clients would find the finished product as satisfying. Therefore, I am careful to protect my clients and to create the actual product in accordance with copyright law. But when it comes to the publicizing of my business, I do cross the line.

Not to be too crass about this, but I'm kind of like the penny-ante marijuana smoker. Yes, the cops could bust me, but they are more concerned about the distributors and the gangs who traffic in it.

Output

The list of possible destinations for a video today is positively dizzying, and ProShow Producer can reach practically all of them. My preferred one is a Flash file that needs only a standard browser to play, like the one for Jamie's video, linked on the previous page. Fades are clean, video is sharp, and music quality is excellent. The file for Jamie's 16-minute video weighs in at 160MB, not exactly loose change, but as a stream, it begins playing almost immediately after the download begins.

There are other output choices, as well:

- For Windows users, you can create an executable (.exe) file that requires nothing else to run. Simultaneous fades (one image fading out while another fades in) are a bit rough, but quality is otherwise excellent. Many corporate firewalls will forbid the downloading of an .exe file, so the smart play is to tuck it into a .zip file and send that. The file is incredibly compact—half the size of the Flash file.

- iPod Video, iPod Touch, and iPhone

- Palm, Blackberry, and most other mobile formats

- Direct support for Apple QuickTime

- Express upload to YouTube

- Standard DVDs and BlueRay discs

- Videos for XBox, Wii, and Playstation

- Export to TiVo format

ProShow is addictive software, so watch out...

Our Toolbox

In addition to the two main programs described here, I regularly call upon the following applications when creating movies:

CorelDraw Graphics Suite

For a fraction of the price of Adobe Photoshop, you get an excellent image-editing program and a best-of-breed vector drawing program. The perfect creative suite for digital movie makers. www.corel.com

SnagIt

No self-respecting software trainer can get by without the ability to capture screen images or create video of a program being driven, and Snag-It from TechSmith is our choice. www.techsmith.com

WavePad

An excellent wave file editor, and completely free. www.nch.com.au/wavepad

Any Sound Recorder

See my sidebar rant about songs copy-protected by iTunes... www.any-sound-recorder.com

Audacity

Another good and free sound editor that will also record music from iTunes and other sources. http://audacity.sourceforge.net.

Chapter 30

Junk & Miscellany

Even across 30 chapters, I seem to be unable to write a book in which all the topics I wish to cover fall neatly into categories. Good thing, too—these potpourri chapters are usually the most popular. I always save them for the end and add to the list of topics as I write the book. And now, as I sit poised to compile this final chapter, I wonder if I shouldn't just wait and save it for an entirely new book. I can see it now on the shelves: *PowerPoint Junk and Miscellany*, by John Doe (would you put your name on that book title?).

Without further ado, here is a loosely organized collection of thoughts, advice, commentary, tips and tricks, and miscellaneous junk about PowerPoint.

Version 2007

Here we are—halfway through 2009 and over three years removed from first laying eyes on the current version of PowerPoint—and still most users are not sure what to do with and make of version 2007. Unlike the first edition of this book, in which it got second billing, V07 has been a full and equal partner this time around, with all discussions of strategy and technique being applied to both V03 and V07. (Except this discussion here—there is no place in this book where we wonder publicly about what to do with version 2003.)

There is a lot to like in PowerPoint 2007 and it is easier to make a legitimately attractive slide deck with it than with any previous version.

Figure 30.1
These photos were controlled by a slide master in 2007 and are now just slide elements when converted down and opened in version 2003.

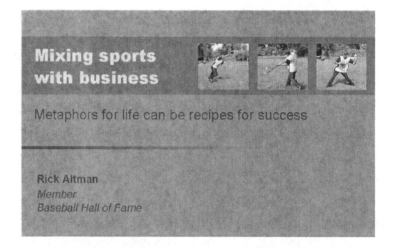

Figure 30.2
Earlier versions of PowerPoint convert 2007's custom placeholders to standard placeholders.

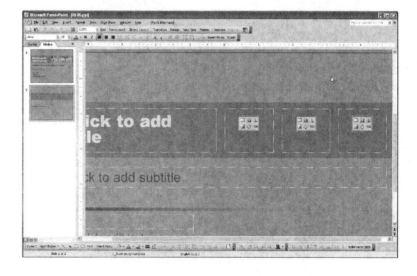

But if I'm being completely honest, I would have to admit that I have no plans to switch to it exclusively.

I love what Microsoft has done with slide mastering, and the new graphics engine is terrific. On more than one occasion, I have started a project in 2007 to take advantage of the new features, and then saved it down to 2003 and continued there as required by a client.

Figure 30.3
Photo effects in 2007 convert down to transparent graphics.

Presentation files degrade quite gracefully, too. Figures 30.1–30.3 show two new features completely foreign to earlier versions, nonetheless performing quite well in version 2003. Figures 30.1 and 2 show a special title slide layout that I created, with the photos that I place on one title, and a blank title slide awaiting my input. The intelligence that we built into the slide master in 2007 was removed, but they were converted down to something that makes sense (placeholders on the slide itself).

Version 2007 layouts are converted to V03 slide masters and that can become messy, but in terms of functionality and peaceful degradation, Microsoft got it right. Meanwhile the photo manipulations in Figure 30.3 are no longer dynamic, but they look every bit as good.

As impressive as the backward compatibility is, why do I resort to it? Because my ability to crank out slides in version 2007 is impaired by the Ribbon and by the inflexibility of the interface. To be fair, the Ribbon is no worse than the old paradigm of a Menu bar...unless you are accustomed to moving quickly with a combination of mouse clicks and keystrokes. Then you would be utterly frustrated if you, say, had two objects selected and you wanted to bottom align them. In 2007, that maneuver requires three clicks and a trip almost all the way across the screen.

I respect Microsoft's desire to cater to new and occasional users, and to be sure, the Ribbon is better than a factory-configured Menu bar that hides over 70% of its commands, as a fresh install of Office 03 does across all of its applications. In moving in this direction, however, without providing provision to create access to commands to which they have grown accustomed, advanced users feel slighted.

This is mitigated by the techniques discussed in Chapter 26, but not enough to bring a groundswell of conversion. We should not have to resort to blind keystrokes or third-party add-ins, and that suggests that Microsoft, however unintentionally, is ignoring an entire sect of its user base. Of course, we only have to return to Chapter 1 to understand the company's logic: it considers its primary target audience to be the 30-minute set—the ones who only learned the first 30 minutes worth of the software. That's probably 90% of its base!

I have come to embrace the new features; I have not warmed to the interface. Therefore, I expect to remain, along with countless others, a dual-version user for the foreseeable future.

Never Paste Again!

Do you actually know what goes on when you use the Clipboard to transfer text or a graphic from another application? Do you know what you are really asking for when you press Ctrl+V or click the Paste icon?

Most don't. If they did, they might never do it again.

The Windows Clipboard is a more sophisticated tool than most know, able to carry many formats of an element at once. In fact, when you copy something to the Clipboard, you are usually placing the object there in many different formats. Furthermore, the default choice—the one you get when you ask for Paste—is often problematic:

■ With a graphic, the default choice is an OLE-linked graphic that will attempt to open the native application if you double-click the graphic. If you share this with others, who do not own that application, fireworks could result.

■ With text from a word processor, it is HTML-formatted rich text in the size and typeface of the original. If you are pasting text into a list of bullets, that might be the last thing you want.

■ Even with text from another location within PowerPoint (from title to bullet, text box to title, etc.), PowerPoint will keep the original formatting intact, even though the destination location will have formatting established of its own.

Sometimes the default choice is correct. And sometimes PowerPoint provides a safety net via its Smart Paste feature, if turned on in Options. But we don't want you playing roulette with your slides. We want you to make informed choices when you transfer information onto a slide.

We want you to use Paste Special.

The Paste Special dialog box shows all of the flavors available to you, enabling you to choose the right one. It's not always obvious which is the right one, but with experience you'll get better. Take the case of this CorelDraw graphic:

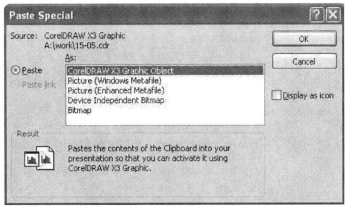

The default choice embeds the entire graphic, editable from a double-click. This sounds attractive, but since OLE was first introduced in 1992, it has never lived up to its promise, remaining fraught with stability problems.

If the graphic you created is made up of vector objects, you would want to choose one of the Picture options, Windows or Enhanced Metafile. The EMF format can hold 32-bit graphics, but that distinction is rarely relevant within PowerPoint, making these two flavors essentially similar. If the graphic is mostly bitmap data, you would want to choose Device Independent Bitmap.

In the case of text, if you are pasting lines of text into a series of bullets, you would most likely want the text to conform to the format you have established for those bullets. That means choosing Unformatted Text from Paste Special.

Practice and experience make perfect here, so start invoking Paste Special instead of just pressing Ctrl+V.

On my customized interface, I have removed the Paste icon from the Standard toolbar and replaced it with Paste Special.

Heading Out the Door

With the exception of Chapter 19, Designing Presentations for Remote Delivery, most of this book assumes that you are creating a presentation that lives on your notebook and will be delivered from your notebook...by you. Indeed, distributing a presentation remains a mystery to many. I have a colleague who wants to write an entire book on this subject; imagine how he will feel when he realizes that I'm stuffing the subject into a junk chapter at the end of the book. Oh well, one less free copy I have to send out...

How wide an audience?

The first question to address will go a long way toward helping you devise a strategy: the people to whom you are distributing your presentation—do they own PowerPoint?

- Are they colleagues at your workplace, where you can safely assume they own Office?

- Or is this going on a web site or some other point of mass distribution, where anyone might download it?

If you can answer Yes to the first question, your life just got easier: you distribute a PowerPoint file. You still have questions to address, but at least you know what it is you are sending out. If your presentation requires the use of exits, motion paths, or simultaneous animations, you will need to try to measure the likelihood that a PowerPoint 2000 user might try to view it (who would see none of those effects). And if your presentation requires specific typefaces, you'll need to find out if you are allowed to embed them within the presentation.

The simpler you can make your presentation, the greater chance of distribution success you stand:

- Can you just use Arial or Tahoma? If so, do.

- Can the slides just advance, without the need for fancy animation? If so, let them.

- Can you do without macros? If so, do without.

Now your PowerPoint universe is about as wide as it can be.

No PowerPoint? No problem...

If you cannot count on your audience owning PowerPoint, the situation is a bit more complicated, and again there are two questions to address:

Figure 30.5
Browsers are better than you might think at preserving the look and feel of a PowerPoint presentation..

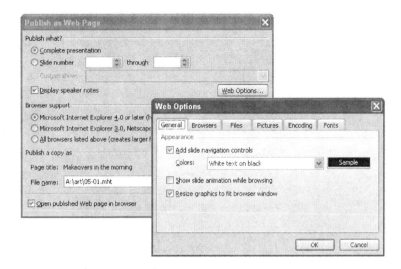

- Do you send your presentation in a different format?

- Do you try to give them PowerPoint?

If you determine that you can live without PowerPoint, there are three almost-universal formats to help you. The place to start is HTML, because every computer built since 1996 knows what to do when you double-click an .htm file. And if you have never saved your presentation to HTML, you might be surprised at how much is preserved. Typefaces, animations, and transitions can all be maintained to some degree, and Figure 30.5 shows some of the controls available to you.

A second possibility is the Adobe PDF format. PowerPoint 2007 users can create a PDF straight off of the Save As flyout; V03 users will need to own Adobe Acrobat or another PDF-creation tool. With Acrobat's Document Properties settings, you can ask for the file to be opened full-screen, and from Edit Preferences | Full Screen, you can choose a default transition and an auto-advance interval.

If your colleagues can't open a PDF file, you work in a very obscure industry. Even my father—the 89-year-old semi-retired rocket scientist who still uses Lotus 1-2-3 for his propulsion formulas—can open a PDF file.

And a third is Flash, the rich format of the Web. If you're just showing slides, go with HTML or Acrobat. But if you need a more robust offering of your ideas—audio, mood-evoking transitions, careful sequencing of images or text—Flash would answer the call for you, and there are numerous companies taking up the challenge of accurate conversion from PowerPoint to Flash.

Part Five: Working Smarter

It would not be completely objective for me to proclaim that PointeCast (www.pointecast.com) leads the charge on this front, seeing how the company has been a PowerPoint Live sponsor for the past four years. But PointeCast Publisher has garnered much praise among end-users with whom we regularly communicate. WildPresenter Pro (www.wildform.com) is also well-regarded for its conversion tools, as is TechSmith's Camtasia (www.techsmith.com).

Through it all, though, the best way to faithfully represent a Power-Point file is with PowerPoint itself. Microsoft freely distributes its so-called Viewer for those who want to send a PowerPoint file without regard for whether the recipient owns the software.

The gateway for using the Viewer is the poorly-named Package for CD function (most people who use it regularly use it to copy a presentation to another folder, not to a CD). It gathers up all of the components of a presentation—linked audio clips or movies, embedded fonts, and any other file you designate—and copies them to a location of your choosing, along with the Viewer files.

Name	Size	Type ▲	Date Modified
pptview.exe	1,638 KB	Application	7/7/2005 3:57 PM
gdiplus.dll	1,732 KB	Application Extension	7/5/2005 12:05 PM
intldate.dll	64 KB	Application Extension	3/17/2005 1:43 PM
ppvwintl.dll	126 KB	Application Extension	3/17/2005 1:07 PM
saext.dll	207 KB	Application Extension	7/14/2003 10:57 PM
unicows.dll	241 KB	Application Extension	10/30/2002 12:21 PM
pvreadme.htm	5 KB	HTML Document	7/25/2003 12:32 PM
09-03.ppt	892 KB	Microsoft Office Po...	2/27/2007 7:06 PM
play.bat	1 KB	MS-DOS Batch File	2/27/2007 7:06 PM
AUTORUN.INF	1 KB	Setup Information	2/27/2007 7:06 PM
playlist.txt	1 KB	Text Document	2/27/2007 7:06 PM
sound02.wav	100 KB	Wave Sound	12/20/2005 9:08 PM

This group of files all needs to be transported together to the recipient's computer, and that presents challenges of its own. A presentation with external elements cannot be shown from a remote URL; PowerPoint won't find an MP3 or AVI file out on a web page.

The entire group of files must make its way onto a drive that has a letter or a network path, and we have a detailed recommendation about how to perform this task at betterppt.com/editorial/archive/05mar.htm.

Start Me Up...

I expect that most of you know that F5 starts a presentation. If you didn't know that, now you do: pressing F5 from anywhere while in Edit mode automatically switches you into Slide Show mode (i.e. your presentation will run). That beats the heck out of mousing up to the View menu or Ribbon and then clicking Slide Show.

With version 2003, PowerPoint inherited an even better keystroke: Shift+F5. When you're building a presentation, you probably spend a great deal of time checking out how particular slides look and perform. If you're working on Slide 70, you're not terribly interested in starting your slide show from the beginning, and you might have grown to loathe that tiny icon in the lower-left corner called Slide Show from Current Slide. Loathe no more—just press Shift+F5, and you will be whisked into Slide Show mode starting at whatever slide you're on.

But not too many of you know what happens if you press and hold Ctrl while clicking that tiny Show from Current Slide icon. Do you know? The slide show plays in a small window at the top-left corner of your screen:

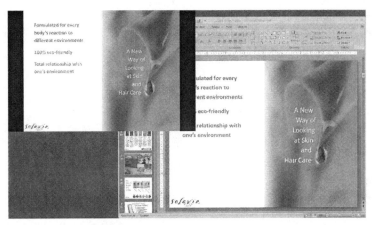

When I first discovered this, I immediately wondered why I couldn't press Ctrl+Shift+F5 to make it happen, but that's because I'm never satisfied and I always search the mouths of gift horses. Still, it's a way-cool trick for times when you want to see how a slide behaves and be able to work on that slide at the same time (changes made in Edit mode are dynamic and immediately show up in the Slide Show window).

So that got me thinking...maybe there are other buried treasures around this part of the interface...so I started poking around...and this is what I found...

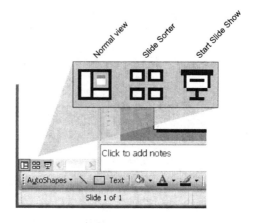

Keystroke	Icon	Result
Shift	Normal View	Enter Slide Master view
Shift	Slide Sorter	Enter Handout Master view
Shift	Start Slide Show	Set Up Show dialog
Ctrl	Start Slide Show	Run slide show in small window
Alt	Start Slide Show	Run slide show in Browse mode*

* *Browse by Individual mode: Slide Show | Setup Show | Show Type | Browsed by An Individual*

Also, don't forget that there are Play and Slide Show icons in the Animation task pane. The Play button plays the current slide right on the slide, to help you with timing and sequencing, and the Slide Show button is the same as the tiny one at the lower-left (but bigger and easier to click on).

It's Midnight—Do You Know Where Your Templates Are?

Back in Chapter 9, we all but mocked PowerPoint's template structure, pointing out that any presentation can act like a template and any version 2003 PowerPoint file can be turned into a template by changing its extension to .pot. (And no, we did not wonder out loud what they were smoking up in Redmond when they chose that extension...we decided to hold that for our junkie chapter, I mean our junk chapter.)

All fine and well...but where should a V03 template reside in order to show up in PowerPoint's Design task pane? That's not so obvious, for three reasons: 1) The Documents and Settings / Users folder can be treacherous to navigate; 2) The folder that you need to find is hidden by Windows; and 3) You can do everything right and still not see your template.

If you want to convert one of your own PowerPoint files into a template, so it can be used from within the application, your course of action should be easy:

1. Open the file.

2. Go to File | Save As and change the file type to Design Template

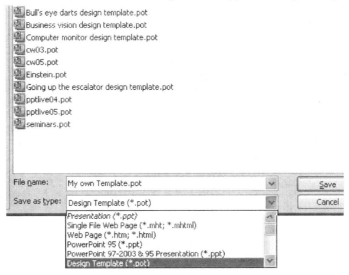

PowerPoint will automatically change the file window to the special Templates folder.

That should be all there is to it...but it's not. In what could only be described as a bug in the program, your new template will not show up in the Design task pane's thumbnails of templates until it is actually used once. (Kind of like needing to have already gotten a loan in order to be granted your first loan.) So the first time you want to use this template, you must click the Browse button at the bottom of the task pane and go find it. Once done, its thumbnail will take up permanent residence in the task pane.

What if you receive a template file from a colleague? Would you know where to place it? As we mentioned earlier, navigating Documents and

Settings (XP) or Users (Vista) is hard enough—once you get there, you should see the Application Data folder (App Data in Vista).

I said, you should see the Application Data folder...where is it??

That folder is hidden by default...isn't that grand? To fix this permanently, from any My Computer or Windows Explorer window, or Folder Options in Control Panel, do the following:

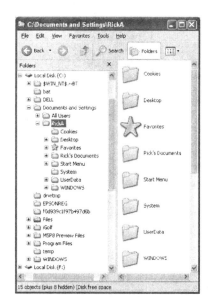

1. Go to Tools | Folder Options | View.

2. Click Show Hidden Files and Folders.
   While you're here, uncheck Hide Extensions for Known File Types, because that is another completely brain-dead default. (What good comes of hiding extensions? Then you end up with file.pps.ppt when you are trying to create a PowerPoint file that runs when you double-click it.)

3. OK your way out.

Now you should see the Application Data folder and be able to navigate your way to the Templates subfolder.

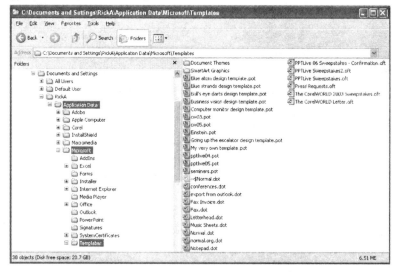

Part Five: Working Smarter

Overheard at the PPT Newsgroup

Diane from Bell South Internet Group asked this question:

I am using Power Point to make simple slide shows for children to advance with a mouse click, as they work independently at the computer. I am narrating each slide. I want the program to ignore inadvertent mouse clicks until the narration is complete, then advance the slide the next time the mouse is clicked (even though children may take varying amounts of time to click the mouse). I do not want to use action buttons, just a simple mouse click where the cursor could be anywhere on the screen.

I find that the children are clicking the mouse and advancing the slides before the narration for each slide is complete. I cannot find any way to keep them from doing this. I don't want to time each slide, because the narration on the slides may be of varying lengths—some with longer narration, some with shorter narration.

This intriguing question got three completely different solutions, each full of merit. First came Ellen Finkelstein, author of the *How To Do Everything in PowerPoint* series of books:

You can disallow clicking to advance slides by choosing (in Power-Point 2002/2003) Slide Show | Slide Transition. In the Slide Transition task pane, uncheck the On Mouse Click check box in the Advance Slide section.

Then set automatic timings for each slide according to the length of the narration. After timing each slide's narration, select each slide and use the same transition to set its timing in the Automatically After text box in the same location I just mentioned.

Next came David Marcovitz, a Microsoft PowerPoint MVP and author of *Powerful PowerPoint for Educators*:

Here is a simple way to do what you want. First, set the slide transition for your slides so that they do not advance on mouse click. Next, create a rectangle that covers the entire slide. Select the rectangle and choose Format | Autoshape to set the rectangle to 99% transparent.

Now, you need to set the animation order. If you have a sound icon, then you already have an animation effect for the sound, so

continued...

Notice that this folder is for all Office templates, not just PowerPoint ones. Copy any templates that you have acquired to this folder and then remember about needing a loan before getting your first one: click Browse to find that template file in the Design task pane. Then its thumbnail will show. Version 2007 users will not have to worry about this nonsense—V07 themes are more refined and better behaved.

Disappearing slide masters

There is one more point of possible angst concerning templates: those with multiple sets of slide masters might be at risk of losing those masters that are not in use. In another example of creating trouble through simplification, PowerPoint will (sometimes) remove slide masters that are not in use.

To be precise, PowerPoint's slide masters (sometimes) default to not being "preserved"—that's the term that Microsoft uses for a slide master that should remain in the file even if it is not being used by any slides. This can be (sometimes) maddening and so you should be (sometimes) vigilant.

It's easy to be (sometimes) glib and (often) sarcastic in the last chapter of your book—why the *sometimes*? Because this doesn't always happen.

...continued from previous page

you need to make sure that the animation effect is set to With Previous.

Next, add an animation for your 99% transparent rectangle and set it to After Previous. To round out the animations, drag the sound's animation (in the custom animation task pane) above the rectangle's animation. Finally, you need to set a hyperlink or action setting for the 99% transparent rectangle to Next Slide.

What this will do is have the sound play and then bring in the rectangle (which the students won't actually see). While the sound is playing, the rectangle is not there, so a mouse click will not work. Once the sound has played and the rectangle has come in, any mouse click will have to be on the rectangle because it covers the whole slide, and the click will take you to the next slide.

Finally, John Wilson of the PowerPoint Alchemy web site (www.pptalchemy.co.uk) offered this suggestion:

In the slide transition pane, set the transition of the slide with narration to automatically after 0 seconds. Make the next slide a duplicate of this slide but with no narration. Set this slide to transition to On Click.

About half the time, PowerPoint automatically preserves the masters. But when it doesn't, you're hosed. So get in the habit of always looking for the little push pin next to the slide master's thumbnail:

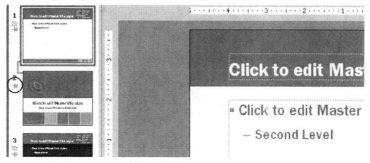

And if you don't see it, right-click the thumbnail and choose Preserve Master.

Bringing Object Order to Chaos

PowerPoint object management is woeful. Objects are given unhelpful names (like Rectangle 23 or Shape 16) and there is no provision to rename them. PowerPoint 2007 finally addresses this situation; users of all earlier versions must purchase third-party tools or just build a bridge and get over it.

And that can be hard, even if you know about the hidden command called Select Multiple Objects, which shows you every object on a slide. In the case of a sequence of rectangles that needs to be animated in turn, you could drive yourself nuts trying to pick out these objects one after the other.

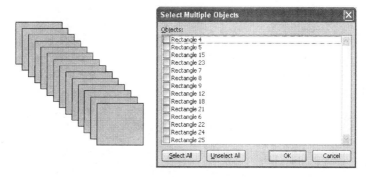

This is a typical situation, in which you did not create the rectangles in order or perhaps moved them around before putting them in sequence, so PowerPoint's names are completely confounding.

This requires a trip to the Format AutoShape dialog (available from the right-click or Format menu) and the seldom-used Web tab. If you create Alternative Text (as if you were going to create web links), that text shows up in the Select Multiple Objects dialog.

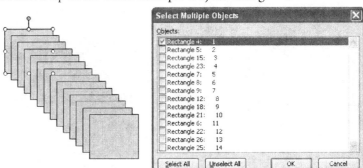

PowerPoint insists on using its own useless name for the object, but as you can see, even a simple Alternative Text entry such as a numeral can help. If you expect to have many overlapping objects, add a bit of Alternative Text (such as "This one goes on bottom!") and it can help you enormously when working through a formatting scheme.

Version 2007 users can enjoy the Selection and Visibility pane, which delivers them from this entire issue. We write about it on Page 155.

Making Peace with Color Schemes

If I had the sense that PowerPoint 2003 users might wake up one day and become enamored and riveted by PowerPoint's engine for controlling color, this would become its own chapter.

I have no such impression. Some very talented presentation designers completely ignore color schemes. But when we show how they are used at Power-Point Live, we turn heads right and left. So here is a brief tutorial on the function that you probably do not use but might wish that you did...

Every PowerPoint template (i.e., every PowerPoint file) has at least one color scheme and most have many.

Each of the schemes here are designed with eight complementary colors that generally look good together. Practicing with them is good for developing your eye, but its use can go well beyond that.

When you apply a color from the color scheme to an object on your slide, you are not just instructing the object to display a particular color. In the case of Figure 30.16, you are telling this circle, "you are to be filled with the color that is assigned to Position No. 5."

Position 5 happens to be a shade of blue right now, but it could be something different if you changed the definition for Position 5, used a different color scheme, or imported this slide into a different presentation.

If instead, you wanted to ensure that this circle is always a specific color, you would manually define that color, either with the standard or custom color palettes found when you choose More Fill Colors from the Fill Color dropdown or popup. Once you choose a manual color, it shows up as a "recent color" on a line below the eight colors in the scheme, as shown in Figure 30.17 on the next page. These colors have a shorter shelf-life: close PowerPoint and reopen it, and they'll be gone.

You can now copy this circle to a different presentation file, move the whole slide there, swap in a different color scheme, or change out the entire template—this circle will remain the shade of blue that it is right now. You can use this knowledge to great effect if you plan for it:

- If the Coca Cola Bottling Company hired you to create slides, you surely would not make Coca Cola Red one of the colors of the color scheme, where the possibility existed that a different presentation

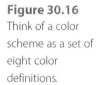

Figure 30.16
Think of a color scheme as a set of eight color definitions.

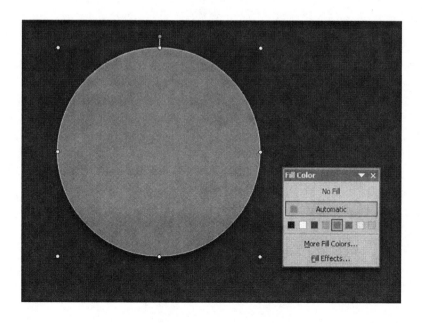

Figure 30.17
This color
assignment will
always be the same
color, no matter
where this circle
goes.

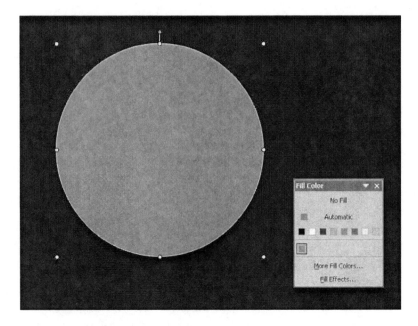

could change it to Pepsi Coca Blue. You would create a custom color, so it would never change.

- If you have designed some nice accent lines between the title and subtitle, you would want their colors to match the rest of the slide and change if you changed the color scheme. For that, you would pick one of the eight.

▼ Download
color_schemes.
ppt for a
demonstration of
how color
schemes operate.

Colors from the scheme can be chosen any time there is a question of fill or outline. I regularly create a gradient fill using two complementary colors so that if the scheme changes, the gradient will still look good. There is plenty more to know about color schemes, but the distinction between the eight colors of the scheme and manually-assigned colors is the part that any user can put into use right away.

version 2007 has vastly improved color scheme dialogs. Maybe as more people migrate to it there will be a wider understanding and use of color schemes. The trickiest part I have discovered about color schemes with version 2007 files is the case of inheriting them from somewhere else: if you want to remove a color scheme from a V07 file, it seems as if the only way to do it is to edit the .pptx file, according to the instructions in Chapter 11. Also, backsaving to V03 is problematic with colors as the sophistication of the V07 color engine doesn't always translate well back to the simpler color paradigms of V03. Best to note RGB values and make sure that when the file arrives in the earlier version, those RGB assignments are maintained.

Ungroup Tables...Always

Like many people who use it, I enjoy/suffer a love/hate relationship with PowerPoint's Table function. It's great to have a mechanism that allows for quick creation of grid-based information——doing it with tabs or separate text boxes would be painful.

However, once you are done creating it, the Table function dumps you right at the point where you would need it most—animating the table. In both V03 and V07, table animation is limited to applying an entrance or an exit to the entire table. That is not how columnar data needs to be built——it needs (often desperately) to be sequenced row by row or column by column.

Unless you are willing to create multiple single-row or single-column tables and animate each one, the solution is to ungroup the table, separate it into logical pieces, regroup those pieces, and animate them. That is why I almost always recommend to clients that they not keep information in a table. This is similar to the advice I offered about ungrouping charts (Page 194), but I am even more strident because there is no other plausible way to animate the information (while it is awkward and frustrating to do, charts can be animated by sequence; it is possible to do it while the chart is still a chart).

So imagine my thrill when I discovered that tables could not be ungrouped in version 2007. Why the downgrade?? I'm still waiting on the answer there, but in the meantime, Paste Special can come to the rescue. If you copy or cut a table to the Clipboard, as we said earlier in the chapter, the information is stored in several different formats, one of which is as a collection of objects (metafiles). The Clipboard essentially performs its own ungroup command on the table. Use Paste Special to retrieve the table, choosing Metafile as the format. That version of the table can now be ungrouped.

Kool Keystrokes

Please note that this is not intended to be an exhaustive list of all of the keystrokes that exist across the application. Instead, this is my list of little-known and/or seldom-used shortcut keys, presented here in no special order. You probably know most of them...but who knows, maybe not all of them. Perhaps you'll find one that might prompt you to raise one of your eyebrows. That would be good enough for us...one eyebrow, up just a touch, as in "Hmm, I'll have to try that one..."

Keystroke	What it Does	Version
Ctrl+Shift+C	Activates Format Painter and picks up format of selected object	03 07
Ctrl+Shift+V	Applies picked up format to selected object	03 07
Ctrl+F1	Toggles Ribbon on and off	07
Ctrl+click	Selects noncontiguous words of text, even in separate text blocks	07
Ctrl+[Ctrl+Shift+<	Size text down by 4pt increments	03 07
Ctrl+] Ctrl+Shift+>	Size text up by 4pt increment	03 07
Shift+F3	Toggles through application of lower case, upper case, sentence case for selected text	03 07
Shift+F9	Toggles view of grid	03 07
Alt+F10	Toggles view of guides	03 07
Ctrl+G	Invoke Grid and Guides dialog	03
Shift+F10	Invoke Context menu	03 07
Ctrl+Shift+Z	Removes all formatting from selected text	03 07
Up, Down, Left, Right	"Nudges" selected objects by small amount in specific direction	03 07
Ctrl+nudge	Micro-nudges selected objects in even smaller amounts	03 07

Working with Groups

The Group command is a terrific tool for maintaining relationships between objects that you have established. If a set of overlapping ellipses have been formatted just so, and are supposed to stay just so, the best course of action is to group them.

The issue arises when you want to adjust the formatting or the content of an element inside of a group; then things are not always so painless, especially in version 2003, where objects inside of groups cannot be moved or resized. And in neither version will animation applied to a group be preserved if you were to ungroup the group. So here are a few strategies and workarounds to consider:

No problem editing text

In both versions, a string of text inside of a group will accept a cursor and allow you to type. If, however, you add a sufficient amount of text in V03 to require that the text placeholder expand, you'll be out of luck. See the previous paragraph: objects in groups cannot be resized.

Try adjusting margins

Your one recourse to the above dilemma (other than shrinking the text, which is usually undesirable) is to use the Format Placeholder dialog to shrink the margins. You just might be able to squeeze enough space out of the placeholder to fit the text.

Changing font, fill, and outline

Both versions allow you to format objects within a group; you just need to click on the object a second time after selecting the group. You will notice a smaller set of handles around the object as is the case with the light gray rectangle here:

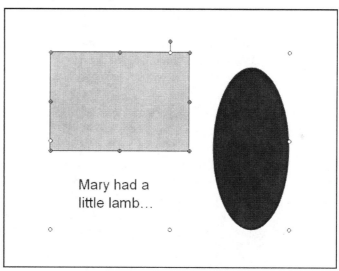

Mary had a little lamb...

In version 2007, when you select an object within a group, you can then do pretty much anything you want to it—move, size, shape, even delete.

If you must ungroup...

If circumstances require you to ungroup a group in order to make substantial revisions *and* you have applied an animation to the group, make a copy of it first. That way, when you have to reapply the animation, at least you'll have the copy for reference.

Dealing with Crappy Slides

What a great headline for the last topic of this book! We refer here to slides that are not necessarily poorly-designed (but probably), and not necessarily poorly-written (but probably), but the slide deck that has been poorly *constructed*. Bullets not in their placeholders... font assignments seven to a page...titles all different sizes...slides formatted one by one instead of through slide masters. That kind of crappy.

And wow do we have a good example to use, as the slides on the following page point out. This presentation was delivered many times several years ago, and ironically, the presenter was so dynamic, he got good reviews despite the fact that his visuals were so bad.

If you were tasked with making this slide deck over, would you relish it or dread it? I was that person, and I did both. Here's a tour:

Slide 1

Quite possibly one of the worst title slides we have ever seen. This presentation was delivered to groups of homeowner associations and the idea of curb appeal was a good theme. But showing the opposite of curb appeal as the title? Not good...

Slide 2

Do we need a separate slide to ask this question? And if we do, must it have that papier mache background?

Slides 3 and 4

Here's the real pain. There were 33 slides just like these that were created using the Blank layouts and floating text placeholders. That means that I was unable to just reapply the slide layout to get rid of all of this hideous formatting. This problem would take some thought...

Slides 5 and 6

These were the first of 10 pairs of comparisons, but there was tremendous potential impact lost by not showing them on screen together. And we won't even talk about the smiley faces...

Slides 7 and 8

These are whimsical and warranted some form of cute treatment. But with the entire slide show feeling like a cartoon, these slides didn't seem to be different. Ironically, they needed to be cutesied up more.

*"It's all in the packaging-
Creating Curb Appeal"*

HARWOOD ROAD
450   4320

Presented to:

ECHO
June 30, 2001

❶

❷

What exactly is curb appeal?

GOAL OF SESSION:

• To create an awareness and understanding of why it is important to maintain the aesthetic appeal and value of your homes.

• To give practical examples of how you can create that appeal.

• To inspire you to action.

❸

❹

• Makes the Community a "desired" place to live

• Safety Considerations

• Breaks downward cycle of deferred maintenance

• Creates emotional involvement by owners (engagement Vs. dial tone)

• *Creates a sense of neighborhood*

❺

❻

Before

After

❼

❽

Fences grow better when watered on a regular basis

The exercise yard at San Quentin???

The makeover

I identified three basic types of slides—normal, before/after, and gotchas—and created slide masters for each. I did nothing fancy; in fact just the opposite: these slides were crying out for a bit of conservatism. Navy blue backgrounds, white text for the regular slides, and black backgrounds for the before/afters and gotchas.

Just about anything would have been an improvement with the title slide. I was horrified to learn that it usually displayed for almost 10 minutes as audience members entered the ballroom. That's a long time for any static image, let alone a terrible one. Instead, I used the technique recommended at the end of Chapter 14 of fading a group of photos one atop the other.

The tricky part was creating the loop, so here's a challenge for you:

> **How do you make one slide loop indefinitely onto itself, and then when you are ready to begin your presentation, proceed to the second slide?**

I'd love to hear from readers who have conjured up other solutions, but here is the one that I came up with:

1. Create two custom shows—one called Intro, containing just the first slide, and one called Main, containing every other slide in the deck, starting with the second one.

2. Go to Slide Show | Set Up Show and tell PowerPoint to run the Intro custom show. Also tell it to loop continuously.

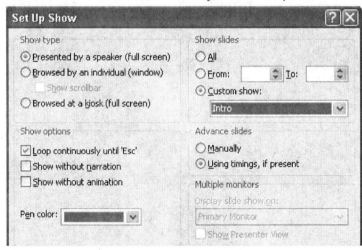

3. From the Transition task pane, choose a transition that fits with the action on the slide and set Advance Slide to Automatic After. For the After value, pick a duration that makes sense. For

instance, my photo fades are six seconds apart, so I told the slide to wait for six seconds before "advancing," which would simply send it back to the beginning.

4. Draw a rectangle over the entire slide.

5. From Slide Show | Action Settings, set the click action to be a hyperlink to the custom show called Main.

6. Set the transparency of the rectangle's fill to 99%, effectively making it invisible.

Now the first slide will loop until the presenter clicks on it once, at which point it will promptly advance to the second slide and then proceed from there.

As satisfying as this was to figure out, this challenge was nothing compared to the task of cleaning up the text. I only showed you two of those ill-crafted text slides back on Page 383; there were actually over 30 of them.

Let's take a moment to frame the problem. Having created a slide master for text slides, now I had to make all of the text slides conform to it. But none of the bullet slides was created using the standard text placeholders; the creator drew text boxes on blank slides and formatted them. As a result, reapplying the Title and Text layout would have no effect except to create empty title and text placeholders.

It would seem that my options were to retype the bullets into the proper placeholders (out of the question!) or try some cut-and-paste maneuver, which, even with a script to automate it, was also unacceptable.

As with the loop, I'm not sure that there isn't a better way to solve this, and I hope to hear from others who have their own ideas. Here was mine, requiring an installed copy of Adobe Acrobat:

1. Print the entire presentation to a PDF file.

2. Open the PDF file in Adobe Acrobat and immediately perform a Save As to plain text. Call it anything, like makeover.txt.

3. Open makeover.txt in Notepad and find your titles and bullets. Enter tabs to identify bullets.

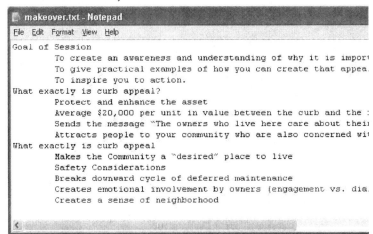

This presentation does not have any second-level bullets, but if it did, you would have entered a second tab for each of them.

4. Save and close the text file and return to PowerPoint.

5. Open the presentation file that has the redesigned slide masters and place your cursor where you want to insert the bullet slides.

6. Go to Insert | Slides From Outline and find makeover.txt. Voilà...

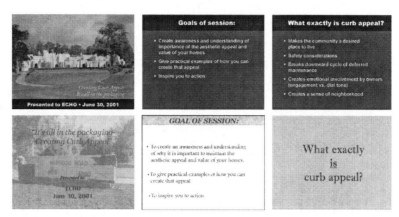

The top row of thumbnails are new slides; the bottom row are old ones. What I particularly like about this conversion technique is that it makes no distinction between types of text. Like the funky GOAL OF SESSION title that is stuffed into a filled rectangle—it all comes out as text, at which point I can delete unwanted text quickly and format bulleted text many, many times faster than I could have had I performed a cut and paste.

Download before.ppt and after.ppt to experience the agony and the ecstasy for yourself.

I converted 33 brain-damaged bullet slides and made them all conform to a redesigned slide masteer in less than 10 minutes. I don't even want to think about how long it would have taken to have fixed them the conventional way. The only caveat is to watch for double-spaces and weird line breaks that Acrobat inserts. You'll want to go on a search-and-destroy mission for them.

There are other ways to extract all of the text from PowerPoint, including special print drivers that create text files and OCR-type screen capture programs. However you do it, the key is to get all of the text into a text file, where then you can create a simple tab-based hierarchy to identify titles, bullets, and sub-bullets.

If you prefer, you could extract the text into Word or another word processor and format it with heading levels. PowerPoint will recognize that as an outline also. And remember, you need to use the Insert Slides from Outline command.

And In the End...

In order to create Chapter 24, I asked several people open-ended questions about the ingredients that make up a successful presenter or presentation. My good friend Korie Pelka, who crafts them for a living, had the shortest and perhaps the most apt response.

"Knowledge and passion."

How perfect is that? Without them, not much else matters. With them, not much else is needed! To circle all the way back to where we started, this book cannot help you with that first ingredient: you have to know your stuff before you can put to use a single paragraph that we have written here.

Passion, on the other hand, can be found in many forms and the best presenters ensure that audiences feel their passion. It is the key to all that is good about designing and delivering presentations, and 388 pages later, it is our hope that we have fueled your passion for creating your next one.

Index

X

Z

CPSIA information can be obtained at www.ICGtesting.com

230258LV00003B/82/P